1

"This book is a lively combination of ancestral imagination, mythology, and historical reality. The author introduces a series of ecstatic trance postures that have been identified elsewhere as having ancient use for facilitating a variety of meditative inquiries and are frequently represented by some of the earliest known sacred figurines from around the world. The author, as he should, leaves the reader to form his or her own opinion as to the degree to which the story can be taken literally or as metaphor, as reality or imaginal fantasy, as personal or collective. Either way, James Hillman suggested that imagination and soul are fundamentally the same thing, and in that sense this book is a soul-focused journey into some of the long-ago roots of modern civilization."

RAYMOND HILLIS, PH.D., PROFESSOR EMERITUS OF COUNSELING, CALIFORNIA STATE UNIVERSITY, LOS ANGELES

"For millennia ancient societies depended on their shamans to bring back information through trance states that was needed for their continued survival and evolution. Now, as we enter into the dawning of a new age, Nicholas Brink is one of those rare individuals bringing us once again into altered states of awareness through the correct use of postures that deepen the trance state. This is a must read for anyone on this path of awakening."

RAHASYA POE, C.HT., AUTHOR OF *TO BELIEVE OR NOT TO BELIEVE* AND *THE 12 SPIRITUAL LAWS OF RECOVERY: AND MEDITATIONS FOR THE 12-STEP PROGRAM* AND PUBLISHER OF THE LOTUS GUIDE MAGAZINE

"*Baldr's Magic* is for anyone who loves mythology and myth-making. They will find themselves interested in one fine man's personal tale in addition to his take on today's society. *Baldr's Magic* gives us hope and encouragement that our time is being reborn into the values of the ancient Great Mother, the values of compassion, nurturing, and peace.

His "Lost Eddas" show the magic, enchantment, and compassion of the Vanir gods, and they show the strong, bold Æsir gods, whose life is war. Do not miss the last part of the book, "The Teachings of the Vanir," and final comments."

LISA N. WOODSIDE, PH.D., PROFESSOR EMERITA
OF HUMANITIES, HOLY FAMILY UNIVERSITY,
AND CERTIFIED TEACHER OF ANCIENT RITUAL POSTURES

"*Baldr's Magic* brings alive the world of the ancient Nordic people during a time of prehistory when the Great Mother was worshipped, the time of the Vanir, the gods and goddesses of fertility, a time of peace when mankind lived sustainably on Earth. Then something happened. Men began to control the world, began to value physical strength, began to fight among themselves, and worshipped the Nordic gods of war, Odin and Thor. This book is about this time of transition. Nick Brink shows a real command of the ancient Nordic beliefs and fills in the missing beliefs or the beliefs that were never recorded: the lost stories of the Vanir. With the use of hypnotic and ecstatic trance he journeys back in time to recover these stories that offer us the picture of what the world was like when the Great Mother was worshipped, a world of peace and cooperation, a world of magic that provides us with guidelines for the coming new age."

MICHAEL BELL, PH.D., RETIRED PROFESSOR OF MEDIEVAL
AND FOLKLORE STUDIES, UNIVERSITY OF COLORADO

"An inspirational piece of work. Reading this book will bring you through the tale of the old gods of the Vanir as we know them from Norse mythology: a peace-loving society in balance with nature and the Great Módir, Mother Earth. With the tools of ecstatic and hypnotic trance, the author assesses the ancient world of the gods and people from the old Norse world. He tells us the tale of Ragnarǫk, and the survival of the Vanir, and he shows the reader the new peaceful world that is to come."

MONICA STEENSDATTER,
REGISTERED PSYCHIATRIC NURSE, NUUK, GREENLAND

BALDR'S MAGIC

The Power of Norse Shamanism and Ecstatic Trance

NICHOLAS E. BRINK, Ph.D.

Bear & Company
Rochester, Vermont • Toronto, Canada

Bear & Company
One Park Street
Rochester, Vermont 05767
www.BearandCompanyBooks.com

Text stock is SFI certified

Bear & Company is a division of Inner Traditions International

Library of Congress Cataloging-in-Publication Data

Brink, Nicholas E., 1939–
  Baldr's magic : the power of Norse shamanism and ecstatic trance / Nicholas E.
Brink, Ph.D.
      pages cm
  Includes bibliographical references and index.
  Summary: "A guide to using ecstatic trance to connect with your ancestors,
rediscover your extrasensory powers, and reclaim the peaceful nature of humanity"
— Provided by publisher.
  ISBN 978-1-59143-184-8 (pbk.) — ISBN 978-1-59143-764-2 (e-book)
  1. Ecstasy. 2. Trance. 3. Mythology, Norse. 4. Shamanism. I. Title.
  BL626.B76 2013
  293—dc23
                                                                    2013028688

Printed and bound in Lake Book Manufacturing, Inc.
The text stock is SFI certified. The Sustainable Forestry Initiative® program
promotes sustainable forest management.

10 9 8 7 6 5 4 3 2 1

Text design and layout by Priscilla Baker
This book was typeset in Garamond Premier Pro with Alliance, Legacy Sans, and
Gill Sans used as display typefaces
Artwork by M. J. Ruhe
"How the Ravens Came to Be Black" by Michaela Macha used with permission.

To send correspondence to the author of this book, mail a first-class letter to the
author c/o Inner Traditions • Bear & Company, One Park Street, Rochester, VT
05767, and we will forward the communication, or contact the author directly at
www.imaginalmind.net.

CONTENTS

PART THREE

The Myths and Beliefs of the Ancient Ones

Learning from the Nordic Gods through Hypnotic Trance

ACKNOWLEDGMENTS

I need to begin by thanking three of the instructors of the Cuyamungue Institute who have assisted me on my journey with ecstatic trance and in writing this book. I thank first Belinda Gore, the instructor of instructors, for her continued support in mentoring and encouraging me on this journey. Then thanks goes to James Lawer and Lisa Woodside, who, with their knowledge and understanding of both Ecstatic Trance and Nordic Mythology, read early drafts of *Baldr's Magic* and offered me their thoughts, and especially to James who wrote its Foreword. Mike Bell with his knowledge of Old Icelandic assisted me by correcting my use of several Old Icelandic words, thank you. I also thank Martha Ruhe, the artist of the book's illustrations and Sabrina Kirby who read and edited an early draft. Finally, I greatly appreciate the work of my project editor, Meghan MacLean, and the staff of Bear & Company with whom I worked to bring this book to print. Thank you.

FELICITAS GOODMAN AND THE CUYAMUNGUE INSTITUTE

The Cuyamungue Institute promotes the original research and findings of Felicitas Goodman. Dr. Goodman's work, known as the Cuyamungue Method, focused on the use of ancient sacred practices and postures that, when properly used, provide an experience that creates a doorway to an ecstatic experience of expanded reality.

Dr. Goodman captured the essence of her work and findings in the book *Where the Spirits Ride the Wind*. I received formal training in the history and proper usage of the Cuyamungue Method at the Cuyamungue Institute in Santa Fe, New Mexico.

To learn more about Dr. Goodman's original work in ecstatic trance and her development and use of the Cuyamungue Method visit the Cuyamungue Institute's website at www.cuyamungueinstitute.com.

FOREWORD

By Reverend James Lawer

Fortunately for us, the rise of narrative structure as a legitimate form of analysis and psychological inquiry oversees an increasingly expansive realm across our academic disciplines. No longer is the chirping mockery of reductionism firmly holding sway, as when someone says (as I once heard spoken to an entire room of professionals), "All you used to do was tell stories." Such ideas segregate myths, sagas, folktales, and personal experiences into a bizarre corral labeled "literature," and worse (as far as their intentions to segregate and diminish), "fiction." It is as though the only allowed truth has to be measurable, and that "facts" (such as a blood pressure or heart rate reading or a medical diagnosis) are the only acceptable way to report on what has formerly been known as a human being. To this day such expressions are dark clouds drifting over humanity.

The restoration of story to human dignity is an ongoing and necessary evolution. People around the world are quickly losing trust in their identity. It's particularly telling when cultures are forcibly severed from their land. Because land and story are interwoven, the loss of one leads to loss of the other. Restoration of story, therefore, has broad implications for our relationship to the earth.

We are far from plumbing the riches of narrative, in part because the current state of storytelling in movies and on TV is largely thought to be "entertainment." And when stories are thought to be mere entertainment, that thought itself can be a form of dismissal. It's a rare writer who leaps headlong into a story knowing that what is at stake is the erasure of human complexity due to the rise of capitalized diversions. Indeed, it seems that the bulk of storytelling these days is largely a diversionary tactic to avoid any kind of raw encounter with authentic, fully human psychological truth, a truth that has its roots in the mud and the dust. Forced emigration of our ancestors demonstrates this, and the descendents of immigrants often keenly feel this rupture. In this vein it is important to note that the author of this book is a psychologist working with those who are adrift.

We are very far from a healthy restoration of story because of two other factors: most of us are disconnected from nature, and we are devoid of relationships with our ancestors. Although many people I have met deeply feel this disconnect and would set out to repair it—and there are many writers and seekers who travel this healing route—our culture has a lengthy history of disassociating humankind from the natural world around us. Even with the increasing numbers of books that would weave us back in, what is often missing is some kind of living example of people who have successfully rewoven themselves back into their ancestral lineage, into their ancestral story, so that their lives have meaning in that larger cloth we call our spirituality. What is implied throughout this book is that truth is not fundamentally about beliefs, but is about actual engagement.

When, therefore, someone (as Nicholas Brink has done) makes a personal encounter with the stories of his blood roots, such a journey might appear to be lacking in both appropriate boundaries of fiction as well as in the discursive remove of an essayist. Instead, Nicholas Brink's journey seems audacious and perhaps even a bit weird to some people. At worst, I groan to realize that some will say that it is very "New Agey," thereby entirely missing the historical antecedents that are percolating under the surface of his writing. What he has done here is as old as when humankind listened to stories: he is assuming that the mantle of bardic and skaldic encounters with our past belongs to each and every one of us. He has made the journey into story and has shown us how he did it, and how he wrested contemporary meaning from the ancient past.

Nicholas Brink is part of a select group of persons who have chosen, personally and in therapy sessions, to use the trance state as a path along which to meet and listen to ancestral voices. This ability is as old as storytelling itself. He is fortunate in that his Norse/Viking ancestors left behind not only their stories, but also their physical postures in statues and drawings that were used by them to access spiritual wisdom. So he has used the very means of his ancestral heritage to engage the remarkable wisdom hovering within those old cultures. Those ancestors have not disappeared altogether; they live in our blood. Following the line of our ancestors back and back and back, through our mothers and fathers and beyond, takes us to hopes and dreams that we ourselves still hold. The return of Baldr itself refers to an "end time" that may finally be upon us, an end time that may refer to a rebirth of honor.

Encapsulated in each of the trance journeys Nicholas Brink has made is a current of perception we very much need today, which needs to be articulated again. Furthermore, for anyone who wants to be revived by their own heritage, he has shown us how he did it. It is an honorable exercise to allow our ancestors to be revealed to us in all their pride, their clumsiness, their disjunctions, their wrongfulness, their accomplishments, and their muscular (and sometimes sexual) ripeness for achievement. They have much to teach us. The gods and the ancestors are revelatory when we ask them to be.

The distinction of this book is that it demonstrates how the deities in our blood can be approached and questioned. Their voices can again be listened to in a world that today is as split between the forces of the Æsir and the Vanir as that portrayed in Norse mythology. The writing, therefore, builds a sturdy bridge over an unfortunate chasm hacked between pieces of research and living myth. The Old Norse had their demons, dragons, vices, and heroes with temptations to cowardice. We have our own, too.

In another narrative treasure, Beowulf swims down into the depths of murky waters to wrestle with uncannily monstrous forces that have taken up residence in the land, and from that bloated home have wreaked havoc on the land and all its inhabitants. I am referring, of course, to Grendel's mother. It is another kind of mother who inhabits this book, a mother to whose dwelling we are invited. It's a familiar theme: the poetic journey for the restoration of beauty and ecstatic living is called up from the deep. It is not far off the beam to say that this is exactly the journey that Nicholas Brink would have us embark on for our own well-being, until we understand that the bones of our ancestors are still singing songs that please all growing things.

REVEREND JAMES LAWER practices contemporary, animist Druidry. He is the provost of Druid College and an instructor of the Cuyamungue Method as well as the New York City representative for the Cuyamungue Institute. He is the founder of the Earth-Centered Healing and Spirituality center in New York City, where he offers ritual trance induction, ritual counseling, and Druid apprenticeships. You can learn more about his work at **druidwalker.org**.

PROLOGUE

OUR RELATIONSHIP TO THE GREAT MOTHER

Now is the time for the rebirth of innocence, for the rebirth of compassion, creativity, and magic, and for bringing alive the enchanted earth. A new age of peace, an age of veneration and caring for our great and nurturing Mother Earth is on its way. As we will see, this rebirth was predicted by the ancient Nordic gods and goddesses at the time of the final battle, Ragnarǫk, with the rebirth of the gentle and compassionate Baldr. This ongoing battle began 10,000 years ago, when we began to move from being hunters and gatherers to being agriculturists; and this battle has continued with our attempts to control the earth through cultivation of its flora and domestication of its fauna. This so-called progress in civilization is now coming to an end with the realization that our dominion over the earth is leading to its destruction and our extinction.

The earliest matriarchal society of the North, which venerated the Great Mother, Moðir, and her progeny, the Vanir, was a peace-loving and nurturing society. One of her daughters, Idunn, watched over Mother Earth's garden—the Garden of Idunn—and she taught us to pick the fruit, nuts, vegetables, and herbs of her garden for our health and sustenance.

According to linguist and anthropologist Felicitas Goodman, the hunter-gatherers arrived on the scene no earlier than 200,000 years ago. She explains:

> In a very real way, the hunters and gatherers open the first chapter of our human history. And fittingly, this dawning was as close to paradise as humans have ever been able to achieve. The men did the hunting and scavenging, working for about three hours a week, and the women took care of daily sustenance by gathering vegetal food and small animals. It was such a harmonious existence, such a successful adaptation, that it did not materially alter for many thousands of years. This view is not romanticizing matters. Those hunter-gather societies that have survived into the present still pursue the same lifestyle, and we are quite familiar with it from contemporary anthropological observation. Despite the unavoidable privations of human existence, despite occasional hunger, illness and other trials, what makes their life way so enviable is the fact that knowing every nook and cranny of their home territory and all that grows and lives in it, the bands make their regular rounds and take only what they need. By modern calculations, that amounted to only about 10 percent of the yield, easily recoverable under undisturbed conditions. They live a life of total balance, because *they do not aspire to control their habitat; they are a part of it.*[1]

As we moved from the hunting and gathering era and into the era of the agriculture, of cultivation of the flora and domestication of the fauna, we began to think that we knew a better way to live; we began to think that we had the knowledge needed to control the earth to our advantage, and we threw Idunn out of the garden. We thought our ways of cultivation and domestication were better. We began to see ourselves as superior to other life forms. We thought of our evolution as reaching its final conclusion, rather than seeing ourselves as one small step in the process of a continuing evolution and one small piece in the sustainability of the earth. We took upon ourselves the role of dominionist in our destruction of the earth.[2]

Hopefully, we have not gone too far in this destruction of our Mother, and we can reverse the process for her recovery and health. As more and more of us accept the failure of this experiment in so-called progress, and as we begin our search for ways to reestablish our relationship with our Great Mother, we will find many needed answers by turning back the pages of history to the earliest times, when we lived by hunting and gathering, when we lived in the Garden of Idunn. We will leave behind the greed that grew through our attempts to control our environment and the greed of capitalism, and we will join others in seeking ways for a new and sustainable life that values and venerates Mother Earth. In so doing we will leave behind the loneliness of competition and find cooperation and nurturance in being close to her.

We are moving toward this new world. A growing number of us are showing our commitment to our Mother Earth by fighting on behalf of the environment, fighting against the causes of industrial pollution that has contributed to global warming and fighting against the unnatural manipulation of our plant stock by for-profit corporations. This fight is on many fronts. We are demonstrating, with a willingness to be arrested, to stop the Tar Sands Oil Pipeline that is planned to run from Alberta, Canada, to the coast of Texas. My wife was one of those arrested to stop that pipeline. We are protesting the process of fracking to extract natural gas from our Mother's belly. Decreasing our carbon footprint has become an issue for many of us. We are increasing the insulation in our homes and adding solar panels to our roofs. We are buying more fuel-efficient cars and driving less. We are shopping for and growing our own organic foods. We are supporting farmers' markets and sustainability by shopping for what is grown locally. Permaculture and forest gardens, where we can again forage and gather much of what we eat, are being planted, and worker-owned businesses and cooperatives are increasing in number. I believe a critical mass has been reached, and this movement cannot be stopped.

To promote this change at an even deeper level, we need to rediscover the power of listening to and hearing the spirits of the earth. How can we hear these spirits? The power of trance, whether ecstatic or hypnotic, can bring us into direct communion with the spirits of Mother Earth, and we can experience the healing powers of these spirits. Many of these spirits are of the flora and fauna of the earth, and when we discover what they have to offer and teach us we will no longer see the flora and fauna as subordinate to us; we will instead become one with them. We will find ourselves just one small piece in sustaining Mother Earth rather than in destroying her. Yet we will not feel small when we are a part of her, feeling how she cares for us and nurtures us. In such a state we will again be part of the Garden of Idunn.

Philosopher Jean Gebser sees this change as one of moving beyond the restrictive nature of the rational mind and into a new world of a time-free and transparent consciousness. Still within us is the magic of what Gebser defines as the magical structure of consciousness, an ancient era of our distant ancestors, in which events, objects, and persons were magically related, and in which, for example, symbols and statues do not just *represent* those events, objects, and persons, but *are* those same objects and persons.[3] This magic came to be suppressed by the rationality of the mental structure of consciousness, with its emphasis on logic and linear thinking, resulting in our false sense of superiority and by our attempts to control our environment. Only now, as our consciousness increasingly becomes time-free and transparent, is our magical consciousness breaking through, in the rediscovery of our innate extrasensory powers and our ability to access the universal mind. The power of trance, whether ecstatic or hypnotic, and the altered state of lucid dreaming provides us with this ability. Trance can take us back to the ancient world to learn what we have forgotten over the last 10,000 years. In short, trance reestablishes our relationship to the Great Mother.

I discovered this ability back in the 1970s and '80s, when I first learned clinical hypnosis in my private practice of psychology. It was then that I realized I could experience, or was experiencing, what my clients were experiencing when I led them into hypnotic trance. I first experienced this when I would see a client's shock after I reflected back to them something of their trance experience that they had not told me. On one particular occasion a client was relating to me her experience with her twin sister when out of curiosity I asked her what nursing school her sister had gone to. My client was surprised because she had never told me her sister was a nurse, but from being part of her experience I just knew this to be the case.

My experience with this extrasensory ability was validated and I found the confidence to believe in it while at a workshop on neurolinguistic programming in the 1980s. At one point during this workshop the participants broke up into small groups of three people each. The workshop instructor offered us six imagery experiences. I still can remember several: "sitting in a comfortable chair after eating a big Thanksgiving dinner"; "waiting at an airport for a plane that is an hour late"; "putting on a fresh shirt with a heavily starched collar"; "walking on a cold, snowy evening." One person in the group was to lead another in the group through these six imagery experiences, while the third person was to carefully observe the person doing the imagining for changes in breathing rate, body tension, skin coloration, and any other clues that were noticeable. Then the imaginer was to select one of the experiences and reexperience it while the observer was to attempt to identify which of the experiences it was. Only two of us in the workshop of about thirty people had extensive experience with hypnosis, and both of us had no trouble identifying the reexperienced experience. In fact, I was able to report that the person I was observing switched from one experience to another after a minute or so, and I was not specifically aware of changes in the physiological clues; I was just experiencing the experience with the other person, with my eyes likely either closed or partially closed. The two of us with experience in hypnosis, whether our perceptions were truly "extrasensory" or not, were clearly gaining access to the inner experience of others to an extent that defies rational explanation. Since then I have become aware of many more of these extrasensory experiences while using hypnotic trance.

Then in 2006, after reading Felicitas Goodman's *Where the Spirits Ride the Wind,* I learned of the altered state of consciousness of ecstatic trance induced by rhythmic stimulation of the nervous system and her additional discovery that certain body postures give predictable direction to the trance experience. I have cultivated this ability to the point that I can very easily go into trance and have found that in this way I can at will access the memory of the universal mind to journey back in time and visit my early ancestors. I have used this learned ability to gain an understanding of how my Nordic ancestors lived and survived and of their mythic belief system, from the earliest time when their consciousness of the world was magical up through the mythical era, and also through the rational times when this magical consciousness was suppressed. Visiting these times in a state of ecstatic trance I have followed their lives, starting from before the time of transition, when they believed in the Great Mother, to the more fragile time of Viking chieftains, warriors, and constant battles, to a time when we now talk of valuing peace but seem unable to attain it.

Understanding the magical consciousness and the life ways of my ancestors in those earliest times before 2000 BCE, when they still worshipped Mother Earth (i.e., Moðir), gives us a glimmer of what this new era now unfolding can be like—an era of enchantment, nurturance, and compassion.

I am only able to place roughly in prehistory my ecstatic experience of going back to my distant ancestors. From the above quote of Felicitas Goodman, the era of worshipping the Great Mother most likely occurred during the hunting-and-gathering era of paradise, which for Scandinavia was after the end of the Ice Age, between 4600 and 3800 BCE, the era of the Ertebølle.[4] The earliest pottery in Scandinavia dates from around 4600 BCE.[5] Farming began around 3900 BCE;[6] this was the beginning of when humans began their attempts to control the earth. It was later during this era that I believe the beliefs in the power of the masculine warrior gods Odin and Thor began. Only since the Bronze Era, around 1700 BCE, have metal implements been excavated.[7] The petroglyphs found around Tanum, Sweden, have been dated to this time, between 1800 and 500 BCE. One set of petroglyphs in particular, across the parking lot from the museum in Tanum, shows a battle scene with axes and swords of iron and a figure of Thor being pulled in his goat cart above the battle scene, thus suggesting that the people at this time already believed in the gods of the Æsir,* or at least in the warrior god Thor (images of these Tanum battle petroglyphs are available at my website, www.imaginalmind.net). I expect, though, that the worship of the Great Mother, the earlier time of the Vanir, continued into the farming era and only gradually evolved into the time when people worshipped the Æsir. Given this rough timeline, I estimate that my earliest ecstatic experiences of the time of the worship of the Great Mother were from around 2000 BCE, and the experiences of the time of transition were from about 1800 BCE, followed soon after by experiences from the era of the Nordic warriors.

I have the hope and belief that the turmoil of our current time is a sign of the final struggle of those who seek to hold on to the old ways because of their fear of this coming new age, and that I have a few more years left to see the dawning of this age.

---

*In Norse mythology, there are two pantheons, the Vanir and the Æsir, the latter of which includes the gods Odin, Frigg, Thor, Baldr, and Týr. According to myth, the two pantheons waged the Æsir-Vanir War, which resulted in a unified pantheon in which the Vanir became a subgroup of the Æsir.

The Scandinavia of my ancestors

PART ONE

The Universal Mind

Understanding Trance

All that happens in one place happens also in other places; all that happened at one time happens also at all times after that. Nothing is "local," limited to where and when it is happening. All things are global, indeed cosmic, for all things are connected, and the memory of all things extends to all places and to all times.

This is the concept of the in-formed universe, the view of the world that will hallmark science and society in the coming decades.

ERVIN LASZLO, *SCIENCE AND THE AKASHIC FIELD: AN INTEGRAL THEORY OF EVERYTHING*

1

THE LOST POWERS OF THE NORDIC PEOPLE

This book is three-dimensional. First, many writers believe that we are on the verge of entering an exciting new age, an age of peace and of going beyond the sterile world of scientific rationality to recapture a world of magical enchantment. This new world is predicted by the Mayan calendar and by many other world traditions. This book examines the coming of this new age through the ancient myths of the Nordic people, specifically the second coming of Baldr.

Second, this book demonstrates, in part 1, the power of the ecstatic postures and ecstatic trance to access the lives of the ancient Nordic peoples; and in part 2, the power of hypnotic trance to access their beliefs and myths. These two vehicles of the trance state can allow us to go back in time to learn more directly and deeply from our distant ancestors. Such access can illuminate the evolving cycle of human consciousness: from the nurturing and peaceful era when the Great Mother goddess was the center of life; through a transitional period to a world of aggression and violence centering around a masculine god; and now the return to a new age of peace and nurturance with newfound respect for the enchantment of our earth.

Third, this book is very personal. My own ancestral roots are among the ancient Nordic people, and I believe that my trance journeys back in time reconnect me with my blood ancestors. In this sense, this book is genealogical and offers me a sense of greater self-understanding. This kind of trance journeying can be undertaken by anyone, though it takes practice. Going back to the era of worshipping the Great Mother will be different depending where your ancestors came from. For instance, these journeys will go considerably further back in time for those with Middle Eastern ancestry since farming and the domestication of animals began there around 10,000 years ago. But time lines and ancestry make no difference in what we gain from our experience of trance journeying as we are in this new age of time-free transparency.

Hans-Peter Hasenfratz, professor emeritus of the history of religion at the Ruhr University in Bochum, Germany, and the author of many works in German on ancient cultures and religions, provides a fascinating picture of the spiritual world of the ancient Nordic people in his 2011 book *Barbarian Rites: The Spiritual World of the Vikings and the Germanic Tribes*. He describes a dimension of this ancient people that is most important to me, with my deep interest in ecstatic trance and with my Nordic roots, as in my interest in all the mythologies of the world I have found that I resonate most profoundly with the stories of the Old Norse. But one piece in Hasenfratz's picture of Nordic spirituality is missing, and I seek in this book to reclaim this missing dimension.

What is this missing dimension? Beyond Hasenfratz's description of the rites of this ancient spiritual world he suggests that the Nordic people found value and power in these rites. For example, in defining the rite of passage of Männerbund, the initiation rite of admitting male youth to adulthood, he states that this rite "grants access to a spiritual reality that was distinct from the world of normal experiences," and that the rite is a "holy mystery."[1] Later in the same chapter he writes of "inducing ecstatic experiences . . . through ascetic and meditative practices, *specific body postures* [italics added], dance, various intoxicants and narcotic drinks."[2] I hope I can bring alive the validity and power of these ecstatic experiences in this new and distinct spiritual reality through the spiritual practices of these Germanic and Nordic people.

This new spiritual reality, as necessary to us today as it was to the ancient male youth, is available to us now in the twenty-first century; it can take us beyond the emptiness and limitations of the rational world in which we have been stuck for nearly two millennia to a new world of time-free transparency, to use the terminology of Jean Gebser.[3] This coming new world is one of real magic and real powers of healing, as used by the ancient Nordic shamans, or vǫlvas, in their practice of *seiðr*. *Seiðr,* an Old Norse word for sorcery or magic, is found throughout the Icelandic sagas. Such sorcery was performed by the sorcerer while lying on a high platform, and from this position seeing into the future or finding answers to specific questions. Those who choose to be entrenched in the rational mind would call these powers of magic mere superstition, but there is growing evidence of their power and validity— a power that I believe we must experience and regain in order to survive the current state of our world. I will provide evidence of and demonstrate these powers as this book progresses, but only briefly introduce them for now. They are the powers of the shamans, ancient and current, to heal; to divine; to journey into the Lower, Middle, and Sky Worlds; to shape-shift; and to die and be reborn.

The Icelandic sagas and other ancient Norse sources provide many specific examples of the use of these shamanic powers. English archaeologist Neil Price says these include foretelling the future (divination); bestowing good fortune (blessing); bestowing bad fortune (cursing); manipulating the weather; attracting game animals or fish; healing the sick; sexual enhancement (attracting the opposite sex, curing impotence, etc.); sexual detraction (warding off love spells, causing impotence, etc.); causing mild harm to people, animals, or property; communicating/mediating with the dead; communicating/mediating with unseen world(s); and communicating/mediating with the gods.[4] The list goes on to include a very specific catalog of war charms, the magical skills of Odin: instilling fear and confusion, conferring courage and clarity of mind, instilling physical weakness, conferring physical strength, magically hindering the body's movements, improving dexterity, breaking or strengthening weapons and armor, providing invulnerability in battle, killing people, resurrecting dead warriors to fight again, providing protection from sorcerers (countermagic), and fighting or killing sorcerers. In Hasenfratz's chapter on magic he provides his own list of magic that includes incantations, runes, death, divination, cursing, and destruction.[5]

The power of death/rebirth experiences and the power of divination will be the focus of the first half of this book, along with the powers of healing, spirit travel, and metamorphosis (shape-shifting). I have learned these powers through my experiences with the ecstatic postures and ecstatic trance, trance induced not through the use of spoken language, but with the rhythmic stimulation of the nervous system. The powers of incantations and the runes as found in the ancient myths of the Nordic people involve the use of language. Since spoken language is central to the induction of trance through hypnosis, the use of these powers will be included in part 2 of this book.

Hasenfratz hints at and opens the door to the power of shape-shifting and the power of healing in his discussion of the powers of the gods and goddesses,[6] with Idunn's power of healing and helping the gods maintain their youth, and with Loki's, Freyja's, and Frigg's power of shape-shifting.

Drawing from another source, Barbara Hand Clow used a few of the techniques mentioned by Hasenfratz (i.e., meditation in the form of ecstatic trance and body postures) to find a deeper understanding of the Mayan calendar in her 2007 book *The Mayan Code: Time Acceleration and Awakening the World Mind.* I will use and demonstrate these same techniques here to uncover and demonstrate the real magical power of the ancient rites of barbarian Northern Europe.

THE NEW WORLD

As we evolve into Gebser's new world of time-free transparency, we will find that we indeed have the psychic powers of mind-reading, of seeing into past and future free of the constraints of time, and the ability to become transparent to other realities. Such powers of the Native American medicine men were aptly described by Native American theologian and historian Vine Deloria in his 2006 book *The World We Used to Live In*. What will this new world be like? Scholar and social activist Riane Eisler believes that until about 7,000 years ago the people of the ancient world around the Eastern Mediterranean worshipped the Great Mother and were peaceful and unwarlike.[7] She associates femininity in this earlier era with "justice, wisdom and intelligence."[8] Thus, in our new, evolving world of peace, a world that reclaims justice, wisdom, and intelligence, there will be no place for Hasenfratz's described last two magical powers, the magic of cursing and destruction.

In our current world of great and unprecedented turmoil, transformation *is* occurring. There are those, as epitomized by the incessant chatter of 24/7 talk radio, who fearfully rattle their swords against this emerging new world. Resistance is strong and expected, since those who continue to hold tightly to the old ways live side-by-side with this coming new age. This new age is being described in many different ways. As noted previously, Gebser sees that we are moving into the era of time-free transparency. In this era we will be free of the limits of linear time, a freedom that allows us to see transparently into and reexperience the past, to see into the future, and to even see what is beyond our rational field of vision. As Gebser explains, "During the era of the magic structure of consciousness, magic was "doing without knowing . . doing without consciousness."[9] During the era of rational consciousness magic, though still part of us, has been denied, deemed superstitious. But now during the era of time-free transparency, as man becomes whole and integrated, magic "becomes transparent and conscious to him. . . . He has perceived its effect on his life and destiny, and mastered the deficient components by his insight so that they acquire the degree of maturity and equilibrium necessary for any concretion."[10] Whereas the characteristic of the magic structure of consciousness is emotion and of the mythical structure is imagination, the characteristic of the mental or rational structure of consciousness is abstraction.[11] Now the time-free transparent structure of consciousness is characterized by concretion.[12] As we recapture the era of magic with a new concrete understanding, we leave the current era of rational consciousness, an era that brought us a great new understanding of the universe through the development of scientific methodology but in which we suppressed the powers of the earlier two eras, the power of magic and the power of mythology. Only now are we beginning to appreciate once again these earlier two eras, which have continued to exist, albeit subliminally, thoughut the era of rational consciousness.

Others writers of this new world, some already mentioned, including Richard Tarnas, Riane Eisler, Marija Gimbutas, Carl Johan Calleman, and Barbara Hand Clow, each add other dimensions to the description of this new era. Barbara Hand Clow proposes that this new world is one of *Homo pacem* (as we leave behind or evolve past the world inhabited by *Homo aggressus*), a world where people will live together in harmony and peace.[13] Cultural historian Richard Tarnas, in *Cosmos and Psyche*, is hopeful that we are beginning to rediscover the world soul, or *anima mundi,* ushering in an era in which we will no longer feel separate from the world but part of it.

With our rational thinking we have separated ourselves from the world around us, seeing this world as something to research but personally meaningless and random, a world that we abuse and from which we have become alienated. As we move full circle, we can never really go back to the way things used to be millennia ago, but we can again experience the world that we are part of as dynamic, as having meaning and enchantment. We can again appreciate the nurturing of Mother Earth, the Great Mother. Riane Eisler in *The Chalice and the Blade* and Marija Gimbutas in *Goddesses and Gods of Old Europe* bring this new world alive with their descriptions of the way the world was 7,000 to 10,000 years ago, when our ancestors worshipped the Great Mother, an era in which human energies were put into creativity rather than destruction, an era in which justice, wisdom, and intelligence were associated with the feminine. Carl Johan Calleman sees this new world as one in which the dualities of the old world that have caused us conflict and chaos are unified, and with this unification harmony will be possible. We will live in "a timeless, enlightened state of cosmic consciousness" wherein "humanity will live in true freedom, joy, and peace."[14] These writers and others hold great hope for the future, but they also recognize that for many, giving up the old ways of the last 2,000 years is terrifying, and so this evolution is going to involve great turmoil and dissension.

THE REBIRTH OF BALDR

From another perspective, that of ancient Nordic mythology, this new world is the rebirth of Baldr.[15] Who is Baldr? Baldr is a son of Odin and Frigg and is the most beautiful, gentle, and beloved of the gods. As the son of Odin, the high god of the Æsir, he is descended from the pantheon of warrior gods. Although his mother, Frigg, is a goddess of the Æsir, I believe that his mother has roots among the Vanir, the earlier gods and goddesses of fertility and nurturance, the gods and goddesses with the power of magic. The Vanir era of magic, I suggest (with some support from others), precedes the Æsir in time, originating before the Bronze Age, which began around 3800 years ago in Scandinavia.[16] Frigg was one of the goddesses carried over from this earlier time. As noted by Anna Malmborg, student of comparative religion at the University of Stockholm as well as student of archaeology and history, "Some scholars argue that the fertility cult, i.e., the Vanir, is an older strain"[17] of gods and goddesses. The *Prose Edda* and the *Poetic Edda,* two Old Norse compilations made in Iceland in the early thirteenth century comprising the major store of pagan Scandinavian mythology, tell of the continued war between the Æsir and the Vanir that ended in a stalemate. The physical strength of the warriors of the Æsir, with such warrior gods as Odin, Thor, and Týr, was unable to overcome the magic of the Vanir. Only through deception did the Æsir finally win, and with this victory the Vanir god Njord and his son and daughter, Freyr and Freyja, became part of the Æsir. Nonetheless, the values of the Vanir continued. Baldr married Nanna, and the goddess Idunn, with her magic apples, was able to keep the Æsir gods young. As we will see in chapter 10 of this book, I believe that both Nanna and Idunn had their roots among the Vanir. This is supported by mythologist Rudolph Simek, who says that because the apples of Idunn are considered a fertility symbol, she "belongs to the fertility goddesses"[18] and thus is one of the Vanir.

But back to Baldr. Loki, the trickster god of the Æsir, enjoys stirring up trouble by continually confronting the gods and goddesses on their hypocrisy. In the likely words of Loki, "How can the gods who fight daily also love and cherish Baldr because of his gentleness?" Because of the gods' deep love of Baldr, when Baldr has a dream of his own death, Frigg, his mother, searches the world to obtain oaths from all substances that none will harm her son. With this assurance it becomes a sport among the gods to throw these substances at Baldr, knowing that he will not be harmed by them. But Frigg missed receiving an oath from one substance, mistletoe. Through his powers of shape-shifting and deception, Loki learns of this overlooked substance, makes a dart out of mistletoe, and gives it to Hǫðr, Baldr's blind brother. With Loki's help in aiming his arm, Hǫðr throws the dart that kills Baldr. It is this act of Loki's that leads the gods to search for and imprison him, an act that is the start of the three endless winters that lead to the final battle, Ragnarǫk. At Ragnarǫk all the gods die, and Baldr is reborn to become the new god of gods. Baldr, the nurturing, beloved, and gentle son of Odin, but also of the lineage of the Vanir through his mother's side, brings us into a new age of nurturance and compassion, a world that again values and reveres the Great Mother. We will learn more of these ancient Nordic stories as this book progresses.

The rebirth of Baldr has taken place for centuries in our own individual and personal cycles of death and rebirth. Now that we are on the verge of a new enchanted world of peace and love, it is now the time for the rebirth of Baldr in Nordic mythology, and in the larger world, paralleling the ending of the Mayan calendar and the second coming of Christ.

FINDING HOPE IN THE CURRENT STATE OF THE WORLD

There are those who, clinging to the old ways, would deny that we are on the verge of this new age, an age of harmony through the unification of the dichotomies that have caused our present turmoil; an age of reconnecting to our roots in Mother Earth instead of raping her in the hope of finding fulfillment in materiality; an age of appreciating the feminine nature of justice, wisdom, and intelligence; an age of the power of seeing into the past, future, and distant places in the present, not limited by time or distance; an age of the power of using ecstatic postures to attain ecstatic trance states. We see these clingers to the past all around us: when threatened by these progressive thoughts they use fear to control others to maintain their obscene material wealth. They have their proponents in many governmental, religious, and other institutions. When Gebser's book was first published in 1949, he offered a fascinating description of these sword-wielding clingers to a fast-fading age:

> Soon we will witness the rise of some potentate or dictator who will pass himself off as a "savior" or healer and allow himself to be worshiped as such. But anyone who does this in the days to come, and is thereby confined to time and is visible in it, has nothing to do with the true manifestation of the one who, in time-free transparency, will make the "future" present. The one who remains confined in time will thus be less than a mere adversary; he will be the ruinous expression of man's ultimate alienation from himself and the world.[19]

How many of these potentates do we hear today on TV and the radio?

As the years pass, it is apparent that this evolution of consciousness and enlightenment that is taking us into a new age cannot be stopped, because according to Calleman, this evolution comes not from our personal decisions, but from beyond us, from the flow of a cosmic plan that was predicted in the Mayan calendar.[20] With faith in this unstoppable evolution it becomes easier to watch those who try to stop the cosmic flow with a smile on our face, knowing that this duality will dissolve into unity when we accept the rebirth of Baldr, or for some, the return of Christ—when literal interpretations of these myths are transcended and we realize that such miracles happen each day with the setting of the sun and the "rebirth" of a new world with every sunrise.

2

THE POWERS OF
ECSTATIC AND
HYPNOTIC TRANCE

Hans-Peter Hasenfratz, with his wealth of knowledge of ancient Nordic literature, identifies among the ways of inducing ecstatic experiences the use of specific body postures.[1] Barbara Hand Clow, a student of Felicitas Goodman and a certified instructor of the Cuyamungue Method of inducing ecstatic trance, uses ecstatic body postures "to penetrate the consciousness" of the worlds of the Mayan calendar. She says her work with the ritual postures has given her "the best insights about the regional people.[2] I too am a certified instructor of the Cuyamungue Method and have found that the ecstatic experiences I receive while using these ritual body postures have given me new insights into the consciousness of the ancient people of Northern Europe. This chapter will present a summary of Felicitas Goodman's research using ecstatic body postures, research that validates Hasenfratz's recognition that ecstatic experiences can be induced through the use of specific body postures. What I have learned from Goodman's research has provided me with the means to attain the ecstatic trance experiences that I present in the first part of this book.

FELICITAS GOODMAN'S RESEARCH

Felicitas Goodman was born in Hungary and educated in Germany. She was fluent in many languages, so when she came to the United States after the Second World War she initially worked as a translator. In 1965, at the age of fifty-one, she decided to return to academia to pursue a graduate degree in cultural anthropology at Ohio State University. There she met Dr. Erika Bourguignon, a professor of anthropology who was researching religious trance states in small societies. Her research caught Goodman's interest, and Felicitas pursued religious or ecstatic trance as her doctoral dissertation goal. The subjects of her research were members of several Apostolic churches of the Spanish- and Mayan-speaking cultures of Mexico. She sought to determine the necessary conditions that led the members of these churches to be possessed by the Holy Spirit such that they spoke in tongues. She concluded that there are five such conditions:[3]

1. Participants need a private physical space separate from their activities of everyday life.
2. They need to come to that space with the expectation of a non-ordinary state of consciousness.
3. They need to believe that the experience is not crazy, but normal, enjoyable, and pleasurable.
4. Meditative techniques need to be offered to help each participant concentrate, such as the technique of counting one's breaths.
5. Rhythmic stimulation of the nervous system is required, such as that provided by the clapping of hands, the shaking of a rattle, or the beating of a drum.

Upon returning to her students at Denison University, where she taught subsequent to receiving her doctorate, Felicitas attempted to use these criteria with her students, but with limited success. She then discovered a journal article by the Canadian psychologist V. F. Emerson on the physiological changes in a person as a result of different meditative body postures or positions. This discovery led Goodman to consult books and journals depicting ancient and contemporary primitive art, seeking postures she believed were used by shamans. She eventually identified four or five dozen such postures, which she then used successfully with her students. This experience led her to develop a procedure that included the above necessary elements plus the use of specific body postures, a procedure that follows five steps:[4]

1. Preparation: Upon entering the meeting space, participants are instructed as to the appropriate attitude. This preparation may take many different forms but may include time for each person to express his or her personal concerns or intent. During this time of preparation, the facilitator then describes the posture to be used during the ritual portion of the experience, and the posture is practiced by each person in the group. Each person, as well as the rattle or drum being used, are then cleansed using the smoke of a smudging bundle of herbs or of incense.

2. Sacred space: With this preparation, the meeting space is then made sacred through the calling of the spirits of the four directions and of Father Sky and Mother Earth; a gift of cornmeal is offered to these spirits to welcome them to the sacred space.

3. Quieting of inner dialogue: The person's inner dialogue is then quieted with a period of silence (five minutes), during which time the person focuses on his or her breathing. I often suggest that with each breath, as the person inhales, they inhale a sense of calmness, and as they exhale, they let this calmness go deeper and spread throughout the body.

4. Stimulation of the nervous system: The period of silence is then ended with the shake of the rattle or the beat of the drum, and each person then takes the intended posture. The rattle shakes or drum beats at about 210 beats per minute for a period of fifteen minutes to stimulate the nervous system and bring the person into a state of ecstatic trance.

5. The ritual: The intent of the session, as established or defined by the posture, gives direction to the ecstatic trance. The enactment of this ritual in using one's body in a particular posture moves the person into the intended domain of alternate reality.

Following the ecstatic experience, participants are given time to record their experiences in their journals; I usually request that each person record his or her ecstatic experience on a 5x7 index card. The members of the group are then given the opportunity to share their experience, as recorded on the card, with the group. Afterward, I collect the cards, transcribe each person's ecstatic experience into a separate computer file, and return the individual descriptions to each person via e-mail.* This delay of several days in my returning the transcribed accounts to participants allows group members to keep their experiences more alive in their minds.

When I first attempted to replicate Goodman's work in a 2007 International Association for the Study of Dreams workshop, in Sonoma, California, I was amazed at the consistency of the results of her research. Apparently, as Goodman collected more and more ecstatic trance experiences it became clear to her that the different postures produced very specific results: some postures produced an experience of energy entering the body for healing, others were for spirit traveling outside the body, some were for going into the Lower World or underworld, some were for traveling in our earthly realm or the Middle World, and some were for traveling into the Sky World or upper world. There were specific postures for divination and for answering questions or making predictions about the future, for metamorphosis or shapeshifting (in which one would become some spirit animal), for initiation or promoting a death/rebirth experience, and for celebration or calling the spirits.

---

*My notecard collection of more than 1,000 ecstatic experiences led me to write an earlier book, *The Power of Ecstatic Trance: Practices for Healing, Spiritual Growth and Accessing the Universal Mind.*

The ancient and contemporary primitive art on which the ecstatic trance postures are based is found in all parts of the world; frequently a particular ecstatic posture from one part of the world may be found in nearly the same form in other cultures. For this book I have selected art figures found in Denmark and Sweden, a few of which are also found in other parts of the world, while several are unique to Northern Europe. One particular posture, the Hallstatt Warrior, is from Germany. This Realm of the Dead posture, an example of which I also found on the island of Fyn in Denmark, has been one of the most powerful postures, providing me with some of my most vivid ecstatic trance experiences, including my experiences of going back in time to commune with my ancestors. The next chapter will present the specific postures I use to better understand the magical powers of the Nordic people and my personal heritage.

UNDERSTANDING THE INTENT
OF A POSTURE

Felicitas Goodman, the founder of the Cuyamungue Institute, near Santa Fe, New Mexico, and others, including Belinda Gore, a student and colleague of Felicitas, have examined the ecstatic experiences of many people in using each ecstatic posture. From this research they have determined the intent in using a particular posture, for example, whether for going into the underworld, for divination, or for healing. Here I suggest two more steps to best understand the intent of a posture.

First, with each group I ask participants to take and hold the posture during the preparatory segment of the session; while holding the posture I ask group members to put into words what they think the posture is trying to express. I have had many fascinating comments. For example, two of the divination postures, the Mayan Oracle and the Jama-Coaque Diviner, have a raised left arm and hand with closed fingers a few inches in front of the face, a posture not a whole lot different from the Freyr Diviner posture presented in the next chapter. Participants have compared these postures to Rodin's *The Thinker,* except that Rodin's figure's head rests against his fist, making the figure seem more closed, while the ecstatic trance postures are more open— open to thinking outside of or beyond the individual, with more openness to thoughts that might come from beyond. In the Freyr Diviner, the figure uses his left hand to hang on to or stroke his chin or beard— again, a more open posture than *The Thinker.* Thus, each of these postures expresses the deep thought of searching for an answer.

The second step is to put oneself in the shoes—or, more accurately, the bare feet—of the shaman and ask: *If I wanted to find the answer to some question or to look into the future, as with divination, what posture would best express that need?* I think that postures similar to the Mayan Oracle such as the Jama-Coaque Diviner or the Freyr Diviner best meets that need. Other divination postures do not express this feeling as directly, but most do express a sense of alertness.

In the Bear Spirit (see pages 36–38), a healing posture, which is a posture found most frequently in all cultures, the person stands with shoulders back and chest expanded, with the hands resting on the lower abdomen, either flat with the thumb and first finger of each hand forming a diamond just below the navel, or with the fingers folded under. In this posture one can feel one's abdomen rising and falling as you breathe (i.e., if you are breathing correctly, from the diaphragm). From my experience and from the comments of others who have used this posture, it expresses a feeling of growing ego strength, a feeling of self-confidence, and a feeling that each breath brings a flow of energy into the body, energy that can also be considered healing. As a shaman seeking strength and energy for healing or as a warrior who seeks to increase his focus, energy, and strength in preparing for battle, I think this is the posture I would take. One of my early ecstatic experiences suggests that this posture may have been a posture used by the berserkers, the warriors reported in Old Norse literature to have fought in a nearly uncontrollable, trancelike fury, for going into their frenzied fighting trance. The fact that the word *berserk* means "bear shirt" supports this relationship between these warriors and the bear.

The postures for journeying into the Upper and Lower worlds also express the direction of the journey. In the Tanum Sky World posture (one of the postures I uncovered, see pages 40–42), the figure is not firmly planted on the earth, but is instead lying at a 37-degree angle from the horizontal, thus the inherent instability of this posture suggests floating or flying upward. Conversely, with three of the postures for journeying into the Lower World, the person lies prone on the ground. There are two commonly used prone postures for this type of journey: In the Jivaro South American Lower World posture, the person lies on his or her back with the back of the left wrist resting on the forehead and the right arm down to the side. In the Sami Lower World posture, you lie on your stomach with arms extended above your head, with the right arm extended out a little farther than the left, with both palms down. Both these underworld postures express well the direction of the journey for which they are intended. Each time I have used either of these two prone postures I have felt myself sliding or gliding downward into a cave or into water. In 2006 I had an opportunity to spend some time in the area of Tanum, Sweden, studying the ancient rock carvings of the area. There I found a number of hero-warrior figures in the 37-degree pose in their journey to the Sky World, or Valhalla, and one lying horizontal as in the underworld postures, traveling to the realm of those who died of illness and old age.

Another underworld posture, the Hallstatt Warrior (see pages 44–45), from around the fifth century BCE, found near Hirschlanden, in Baden-Wuerttemberg, Germany, takes us more specifically into the Realm of the Dead. In this posture the warrior wraps his arms across his chest as if he is going into a place that is cold and damp, such as the Realm of the Dead, and his posture expresses apprehension about where he is going. It was this posture that provided me with one of my earliest experiences of going back in time to visit a Stone Age ancestor in Germany. I recently found this same posture in a figurine in Denmark.

It has been suggested by my ecstatic posture group that the initiation and death/rebirth posture known as the Feathered Serpent, with the backs of her fingers resting on her hips and her elbows out to the side, expresses defiance or a sense of "I am ready for anything." The Nyborg Man, a posture found near Nyborg on the island of Funen, in Denmark, stands in a posture similar to the Feathered Serpent, much like a figure of Odin found in Southern Sweden. Initially, a person tends to hang on to and fears letting go of that part of him- or herself that needs to die, a part that may in some way be unhealthy and ineffective. But as the person grows in ego strength it becomes more and more apparent that that part needs to die and a new self, with greater health, strength, and effectiveness, needs to be born. Eventually the person faces the situation with a sense of "I am ready," a sense, even, of defiance in letting the unhealthy, ineffective part die. One person suggested that the elbows-out gesture is like feathery wings ready to fly in rising from the dead, while the feet are planted, as the serpent is also attached to the earth. For the shaman who recognizes the need for death and rebirth, this posture would well express this readiness.

In examining the many metamorphosis or shape-shifting postures, we see that in some, such as the Olmec Prince, the person's arms are extended forward as if using them like the forelegs of an animal. The Cernunnos posture (see pages 50–51) seen in an artifact from Scandinavia and which has been found to lead to shape-shifting, does not specifically show this feature. This figure, which appears on a cauldron from around 100 BCE, was found in Denmark and is thought to be the Celtic deity Cernunnos. The figure is sitting cross-legged, with the left leg in front of the right. He holds a snake in his left hand, a torque in his right hand, and is wearing a set of antlers on his head. With all of the other animals standing around him, it is apparent that he is identifying with these animals, and the intent to change shape is likely. As a shaman sets upon changing into the shape of a particular animal, I would likely place myself among animals and even wear something of the animal in question, such as a set of antlers. The Norse goddess

Freyja had a falcon-skin cloak to wear in order to fly like a bird, a cloak that in another story was borrowed by Loki in order to change his shape into that of an eagle.

The power of a posture thus includes how it expresses what a shaman wants to accomplish, i.e., going within to heal; journeying into the Lower World, the Realm of the Dead, or the Sky World, the realm of the gods; shifting shape; preparing to die and be reborn; or seeking an answer to a question or a direction in life.

THE UNIVERSAL MIND

I write extensively about attaining the universal mind in my book *The Power of Ecstatic Trance*. I will briefly describe it here.

My experience with hypnosis has generally been to use it to journey into the realm of the unconscious mind. The experiences that come from the unconscious are in a different language than that of our rational, conscious experience. The unconscious uses the language of metaphor, a language that encodes our life experiences in the shorthand of images. There are times, though, when a person's experience seems to come from somewhere beyond the unconscious yet is still in the language of metaphor. The clearest examples of such experiences from beyond are the frequent mutual experiences that occur in ecstatic trance between members of a group. To offer one example, which I described in *The Power of Ecstatic Trance*:

> Sarah, an early member of our ecstatic trance group, saw my head open up
> as tiny, colorful birds flew out and all around the room. She then felt her legs
> become rigid as she slowly turned into a marble statue. At the same time
> I saw Sarah turning into shimmering colors, and then she began to shrink
> and then expand in length, up and down several times; then the shimmering
> colors flew overhead around the room and out the glass door, beckoning me
> to follow. When we were outside on the hill behind the house, both Sarah
> and I became trees, reflecting a similar rigidness as the marble statue.

A number of other, similar examples of mutual experiences are offered in *The Power of Ecstatic Trance*. Such experiences suggest mental telepathy or extrasensory perception, with the perception of accessing the thoughts of another person. This has happened frequently enough for me to become a believer in the fact that we can access thoughts from beyond our own mind, whether consciously or unconsciously, thoughts that come from what I call the *universal mind*.

What is the form of this universal mind? Rupert Sheldrake, author, parapsychologist, and former biochemist and plant physiologist, suggests that everything possesses an energy field, which he calls a *morphic field*.[5] He relates the concept of the morphic field to the well-documented gravitational fields of astrophysics and the electromagnetic fields of particle physics. It logically follows that since our body is composed of atoms, and since each atom has its own field, then each cell of our body has its field and each organ would therefore have its field. Thus, we have a liver field, a spleen field, etc. Our whole body has its field, and the collection of all humans has its field. Sheldrake believes that these fields hold memories, and we have the ability to access these memories, past, present, and future. He offers many examples, but one fascinating one that everyone has experienced is seeing a flock of birds diving and turning in unison; he attributes this ability to act in unison to the field that surrounds the flock of birds.

Integral theorist and philosopher Ervin Laszlo suggests that this field, which he names the *Akashic field,* contains all the information that exists from the beginning of time. He suggests that it is holographic in nature, that it can be accessed from anywhere, at any time, and that we can learn to access it. He suggests that the cytoskeletal structure of our brain, which has been thought to be simply a structure that holds the neurons in our brain in place, is composed of the receptors that allow us to access this Akashic or morphic field—what I call the *universal mind*.[6]

Various writers offer many examples of accessing the universal mind. In *Entangled Minds: Extrasensory Experiences in a Quantum Reality,* parapsychologist Dean Radin offers many examples that demonstrate the power and reality of extrasensory perception and psychokinesis. When the theories of modern physics are applied to human consciousness, as is done convincingly by Fritjof Capra in his best-selling book *The Tao of Physics,* the reality of the universal mind and our ability to access it cannot be denied.

Characteristics of the Universal Mind

The universal mind expresses itself in the language of metaphor, as does the language of the unconscious. Metaphor may be a simplifying way of organizing this mass of information, yet at times what we experience from the unconscious and universal minds is very concrete or rational. For example, in college I awakened one morning with the solution to a trigonometric proof that I had been unable to solve the evening before. In Laszlo's book *The Akashic Experience,* psychologist Stanley Krippner recalls the moment he realized that a close friend had died. Krippner had developed a close relationship with the Native American medicine man Rolling Thunder and his wife, Spotted Fawn. Fourteen years into this relationship while at a conference in Mexico Krippner had a dream that he arrived at Rolling Thunder's ranch, and as he arrived he saw Rolling Thunder driving away with a somber expression on his face. When he stopped and asked Rolling Thunder about Spotten Fawn, Rolling Thunder pointed to the back of the truck where laid a wooden casket. The next morning Krippner also had a hypnopomic image in which he heard Spotted Fawn's voice telling him, "You know, I won't be seeing you any more." Upon returning to the states he learned that Spotted Fawn had died the same night as his dream.

Native American historian Vine Deloria, in his last book before his death, *The World We Used to Live In,* compiled many stories of the extraordinary experiences of the indigenous people of North America. To offer just one example: Siya'ka told the story of when he lost two horses. White Shield, using his way of knowing, told Siya'ka that his horses were fifteen miles west of Porcupine Hills, at the fork of

Porcupine Creek. He knew that a traveler was coming from that direction and would return the horses. This proved to be true—a neighbor of Siya'ka had been on his way home when he recognized the horses and brought them back.[7] Such information was gained not through the five senses, but through what we might call extrasensory perception or the universal mind, and it was expressed in a very concrete, and not metaphoric manner.

To access the universal mind, we need to let go of the rational thought process that interferes with or inhibits our openness to the universal mind. Laszlo suggests that the information contained in the universal mind is stored holographically. Psychologist and lucid dream researcher Robert Waggoner asks the question "What is behind the dream?" or "Where does the dream come from?" and receives an experience of seeing blue light.[8] In a number of ecstatic experiences I have collected I have found similar experiences of seeing blue light or energy in a matrix or grid, as strands or fibers. To offer one example, Susanne had the following experience:

> I am a mummy wrapped in muslin. My spirit leaves my body as a snowy white owl. It says "fear nothing." I see huge strands of DNA, vibrating, undulating, intertwining, and moving very fast. The DNA seems like a huge paper Chinese dragon in a parade. I have a strong feeling the DNA is very driven with purpose, the purpose being that of evolution into higher forms of being. It cannot be stopped. As myself doing the exercise, I am shaking and undulating too. I feel energy intertwining, going up my spine. The owl hugs my mummy self and untwines my wrappings. I dance with the DNA.

In what Jean Gebser describes as the mythical era of consciousness, life and the phenomena of the earth and the universe are described metaphorically in the form of the many myths found in all parts of the world. I suggest that these metaphoric myths were experienced ecstatically by our ancient ancestors and recorded during this bygone era when the ways of written language also developed. My journeying with the Hallstatt Warrior has taken me to the Realm of the Dead, as described in the ancient Nordic myths. These ancient Nordic images provide me with a scaffold on which to build my experiences. The experiences are metaphoric; I do not believe in them literally, just as I do not literally believe in the Christian images of a red devil with horns and a hell of fire and brimstone, which I believe are rather the metaphoric encoding of the guilt and self-punishment we experience when we do something we know is wrong.

The story from Nordic mythology of the final battle, Ragnarǫk, and Baldr's rebirth is relived daily with the retelling of the story of the death of Baldr at sunset and his rebirth at sunrise, as well as his death in the winter and rebirth in spring, and of death and rebirth at the times of significant change in our lives, as we experience the death of unhealthy parts of ourselves and rebirth into health. Though many Christians are stuck in a literal world of waiting for the Second Coming in a very real, concrete sense, I believe that the more powerful story would be to recognize that this death and rebirth as described in the Christian tradition is a continued experience that happens daily, seasonally, and with the personal changes in our lives.

HYPNOTIC TRANCE

Whereas in part 1 of this book I use ecstatic trance in my journey to better understand the world of the ancient Nordic people, in part 2 I use hypnotic trance. Whereas ecstatic trance posture work is induced with the rapid beat of a drum or the shake of a rattle, hypnotic trance is induced with soft and slow speech that relies on the concept of what is known as the *yes-set* technique, outlined and pioneered by psychiatrist and hypnotherapy sage Milton Erickson, which refers to inducing a repetitive series of "yes" answers, establishing a habitual compliance on the part of the hypnotic subject.[9]

As a psychotherapist I have used hypnosis over the last thirty-five years. To induce trance I speak to a client in such a way that I have some certainty that the client can answer "yes" to whatever I may say. To give an example: If the client is sitting in a chair with his or her back resting against the back of the chair and hands resting in the lap, I might speak slowly and softly, saying such things as, "Feel the heaviness of your hands resting on your legs, feel the warmth between your back and the back of the chair, feel the tightness of your jeans across your knees, and as you breathe, feel your chest rising and falling, and feel the slight movement of your clothing against your chest." The client can then answer "yes" to all these statements as I speak them slowly and pace my words to the rate of the client's breathing. I then can begin to talk about the client's life and feelings, and I can make certain suggestions, such as asking the person to take certain feelings back through time or down into the unconscious to see when, where, and why he or she first had these feelings. I can then make suggestions as to how these feelings can be dealt with differently. All of what is said is carefully paced and is said with some certainty that the person can continue to answer "yes," affirming the experience. With this technique of induction, the person in trance experiences a time distortion, a feeling of heaviness, and a feeling of deep relaxation. It does not take much practice for clients to be able to subsequently attain these feelings of trance, and they quickly learn to attain these feelings of deep relaxation on their own. Most importantly, as I lead my clients into trance in this way, I am in an equally deep trance myself, and I have discovered that I can trust that I know what they are thinking and feeling because we are experiencing the same thing together.

With so many years of experience with hypnosis, I have learned to quickly go into a deep trance on my own and have had major surgery and several dental root canals without anesthesia by using this ability. It is this very same ability that I use to access the experiences presented in part 2 of this book to better understand the ancient mythology of the Nordic people. These experiences gave me the "lost" myths that describe the values and beliefs of those who worshipped the Great

Mother, Moðir—the values that will return and are returning with the Nydagan, the New Dawn.

Hypnotic trance is physiologically different from ecstatic trance, but both are very powerful and useful. The autonomic nervous system is composed of two opposing systems, the sympathetic and parasympathetic. In hypnotic trance, the parasympathetic nervous system takes over: our heart rate slows, our blood vessels dilate, our blood pressure drops, our breathing rate slows, our skin cools and becomes dry, and our body goes into a state of deep relaxation. Hypnosis leads the person into this altered state of deep relaxation. Sometimes, however, a person may experience something terrifying in hypnotic trance, in which case the sympathetic nervous system takes over. The sympathetic nervous system controls the opposite response to the relaxation response. It is the response to an emergency, when our blood pressure rises. We become very alert, we might break out in a sweat, and in the extreme we could wet ourselves.

What is interesting with ecstatic trance is that aspects of both the sympathetic and parasympathetic nervous systems are stimulated at the same time. The rattling or drumming keeps the sympathetic system stimulated, and we have the unusual response of low blood pressure, a parasympathetic response, and at the same time increased heart rate, a sympathetic response. This unusual combination of two contradictory responses has been seen in the process of dying, and thus may explain why sometimes shamans talk of their ecstatic experience as a near-death experience.

The hypnotic trance narratives of part 2 of this book were written around the year 2000, while I was still using hypnosis and before I learned of ecstatic trance. Only in about 2004 did I first read about ecstatic trance posture work and became fascinated with its power. Thus, with this introduction to the ecstatic and hypnotic trance experiences, we will now examine the postures that will be used in the next few chapters.

3
NORDIC POSTURES

The artifacts that provide us with many of the ecstatic postures described in this chapter were found in either Denmark or Sweden. The Hallstatt Warrior—a Realm of the Dead posture and among Felicitas Goodman's first described postures—and the Danish metamorphosis posture Cernunnos, revealed by Belinda Gore, were found among artifacts in Denmark. The Bear Spirit, the Feathered Serpent, the Lascaux Cave Sky World, and the Jivaro South American Lower World postures were originally revealed and named after artifacts found in other places of the world. The Bear Spirit has also been found in artifacts in Scandinavia, and I have uncovered Nordic versions of the other three postures in Scandinavian artifacts—Feathered Serpent in the form of Nyborg Man, Lascaux Cave Sky World in the form of Tanum Sky World, and Jivaro South American Lower World in the form of Tanum Lower World postures. I also discovered and used for the first time two new postures specific to Scandinavia, the Freyr Diviner and the Freyja Initiation postures.

The ecstatic experiences recounted in the following six chapters are dated as to when they occurred. Those that occurred before November 27, 2011, spontaneously provided Nordic content, but after that date the ecstatic trance experiences were more directed and intentional for this book and thus their Nordic content was more likely. Before that date, some of the Nordic experiences occurred while using postures other than specific Nordic postures, i.e., the Tennessee Diviner, the Olmec Prince, the Mayan Oracle, and the Priestess of Malta. After that date, for the purpose of this book, I used the Nordic postures, presented in this chapter.

HEALING POSTURE

Bear Spirit

Three figurines that stand in the Bear Spirit, a posture that dates from between 400 and 550 CE and made of gold, silver, and bronze, were found near Strängnäs, Sweden.[1] I had the opportunity to see these figures on a visit to the museum at Gamla Uppsala, Sweden. Figurines in this posture have been found in almost every area of the world, including this Northern European region. Felicitas Goodman and Belinda Gore have determined it to be a healing posture, and indeed in this posture participants often experience a flow of healing energy into and through their body. I would add that this healing posture is often used for an increase in ego strength, as mentioned in the previous chapter. I use this posture regularly during the five minutes of centering between calling the spirits from the six directions and the beginning of the ecstatic posture ritual with rattling or drumming. I find that using this posture, while quieting my mind and focusing on my breathing, brings to me a powerful experience of strength. I believe this posture was used by the ancient warriors known as *berserkers* as they worked themselves up into a fighting frenzy.

The Northwest Pacific Coast carving of the Bear Spirit is used as the logo for the Cuyamungue Institute. This Native American wood carving shows a human figure standing in this posture with the spirit bear squatting behind, holding him. This specific carving is what gave this posture its name.

Two other Nordic healing postures need to be mentioned, though they are not a focus for our journey. One is the Snake Woman of Faardal,[2] determined by Felicitas Goodman to be a healing posture, and

The Bear Spirit Posture

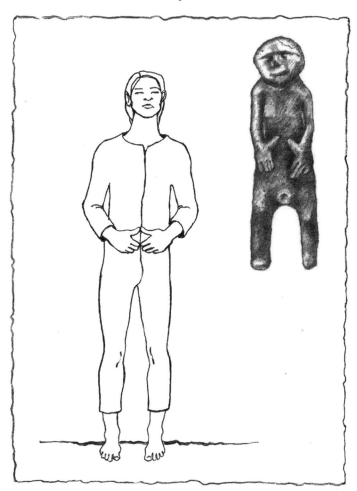

Stand with your feet parallel, about six inches apart, with toes forward and knees not locked but slightly bent. Your hands are resting relaxed on your abdomen, with your thumbs touching and fingers spread apart, flat or together and bent under, such that the first knuckles of your index fingers are above your navel, forming a triangle. Your elbows rest easily at your sides. Your eyes are closed and your head is gently tipped back as though you're looking at a point where the wall meets the ceiling.

the other is a figurine found on the Danish island of Fyn[3] that is standing in the Chiltan Spirit, another healing posture described in Belinda Gore's first book, *Ecstatic Body Postures*.

DIVINATION POSTURE

Freyr Diviner

The posture used the most in part 1 of this book is the Freyr Diviner, taken from a figurine from the eleventh century found in Rällinge, Södermanland, Sweden.[4] Freyr, a Vanir god, the son of Njord and the brother of Freyja, is considered a fertility god, but he is also a warrior in some stories. This figurine is thought to be Freyr because being a fertility god he has a large and erect penis. I have found this posture quite effective in taking me back to the ancient times of the Nordic people, the people whom I believe are my ancestors.

Three other figurines somewhat similar to the Freyr figurine have also been found, in which the figure strokes his beard, though in each case with both hands.[5] Such stroking of one's beard is a gesture of thoughtfulness, and the similarities among the figurines suggests that stroking with both hands may also be an element of a divination posture. I have tried this posture stroking my short beard with my right elbow resting on my right knee, but this required that I bend forward and tilt my head downward. While bending in this slightly awkward way I did not feel as if I was leaving myself open to accessing the universal mind. The posture was more powerful when I raised my elbow off my knee, thus allowing me to sit up straight with my chin up so that my eyes were facing forward.

The Freyr Diviner

Sit cross-legged with the right leg in front of the left. Your left hand clasps the ankle of your right leg, while your right hand clasps or strokes your chin or beard. Your right elbow rests on your right knee if your beard is long enough; otherwise, place your elbow above your knee. Look straight ahead with eyes closed.

SPIRIT JOURNEY POSTURES

According to Scandinavian mythology, when people died there were three places they might go: Valhalla in the Sky World, the Realm of the Dead in the underworld, or with Freyja, who takes half of the fallen warriors whenever she goes into battle.[6] We assume she takes them to her place, Fólkvangr, to Gæfuleysabjarg, the "cliff of lucklessness." The remaining heroes are taken to Valhalla by the Valkyries, where they will fight each day; if they are injured or die in these fights they are healed or brought back to life to again fight the next day.

Those who die "unheroic" deaths due to illness or old age are taken to the underworld, where the goddess Hel looks after them in the Realm of the Dead. For this journey to the Lower World the burial generally involves a ship. The dead are sometimes placed aboard a ship that is set adrift, or the ship may be burnt, or sometimes it is buried in a large mound. At other times they are buried in graves and stones are placed on the grave in the formation of a ship. With this information, let us now consider rock carvings found near Tanum, Sweden.

Tanum Sky World

Among the Bronze Age petroglyphs at Tanum there are at least five figures that are seen rising upward above their ship at approximately a 37-degree angle, similar to the Lascaux Cave posture found among the petroglyphs at the French archaeology site famous for its Palaeolithic cave paintings. The Tanum warriors are carrying swords; their arms either rest at their sides or one (the right) or both are raised above their heads.[7] In one case the man has wings. They are obviously men because they all have penises.

A king or chieftain often had twelve berserkers among his other warriors or retainers who fought for him. Years ago, I heard the story

The Tanum Sky World Posture

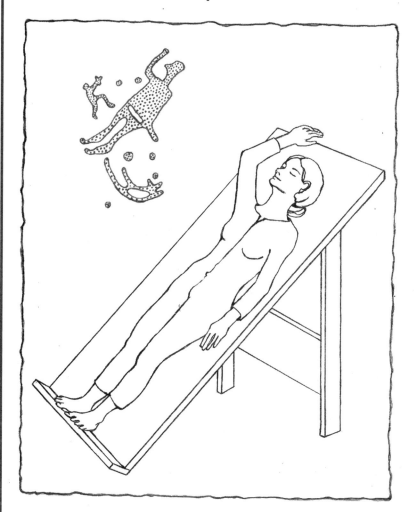

Lie on a launching pad* at a 37-degree angle. Your legs and feet are together. Your arms resting at your side, or one, your right, or both may be raised above your head.

———————————

*The launching pad is a platform slanted at 37 degrees, strong enough to support a reclining person.

that when a berserker worked himself up into a fighting frenzy, the sign that he was sufficiently worked up was his erect penis, suggesting that these fighting men could be berserkers. Yet not all warriors were berserkers. Certainly I would think that an erection would be a distraction to a warlike frenzy, and thus this belief does not make a lot of sense. On the other hand, that might not be true for some men, e.g., aggressive, angry men who become involved in such violent situations as rape; and if true in instances of rape, maybe too for some men in war. When I tried to find the source of this story on the Internet, a lot was said about this belief but no specific source was mentioned. The source may possibly be found in the many images shown in these rock carvings. Similarly, what is the source of the belief that Viking warriors wore helmets with horns? Such horned helmets have never been found in Viking archaeological sites, yet they are shown in some of these same petroglyphs, which date from the Bronze Age, approximately 1800 to 500 BCE, well before the historical age of the Viking raids that occurred between the eighth and the eleventh century CE.

Tanum Lower World

In one petroglyph a woman is kneeling, bending over the head of a reclining warrior. A ship extends from or is attached to the warrior's left foot. Neither arm is visible.[8] This figure is shown off to the left of a scene of battle, and not far above this figure is a man and woman standing, embracing and kissing, and behind the kissing couple is standing a man with a raised ax (see illustrations of these Tanum battle petroglyphs on my website, www.imaginalmind.net). The message seems quite clear that this man did not die a hero in battle, but was distracted from the battle by his attraction to a woman, thus he is on his way to the underworld. For the warrior, everything else in life needs to be secondary or casual, even love. This figure appeared

The Tanum Lower World Posture

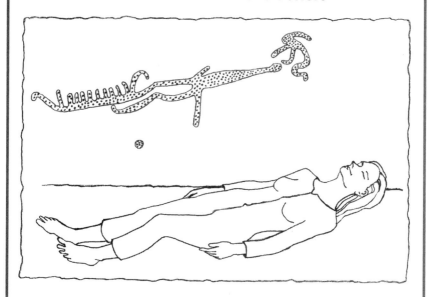

Lie on your back with your arms at your sides close to your body. Your legs are essentially parallel, though your left knee may be slightly raised.

without arms, suggesting a total inability to control his environment. I assume that in this posture one's arms are lying at the side, close to the body. This posture is not greatly different from the Jivaro South American Lower World posture except for the latter's raised left arm with the wrist resting over one's eyes.

Hallstatt Warrior Posture

The Hallstatt Warrior, from Germany, has been very powerful for me in my journeying into the past, providing me with my most distant past experiences. This posture, as illustrated in my book *The Power of Ecstatic Trance,* is from the fifth century BCE, from Hirschlanden, in Baden-Württemberg, and it carries us into the Realm of the Dead. This same Realm of the Dead posture is also seen in a figurine found on the Island of Fyn in Denmark, and though the Danish figurine is missing its right arm, the position of the arm is easily inferred from the position of the remaining right hand as seen at the waist.[9] Because my earliest roots are in Germany before my ancestors migrated northward into Denmark and the Swedish west coast, both of these figurines have been important to me in helping me plumb the depths of my ancestral past.

The Hallstatt Warrior Posture

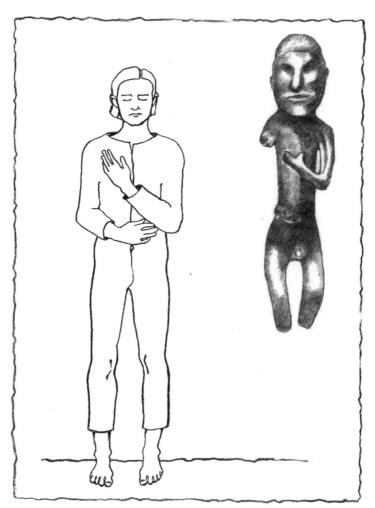

Stand with feet about five inches apart, toes pointed forward. Your knees may be slightly bent as in the Danish figure, or locked as in the Hallstatt Warrior. Place your right arm along your waist with the ball of your hand covering your navel. Your left arm rests up along your torso, with the left hand resting on the right breast with your fingers pointing toward the right shoulder. The Hallstatt Warrior shows more tension in the shoulders than does the Danish version of this posture. Your face is forward with eyes closed.

INITIATION OR DEATH/REBIRTH POSTURES

Nyborg Man

I often use the Nyborg Man posture to facilitate death/rebirth experiences, though I have found at least six other ancient figurines from Denmark and Sweden[10] in the same posture. The gold Nyborg Man figurine is from Slipshavnskogen, near Nyborg, Denmark, and measures seven centimeters high.[11] Another of the Feathered Serpent figurines, thought to be Odin because it has only one eye,[12] is not used as an example in this book because one arm has been broken off, whereas the Nyborg Man clearly shows both arms.

After the Freyr Diviner, this is the most-used posture in this book. I have found the Freyr experiences to be very descriptive in portraying life in the ancient times. The Nyborg Man, on the other hand, has provided more personal, feeling-full experiences of something that has changed within me in the experience—of the death of some part of me and the birth of something new. These have been powerful experiences that have added greatly to the depth of my understanding of what the people of the time were experiencing.

The Nyborg Man Posture

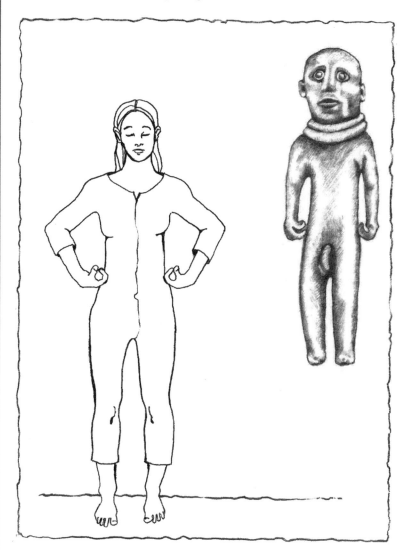

Stand with your feet parallel, about six inches apart, knees slightly bent with toes pointing straight ahead. Cup your hands and place them at your side at waist level with fingers pointing up and thumbs pointing forward, with your arms rounded outward and elbows pointing to either side. Face straight ahead with your eyes closed and your mouth slightly open.

Freyja Initiation

Another initiation/death and rebirth posture used in these ecstatic journeys is the Freyja Initiation posture. Freyja (meaning "the Lady") is a Vanir goddess associated with love, sexuality, beauty, gold, sorcery, and death.[13] She is the sister to Freyr and the daughter of Njord and is considered the most beautiful of the goddesses. She wears a gorgeous necklace, named Brísingamen (from Old Norse *brisinga,* meaning "flaming, glowing," and *men,* "jewelry, ornament"), made for her by the dwarfs. Many of the Nordic stories are of Freyja, who, though a fertility and love goddess, was also a warrior who rode a pig into battle. In an attempt to make peace between the Vanir and the Æsir, the leaders of the two races of deities decided to exchange some of their important personages, thus Njord, Freyr, and Freyja became part of the Æsir, and it was from Freyja that the Æsir learned the magic of the Vanir. She was a shape-shifter, and with her falcon cloak would sometimes become a falcon.

I use this posture when seeking deeper meaning from an ecstatic experience, and each time I use it I became a woman. It leads me, as a woman, to feelings of something changing in my ecstatic life—of the death and rebirth of something important within me.

The Freyja Initiation Posture

Stand with your feet spread hip-width apart and your arms crossed below your belly, right arm above the left arm, with the hand of the right arm clasping the left forearm. Your arms may be holding your pregnant belly.

METAMORPHOSIS POSTURE

Cernunnos

Another important Scandinavian posture is the Cernunnos meta-morphosis posture, described by Belinda Gore and named after the horned god of Celtic polytheism, though nothing is known about this god from literary sources, and details about his name, his cult, or his significance in Celtic religion are unknown. Though the source of this posture has been attributed to Celtic mythology, the figure was in fact found at Gundestrupp, in Denmark, on a cauldron from the third century BCE, an artifact that may be found today in a museum in Copenhagen. The cauldron shows Cernunnos wearing antlers and surrounded by animals: lions, dragons, elephants, boars, wolves, birds, and a dolphin. The torque in his one hand represents the power and authority of royalty, and the snake in his other hand indicates wisdom and sacred knowledge. Gore reports that many of the experiences associated with this posture are of shape-shifting into the world tree, or Yggdrasil.

I have used the Cernunnos posture wearing a pair of horns while holding a fabricated torque in my right hand and snake in my left. I have also used it without these accoutrements and have found each variation invites a different yet equally profound shape-shifting experience. Holding the torque and snake gives my arms a reason to be raised as branches of a tree that can hold life. With nothing in my closed fists, I had quite a different experience, in which my arms felt more like raised forelegs, with the energy of alertly watching, as in the alert energy of an animal. I would eventually find myself rolling forward off my buttocks, bringing my forelegs to the ground and wandering off as a four-legged animal. Thus, whereas without the accoutrements the shape-shifting experience is more like that of an animal, using the accoutrements of antlers, torque, and snake seems to change the experience to one of deeper spirituality, likely related to the world tree, royalty, and wisdom.

The Cernunnos Metamorphosis Posture

Sit on the floor with your legs crossed in front of you. Bring your right calf as close to your right thigh as possible, so that your foot rests in front of your crotch. Position your left leg so that the calf rests in front of your right leg. With your shoulders squared, hold your arms to the side of your body and bend your elbows so that your hands are at shoulder level, creating a V shape with each arm. Face forward, with your eyes and mouth slightly open as though you were preparing to whistle. An option is to wear a pair of horns on your head and hold a snake in your left hand and a torque in your right.

In searching through the pictures of ancient Scandinavia for artifacts showing ecstatic postures, the only posture that remains missing is a spirit journey posture for journeying to the Middle World. Despite this missing posture, the postures for healing, for divination, for journeying into the Upper and Lower worlds, for death and rebirth, and for metamorphosis have been sufficient for me to complete the ecstatic journeys I describe in the following six chapters.

PART TWO

The Lives of the Ancient Ones

Using Ecstatic Trance to Access Nordic Ancestors

Greater male physical strength was here not the basis for social oppression, organized warfare, or the concentration of private property in the hands of the strongest men. Neither did it provide the basis for supremacy of males over females or of "masculine" over "feminine" values. On the contrary, the prevailing ideology was gynocentric, or woman-centered, with the deity represented in female form.

Symbolized by the feminine Chalice or source of life, the generative, nurturing, and creative powers of nature— not the powers to destroy—were . . . given highest value. At the same time, the function of priestesses and priests seems to have been not to serve and give religious sanction to a brutal male elite but to benefit all the people in the community in the same way that the heads of clans administered the communally owned and worked lands.

RIANE EISLER, *THE CHALICE AND THE BLADE: OUR HISTORY, OUR FUTURE*

4

COMMUNING WITH ANCESTORS

An Overview

For the last several years I have used ecstatic postures to explore more deeply the lives of the ancient Nordic people, especially the postures for divination, journeying into the Realm of the Dead, and initiation or death/rebirth. I believe these ecstatic experiences provide useful descriptions of life as it was in the past, even as they address more personal concerns, such as my questions about my direction in life and defining who I am with regard to what life will be like to be living in the coming age with the rebirth of Baldr.

These experiences are, of course, coming from within me while in an ecstatic trance state. Although they cannot be definitively proven to be actual experiences from the past, I believe they do in fact come from the past via my tapping into the Akashic record or morphic field while in a trance state. Though the content is much as I would imagine the past to be, there are many details that have surprised me, details that I did not expect and could not have foreseen in almost every experience. For example, in chapter 6, which explores the transition period between the era of the Mother Goddess society and the era of the masculine warrior society, my experience of December 15, 2011, describes the platform on which a vǫlva, a shaman or seeress, sits to see into distant places or into the future. From my reading of the literature I knew that a vǫlva typically sat on a platform, but it never occurred to me that such a platform would be a regular feature of a home or hut, such that it was hinged and lifted from the wall. Could this detail be the product of my own twenty-first-century imagination, or could it have been a real feature of the huts of these ancestors, given that such visits from vǫlvas were important occasions for any family? In another experience in the same chapter, dated December 1, 2011, in which I was a farmer, I did not expect that my wife would practice divination, a practice I heretofore believed would have been used only by a vǫlva. If it were practiced by those other than vǫlvas, homes may indeed have had such platforms readily available, though in that experience my wife simply sat at the family table.

I found that each of my ecstatic experiences have had a metaphoric dimension that reflected some personal issue, answered a question, or provided direction, whether coming from the unconscious mind or the universal mind. For example, the skeletal faces I saw of my distant ancestor's great-great grandparents in my underworld experience of November 27, 2011, described in chapter 9, were metaphoric but also gave me information I was seeking: that the older world was more magical than the present world. I do not suggest that such experiences are actual experiences from the past of a person actually traveling into the underworld, yet they are real in the sense that in trance one can experience going into the underworld. I believe that these experiences open up a world of possibilities and bring alive the ancient world of the Norse and their extraordinary powers—powers that are available to us today if we cultivate them, powers that I have experienced first-hand in using the ecstatic postures. I expect that as I practice "tuning into" the Akashic or morphic field, I will glimpse images of the past and the lives of my ancient ancestors, or my own past lives.

One distinction between communing with ancestors and connecting with one's own past lives is that a line of ancestors would likely follow specific routes of migration, as happened in my ecstatic experiences, whereas the literature on past lives does not seem to follow such a geographically linear progression. For example, in my book *The Power of*

Ecstatic Trance, I describe how Jan, using the Hallstatt Warrior, which is based on a figure found in Germany from the fifth century BCE, had an experience in which he was an Alaskan native. Now, from what Jan knows of his genealogy he did not think this was his ancestor, but rather that this was a past-life experience. Others whom he met in this apparent past-life experience seem to be in his present life, though the relationships are different this time around: for example, Joe was his brother rather than the friend he is today, and Lois was his mother rather than his current wife. It is not uncommon for people in current lives to appear in past lives, though the relationships may change.

I used the Hallstatt Warrior, a Realm of the Dead posture, for the first in a series of distant ancestral experiences that began on January 17, 2010. With this posture I went back to a much earlier time, probably around 5000 BCE, in Germany, likely one of my ancestral places of origin. I was in a thatched hall, long and narrow, that sat near the entrance of a cave. A man wearing a bearskin was with me—not the leader but the second or third in command. He told me that the group of men in the hall was preparing to go out for a hunt in the morning. Some of the men were drawing in the dirt pictures of animals and drawing spears stuck in them. Others were carving, sharpening the ends of their spears. He then told me that since I was from the future, I must have some wisdom or knowledge that would help in the hunt. I shook my head no, but he was insistent that I was to lead them in the morning's hunt. We slept on the dirt floor around the fire, and in the morning I took the group in what felt to me like a random direction, though we did come to several deer. I motioned for the men, about a dozen of them, to spread out, and we herded the deer over a cliff. They all seemed overjoyed in appreciation, though I still felt as if I had done nothing of significance or had no special knowledge.

If this experience were to happen now, it is very unlikely that we would so casually greet someone from the future, though such encounters could have been more common and acceptable during that more magical era when the boundaries between time dimensions were more permeable. And it is true that the descriptions of the hut and even the practice of herding deer over a cliff could have come from stories that I have likely heard or read over the years. At the time of the ecstatic experience, the personal "takeaway" message to me was to have more confidence in myself. This narrative came during an ecstatic trance that I entered with the awareness that Germany is one of my ancestral homelands, and likely with the unspoken intent of visiting these ancestors. This German connection made this trance experience very special to me.

My next Nordic experience of going back in time occurred later that same year, on December 16, 2010, while again using the Hallstatt Warrior. In that trance journey I was the drummer on a Viking ship, beating the cadence (though drumming too fast) for those pulling the oars. We went along a river off the English Channel in Normandy and came to a dock and pulled in. It was my job to direct the unloading of the boat. The load was mainly animal hides. The chieftain went ashore to the main hall, the largest hut of the village. A teenage boy who turned out to be my son came running to the dock and told me that his grandfather—my father—was dying and that everyone had been waiting for me to get home. I turned the unloading over to someone else and hurried to our thatched cottage and went in. My papa was on the bed, and when I entered he looked at me and reached out his hand. I held it and felt it go limp, whereupon he passed. I looked around the room and saw my wife, who held rosary beads, and a priest. I felt disgusted to see these signs of Christian ways and started shaking a rattle to ward off the evil spirits from entering my father, as I knew he would have preferred it that way. The whole experience felt like the late 900s or early 1000 CE, a more recent time than the previous experience.

It turns out that one of my distant ancestors of twenty-five generations ago, according to my aunt, who painstakingly researched our genealogy, is Sir William de Willoughby, who was knighted by King Edward I in 1295. My aunt's and my mother's maiden name was Willoughby. Records of the origin of names indicate that Willoughby is a Norman name, thus in all probability my ancestry does go back to Normandy, and from there to Denmark. Thus, this experience supports my Norman heritage, though I do not deny that this knowledge of my genealogy could have influenced this ecstatic experience. What was interesting and surprising to me in this experience was the inner conflict I felt about the encroachment of Christianity into our lives and my need to do what I felt my father would have wanted. Another interesting observation, in light of my genealogy, is that my ancestors apparently were secondary leaders in the community. In this case, I had the responsibility of unloading the ship but I was not the chieftain.

My third experience in this ancestral journey sequence occurred on January 6, 2011, while using the Priestess of Malta Middle World posture. On this occasion I picked up from my earlier experience of coming in to the boat dock on a river in Normandy. This time I was going in the opposite direction, up the coast and into the North Sea around Jutland and down the east side toward what is now Germany. It was the beginning of winter, and I was just getting home from my merchant trip. My first concern was whether there were sufficient supplies for my family for winter. Did my sons and daughter do enough in preparation? My oldest son was left in charge. My wife was pregnant and doing little; she was almost due, and my daughter was attending her. The year was maybe the early 800s, several generations before the previous episode.

These three ecstatic experiences establish the range of time for the experiences I describe in the next four chapters—from the earliest time, in the era of the worship of the Mother Goddess, through the time of transition, and into the time of the masculine warrior era. The path of migration of what I believe to be my ancestors begins in central Germany and leads northward, into Denmark, to the island of Fyn, not far from present-day Ladby, where I experienced the peaceful village life of a people who worship the Great Mother. From there, my ancestors migrated to the west coast of Sweden, where they experienced the transition period, and then the beginning of life in which a masculine god was worshipped, a time of fighting as warriors. From there, my ancestors returned to live along the east coast of Jutland, in Denmark, before migrating to Normandy with the Viking invasion, around 900 CE.

In another trance experience, on June 26, 2011, in which I used the Sami Lower World posture, I quickly reviewed my heritage since the invasion of Normandy. In this journey back in time I was pressing my forehead into the ground and going down. My body followed, as if doing forward summersaults, down, down, deeper into the earth. I came to a cave, and my last summersault ended with me lying on my back on the floor of a large cavern, looking up. A phosphorescent stalactite hung down above me. A bear came over and looked down at me, then licked my face. I sat up, and the four men I had been with in several previous ecstatic experiences came in and sat in a circle, looking to me in a questioning way, as if we all were asking, "What do we do? Why are we here? What is going to happen?" Then the scene changed and we were sitting at the entrance of the cave around a fire, looking out into the night sky. A blue haze drifted in front of the full moon. We were looking for the answers to our questions. I had a sense that it had something to do with my ancestors. I saw my father in different parts of the world and my grandparents in the Philippine Islands. I went back to my great-grandparents in Ohio and back to past generations, to New York, the Netherlands, Germany, Normandy, and Denmark. I wondered what the message in the blue haze in front of the moon was—maybe it was telling me that I can experience the experiences of my ancestors.

With this sequence of experiences I made the decision to begin working on this book, and subsequently all my ecstatic experiences become directed toward this goal. An early, key question that informed all these sessions was "How can men who value the warrior gods of the Æsir and women who are nurturing and not warlike relate to each other?" Subsequently, on November 27, 2011, while using a Nordic adaptation of the Hallstatt Warrior I began the following journey:

I am a panther, stalking or walking cautiously along a path, first to the east, then down to the west, to the underworld, to the Realm of the Dead of the Norse, to the place of those who died of illness and old age, seeking an ancestor. I am safe going there as a panther; as a human I could go to the Realm of the Dead, but I would not be allowed to return. I sniff among the dead until I find the right person, sitting under dripping water from a ceiling, looking almost like a skeleton whose nose has water dripping off its tip. I ask this person what he has to teach me. He answers that I need to trust my intuition, not my muscular strength—that my intuition is my strength. He recognizes me as his descendant even though I am in the shape of a panther. I then begin my journey back up out of the underworld, and I return home realizing how the message runs contrary to the common understanding in so much of life, yet there are many who can understand and accept the message. My ancestor was old, and I know he lived life not as a warrior, but as a farmer.

This ecstatic experience began my journey toward understanding the transition period between the Mother Goddess era and the warrior era.

The Mother Goddess era was primarily an era of hunters and gatherers and the very beginning of the era of farming and animal husbandry, beginning around 200,000 BCE and ending during the Neolithic era, around 2000 BCE. Iron was not yet in use except farther to the south in Europe, and lethal aggression was minimal.

A study done by Fry and Soderberg of twenty-one nomadic forager societies suggests that these people cannot be considered especially warlike. Documented incidences of lethal aggression found in reputable accounts spanning the last two centuries indicated that such incidents were rare—only 148 incidents in all, of which more than half involved a single person killing another. Only one-third of these incidents involved conflicts between groups, and most killings were motivated by sexual jealousy, revenge for a previous murder, insults, or other interpersonal quarrels. Assuming that what we learn of the characteristics of contempory hunter and gatherer societies can be generalized to ancient hunter and gatherer societies, the weight of evidence in this study suggests that humanity's origins were, if not exactly peaceful, then not warlike, either.[1]

Other features of hunter-gatherers are their lack of material possessions and lack of interest in attaining material wealth. According to Marshall Sahlins,

> The manufacture of tools, clothing, utensils, or ornaments, however easily done, becomes senseless when these begin to be more of a burden than a comfort. Utility falls quickly at the margin of portability. The construction of substantial houses likewise becomes absurd if they must soon be abandoned. Hence the hunter's very ascetic conceptions of material welfare: an interest only in minimal equipment, if that; a valuation of smaller things over bigger, a disinterest in acquiring two or more of most goods . . .[2]

Chapter 5 explores what life was like during the Mother Goddess era through a series of ecstatic trance journeys in which I commune with my ancestors. I describe various scenarios that take place near what is now Ladby, Denmark, a place I visited in actuality in 2006. I recognized the general location of this place from my ecstatic experiences there, but was able to confirm the location by examining Google Earth. It is protected by virtue of being situated slightly inland from the channel that separates Fyn from Zealand, on a river that connects a small lake, Kertinge Nor, to the channel. In these ecstatic experiences homage is paid to the Great Mother and the other gentle and nurturing gods and goddesses of the era. I experienced these trances as a member of a Nordic family. My life and the life of my wife are described. As the son of that same family in a different trance experience I eventually move across the river to another village to live near the family of my new wife. Celebrating the seasons is central in our lives. Life is hard for some—one young boy who was the only member of his small village to survive the winter joins us. The ritual of how death is dealt with is also described.

Chapter 6 offers a series of ecstatic experiences depicting the transitional period between the Mother Goddess era and the warrior era.

These take place on the northwest coast of Sweden, south of what is now the border with Norway. I have driven through this area of Sweden, an area just south of Tanum, where the petroglyphs of the Upper and Lower World postures I mention in this book were found. In these experiences, I am at first a father of a family at a time before we started valuing the honor of being a warrior, when raiders first come ashore and destroy almost everything in my village. My son and I escape inland, and we eventually find three other farmer families, each living separately in the interest of safety. Eventually, as the farmer's son in a subsequent ecstatic experience, I marry the daughter of one of the other families, and we set up our own homestead. Warriors then begin to visit us periodically to seize half of what we have grown or accumulated in exchange for "protection" by the warrior chieftain whom they represent. This change in life causes us great inner and interpersonal turmoil, as we are required to begin to see life differently from the peaceful times of cooperation we experienced previously in our small village.

Chapter 7 delves into the beginning of the warrior era and provides descriptions of what life was like for a warrior and his family. This sequence of ecstatic experiences covers three generations of a family. First, I am a warrior who is second in command to the chieftain, serving as a trainer of his warriors—a first retainer. I have a wife, but I only relate to her casually when I am in the chieftain's great hall, where I may grab her when she comes by serving the men. When we are not fighting or practicing, we spend our time drinking and are likely quite drunk most of the time. I have a son and daughter I hardly know and who think I don't know who they are. My son and the other boys spend their time watching us practice, and they emulate us, practicing among themselves with wooden swords. When they are old enough they are invited to begin practicing with the older warriors, and my son eventually takes my place after I am wounded and retire from my position of responsibility. In other ecstatic experiences that take place during this warrior era I am this same first retainer's wife, experiencing the role of a woman in relationship to her husband, to the other women, and to her children. I also become the first retainer's daughter and fall in love with another warrior, who eventually dies in battle. Although most women who lose their husbands become no more than servants to all the men and are used by them, I find that in this life I have the power of "seeing" and I withdraw to become a seeress, a vǫlva. One of my sons already has the power of seeing into the future and as a result has become an important person to the chieftain.

I then become this seeress's second, younger son, the nephew to the new first retainer. Finding myself bored with practicing war with the other boys and watching the warriors practice, I decide I don't want to be a warrior anymore, and in several subsequent ecstatic experiences I am this son struggling to decide what I want to do. I eventually decide to become a blacksmith.

Amid these ecstatic experiences of chapter 7, I find myself on one occasion being a farmer's wife living not far from the chieftain's village, pleased that our son decided to be trained as a warrior, knowing that he will be well-fed. This time I do not resent having the chieftain's men take half of what we produce. It is this son who eventually becomes the chieftain's first retainer.

The next three chapters take us from a society that venerates the Great Mother—a society that values peace, cooperation, and nurturance—to a society that worships warrior gods, that values power over others, power maintained by physical strength, violence, and material wealth. Women who were once valued find themselves in a society where their submission is now demanded and they become slaves to the king and his warriors. As we now know, the position of women in society greatly deteriorates over the next two millennia, and the picture of their lives derived from the following ecstatic experiences was just a beginning. Only in the late nineteenth into the twentieth century have women begun to regain their rights—beginning with the woman's suffrage movement and followed by the women's liberation movement of the 1960s. This move toward equal rights for women is a major factor in bringing us to the rebirth of Baldr, to a new age of peace and veneration for our Mother Earth.

5

THE ERA OF THE MOTHER GODDESS

On December 16, 2011, using the Freyja Initiation posture, I asked the goddess, "What do you have to show me or teach me?" Freyja took me back to the very beginning of the world of the Æsir, and then to the time of the transition, where I met my distant ancestors in the domain of Hel,* ancestors who told me of an earlier time, when they worshipped the Great Mother . . .

It takes a while for anything to happen. I feel the drum beating through my body, then I feel myself being pulled forward slowly. I take a few steps and start walking slowly forward. I come to the edge of a sheet of ice and sort of trip or dive forward onto it, sliding on my belly with my arms above my head. I slide down this hill that turns to the right and keep on sliding. When I finally come to the bottom I am sitting next to a high stone wall. I can smell sulfur and hear a dog barking—it's Garmr, the huge bloodstained dog who is the guardian of Hel's underworld domain. Stone steps take me to the top of the wall, where I can see Garmr on the other side. Rather than going down the

---

*Hel is a giantess and goddess in Norse mythology who rules over Niflheim, the underworld where the dead dwell. According to the thirteenth-century Icelandic scholar Snorri Sturluson, Hel, the being, is the daughter of Loki and the giant Angrboða, and therefore the sister of the wolf Fenrir and the sea serpent, Jörmungandr. She's generally presented as being rather greedy and indifferent to the concerns of both the living and the dead.

steps, I sit on the top until he finally stops barking, lays down, and falls asleep. I look out along the wall and see many figures, skin and bones in death. Two of them, a man and a woman, move very slowly over to the wall near where I am sitting, and I go down a few steps to be closer to them. They tell me that they are the great-great-grandparents of a boy who had died in his first battle because he was distracted by a woman, and that this boy is one of my distant ancestors. They report that they had told him that he had forgotten the old ways, and that they want to tell me about these old ways. "We lived a simple life and didn't feel what you would call competition, and we did not even have a word for it. We cared for and nurtured one another and our neighbors. We made weapons of stone, but to be used for hunting, to feed ourselves and our neighbors. Life was peaceful. We had what we needed and there was nothing we really wanted otherwise. We loved one another and everything around us. We enjoyed watching and listening to everything, and through just listening we were told everything we needed to know about how to live . . ."

On December 21, 2012, the winter solstice and the last day of the Mayan Calendar, I was moved to reread the near-complete manuscript of this book. In reading, I felt that the life described by this couple in Hel's domain was limited, and something more was needed. Using the Hallstatt Warrior, I found what that was in a trance experience that proved to be a continuation of the narrative that I mentioned earlier in chapter 4, in my January 17, 2010, Hallstatt Warrior journey. This was an experience that took me to the hunter-gatherer era in Germany, around 5000 BCE. That was the time I first met this ancestor as he and a group of about a dozen men were preparing to go on a hunt, and I, as a man from the future, assisted them in driving a herd of four or five deer over a cliff. On this winter solstice of 2012, the Hallstatt Warrior again quickly transported me back to join the same group of twelve hunters . . .

As I watch, I am very much impressed by the manner in which

the hunters go into action in dealing with the five deer carcasses. They know just what needs to be done and act in near silence. I just watch, not knowing how I can help. One of the men takes off in a hurry in the direction of their home camp near the mouth of the cave about a mile away. The others climb down to the bottom of the cliff and with their flint knives begin skinning, gutting, and cutting up the deer. They move quickly. A couple of the men go off into the nearby woods, bring back poles or branches, and start building an elongated A-frame structure. Over this structure they stretch and tie the skins of the deer with the hair facing out. The deer meat is cut up into fairly thin strips and is hung from the poles inside the structure. One of the men brings wood and with a piece of flint starts a fire. He adds some greener wood to the fire so it smokes, smoke that rises to fill the covered frame structure to smoke the meat.

Soon the man who left to return to the village returns with about ten other men and women who all join in cutting up and smoking the venison. They also bring with them some more hides to complete the covering of the smokehouse. A couple of the women start a fire and hang a piece of the meat, a thigh, over the open fire to cook, and they go out to find the herbs and vegetables they need to put with water into a large blackened ceramic pot that hangs over the fire. I just stand there and watch, still feeling helpless amid all this activity. I shake my head to clear it and think *I need to help,* so I follow the fire-tender out into the woods to help him carry wood from some special trees to put on the fires. Still, everyone is too busy in their excitement to talk much. I realize that some of the people are going off in the direction of their home camp carrying loads of meat, so I grab an armful and go with them. Back at the camp there is another, similar smokehouse, only larger, in which they hang the meat. A couple of the older men who had remained in the camp carry the wood for this fire, which they had started earlier. I then return back to the butchering and see that someone has built a structure under a rock ledge extending out from the cliff as a place for a couple of people to stay for several days while the meat is smoked and the new hides of the smokehouse cure. Next to the shelter is a small rock shelf on which someone has placed a carved stone figure of a fat woman with large breasts, in front of which lies a piece of roasted meat with some sprigs of herbs and flowers. Everyone knows what needs to be done and they are doing it. It is a very busy but joyous time . . .

The next day, December 22, I again felt a need to return to this same place and time, and so I again journeyed with the Hallstatt Warrior, asking, "What more do I need to see and learn . . . ?"

It is around 5000 BCE and I am back at this camp or village. I am with the man whom I first met while trance journeying nearly three years ago, who I thought back then was my ancestor. This time he takes me to his hut made of branches and daubed with mud, which stands near a cliff wall not far from the opening to a cave. It sits among about twenty other similar huts sheltered by the cliff. As we go inside it is fairly dark except for the glow of a central fire. His wife is tending the fire, which has a stew bubbling in a blackened pot hanging over it. The walls are blackened from the smoke that is rising and flowing out of a hole near the hut's ceiling at one end. She has a baby tied to her chest in a soft piece of hide. They have a young daughter who quickly brings me a wooden bowl of the stew. I feel welcomed as an honored guest. There is a sharpened stick in the bowl for sticking the meat and vegetables, otherwise I hold the bowl to my mouth to drink from it like the others. It is delicious, but I stop eating when I see the others, one by one, go to the family altar, where there is a figure of the Mother Goddess that they touch with their hands and thank. I feel real warmth in their love for her and go to her too, touching her with this same feeling of love . . .

What is interesting in reflecting on these experiences is that I knew what was being said when my ancestor asked me to come with him, to come to his home to meet his wife and family. I felt them saying "welcome," but it was more as if I just understood what they were say-ing or as if I was reading their minds. Even in the trance experience of

December 21, 2012, my impression was of how quiet everyone was—not because they were not talking, but because I was just watching, and they were not talking to me but to one another, except on the one occasion when I went to get firewood and the man I followed told me or I just knew that he wanted me to get the wood from only this one particular tree.

I had had previous ecstatic journeys that took me back to the horticulturist era in Denmark, the era of transition when the people were just beginning their attempts to control the earth through gardening and domesticating animals, yet I believe they still worshipped Mother Earth and the fertility gods and goddesses, though with their growing ability to control her through agriculture their appreciation of her began to diminish. One of these experiences occurred on December 30, 2011, the next-to-last day of that year. I was in Santa Barbara, California, visiting my brother-in-law, where I stood on a bluff overlooking the Pacific Ocean. On the horizon I could see the Channel Islands. Using the Nyborg Man, a death/rebirth posture, I found myself standing on the beach at Fyn, in Denmark, looking out into the fjord off the North Sea . . .

It is a sunny day and the water is relatively calm. I am with a couple of other men from our village, an uncle and a cousin. We push our fishing boat out into the water, get in, and push out farther using the oars. Out beyond the surf we row a bit farther, out beyond a rocky point of land, and there I sit with the other men, breathing the fresh sea air and feeling quite at peace. I think of Njord, the god of the sea, one of the Vanir gods and father to Freyja and Freyr. We sing a chant to the god to help us in fishing as we put bait fish on our hooks, and I reach into my pocket and pull out a piece of polished amber and throw it into the sea as a gift to him. I then throw my fishing line into the water, and soon I'm struggling to pull in a fish, a large one. I can feel the strain of pulling in my shoulders and arms. I land it, cut it open, use a piece of its entrails for bait, and soon catch another. I feel very much at peace with the rolling of the water, with being gently lifted up and lowered with each swell. I can hear the water breaking on the rocks some distance from me. It is beautiful. I rest my hand of the sides of the boat and can feel the carvings of fish and sea birds along its sides. I feel that these carvings are also a gift to Njord. After we each catch several fish and sing another chant, a kenning,* in thanks, we row ashore and walk up the beach, up a rise of land to our huts. I can see my wife at a distance carrying a basket, picking herbs and different plants with our young daughter. I take our fish inside and put a couple of pieces of wood on the fire in the center of the hut. The smoke rises and flows out the smoke holes in the thatched roof. The room is somewhat smoky, but most of the smoke rises, and we are used to it anyway. I rake some of the coals to one side, and after wrapping the fish in some leaves and mud, I lay it in the coals. I take some woven reeds we have saved for rope and tie the other fish from the roof rafters above the fire and in the flow of the smoke, to smoke and preserve them for the winter. I feel very much at peace and again thank Njord for providing us with these fish . . .

On January 13, 2012, I sat in the Freyr Diviner posture and soon found myself among a familiar small cluster of thatched huts, sitting with the other men of the Old Norse village . . .

I am speaking, thanking the Great Mother for a dream I had of where we would find a herd of deer. We are preparing for a hunt. We know the way deer wander, and by this time in the morning we know the deer will be somewhere else. We decide to wait until tomorrow morning and count on one or more of us to dream again about the location of the herd. In the morning we will be up before dawn to start on the hunt.

Several of the men do dream of where the deer will be in the morning, and each man sees them in generally the same area. We leave on the hunt and come to this wooded place. As planned the night before, we spread out to encircle the wooded area and begin to move forward.

---

*A type of literary trope common in Old Norse, which uses figurative compounds in place of a name or a noun; e.g., a sword might be called a "wound-hoe."

There are six deer, and we quickly bring down three of them, though one deer I spear gets away. I sit down and stroke my beard, thinking. Stroking my beard seems to bring visions. I "see" the deer lying under a bush some distance to the west, bleeding. I beckon to one of the other men to come with me. When we find the deer, we drag it back to where the others are busy dressing deer in preparation to take them back to the village . . .

This experience illustrates the magical power of "seeing," the power of Odin as expressed in his ability to see great distances from his high seat, and the power of Heimdallr, the god of foreknowledge and keen eyesight and hearing, in being able to hear across great distances. As we shall learn in part 3 of this book, Heimdallr's hearing is so acute that he can hear the sound of grass growing as he guards Bifröst, the flaming bridge that connects the home of the gods to the home of the humans of Midgard. This power that we would call magical was a real, nearly commonplace power of the ancient peoples and of even the more recent native peoples of the world. Recall the story from chapter 2 of the medicine man White Shield finding Siya'ka's missing horses, one of many stories recorded by Vine Deloria in his book *The World We Used to Live In*. This is a power that I have frequently experienced while using the ecstatic postures.

On January 15, 2012, using the Freyr Diviner posture, I asked what life is like when the Great Mother was honored, I found myself again on Fyn, above the south side of a river that flows into the channel between the islands of Fyn and Zealand, near what is now Ladby, Denmark . . .

There are about twelve huts clustered fairly close together, generally in a circle and against the side of a hill. The huts have wattle and daub or mud walls and a thatched roof. It is near evening, and I have been carrying mud up from beside the river to repair some places in the wall. I see my son in our boat polling his way back across the river toward home. He was across the river visiting our neighbors and his girlfriend. He helps me carry the last load of mud in a hollowed-out log up to the hut. My wife and daughter are inside and have been cooking. It is warm inside and the mud will dry fast. After plastering the wall, we all sit down to eat. I can see the reflection of the firelight on the glistening mud on the wall. I then sit by the fire and pick up my prized flint knife and the piece of wood on which I have been carving. I am carving a figure of a fat woman with heavy breasts, an image of the Great Mother that is to be a wedding gift for my son and his new wife. He will be moving across the river to live with his wife, and he has been busy building an addition onto her parents' hut for the two of them . . .

The next day, January 16, I again used the Freyr Diviner to further explore what life was like during the time of the Great Mother, the time of the worship of the gods and goddesses of the Vanir . . .

Idunn appears first, the goddess who in the later times of the Æsir keeps the gods young with her golden apples, the goddess of healing, and the goddess my wife calls on when she collects herbs for healing and for the kitchen. I often see my wife out collecting with some of the other women and with our daughter, standing silently, holding something to her breasts. In this way when she calls to Idunn she receives an answer about the powers of the plant. I don't know much about the herbs except that she often uses the leaves of comfrey and other things to put on my cuts, scrapes, and bruises, and especially on our son's, to keep them from getting red and filled with pus. She sometimes makes teas for us to drink, and some are very bitter. Other women often come to her with questions. She learned a lot from her mother, but she always says that what she has learned has been mostly from Idunn herself. I feel very fortunate to have a wife who trusts in Idunn and our daughter is learning, too . . .

Following that ecstatic trance journey I still had questions regarding the small village and its inhabitants, and so I returned that same afternoon to the Freyr Diviner, asking, "How is this village organized? Tell me more . . ."

I arrive when we are celebrating the summer solstice. People are singing and dancing to the beat of drums. As I look around and feel the warmth, I know here is where I belong. I am related to many, if not most of these people—cousins, second and third cousins, maybe fifty people in all. A lot of them are young children and older youth. There are a few who are not related who have joined our village for various reasons. A couple of young men who had recently joined us had decided to leave their home to explore the world. They had not found a woman near home to marry and were adventurous. We welcomed them into our village, and one has found a wife among us. The spring before last, a hunting party found a boy wandering and confused. They brought him home and my wife nursed him back to health with her herbs and teas. He told his story: that he was from a village much smaller than ours. The people of this village ran out of food as winter went on and most all were sick and died before the end of winter. He was alone and left to find food and a place to stay. He did not remember much after that. We welcomed him. Other men from nearby villages related to us through marriage join us. We feel a kinship with the nearby villages; the one across the river is the closest, but there are others. We are quite close to the one to the east and another to the south because some of our young men have married the women of those villages. Life is peaceful. My wife's parents are part of the village. Her mother is the one whom others look to in making decisions, and her father knows a lot about their environment and a number of crafts, which he shares with the other men of the village. We live and work together in supporting one another . . .

I had other such visions, especially with the Freyr Diviner (thank you, Freyr). It is apparent that these visions were influenced by my extensive reading on Nordic life as well as the opportunities I have had to visit reenactment sites of ancient life in Scandinavia, such as the research center at Lejre, Denmark, the ship burial site at Ladby, Denmark, and the Vitlycke Museum at Tanum, Sweden. Yet these ecstatic experiences were more personal because I was part of or within them. I was living them.

In the next few journeys back in time with Freyr, I found myself as the adult son of the ancestor I was in the previous trance experiences. Going into the trance journey, I asked Freyr to give me more details about the village. I was immediately given the vision of about a dozen huts in a circle or an oval, which encircle two larger huts where the people spent a lot of their time . . .

I understand that one of the large huts before me is for the men and the other is for the women, though the men and women freely go back and forth between these huts. The men's hut is more for the men's crafts of spear- and knife-making. There is one old man who still knaps flint for blades, spears, and arrow points, but flint is very rare so quartz is often used. The men also meet there to plan for hunting and fishing expeditions. The women's hut is more for food preparation and preservation, and the women's crafts of carding wool, breaking flax for linen, spinning, weaving, sewing, and basket-weaving. Many of these tasks are done outside, weather permitting. There are a few other structures somewhat separate from the center of the village, such as a kiln for firing clay for bowls and pots of various sizes, and a shelter for the sheep during the summer. There is a story I have heard told about my grandfather's father, or maybe it was about his father's father: one day he was out hunting and found an injured lamb that he brought home, and with his wife's milk they nursed it back to health. It could not easily walk. It stayed near the village, and when the grandfather was home it would stay near him. I've heard this same story told by others about their grandfathers, too.

Each individual hut is generally rectangular with a hearth fire in the center, with smoke rising out of the holes at either end of the thatched roof. Each hut has a penned-in area at one end for the family to keep their one or two sheep during the winter for their protection and also to add some warmth to the hut. During the summer these sheep are led up the hill during the day to graze, and in the evening they are brought back to the pen, where each family comes to milk their own two or three summer sheep. Next to the hut is a stack of hay for the sheep during the winter. Grain is kept in large pots to protect it from rodents, grain that is used for making bread and a little may be given to the sheep during the winter. The hut has wooden platforms around the edge on either side of the hearth with straw for beds or to sit on to be close to the fire, sufficient chairs for the number of people in the family, and a table at the end opposite the sheep pen. Some of the huts are larger, with an addition or extension for an extended family of daughter, son-in-law, and children, with its own hearth and beds, though the families generally work and eat together. Tending sheep is an important activity of the village, as sheep are an important part of life during this time when we worship the Great Mother. My son, along with the young boy our village rescued from the long winter, along with the boys' dogs, are the primary shepherds for the village . . .

I have found that by using the Freyr Diviner, my journeys more clearly answer my questions concerning the details of what life was like in these ancient times. On the other hand, the initiation and underworld postures, I have found, provide different kinds of explorations, usually revealing stories concerning the gods or other ways of experiencing life. But because I wanted to learn still more about village life in the time of the Great Mother, I once again used the Freyr Diviner on the morning of January 17, 2012. I entered a trance and quickly found myself sitting on the hill above the ancient village . . .

I see the village below me and across the river and downstream a little I see the village of our neighbors. Next to me is my dog and close by is my friend, a boy about my age, though he does not know his exact age. We call him the Wanderer, because he was found by a hunting party in the late winter, confused and wandering. They brought him back home, and my mother took him in and worked to bring him back to health. He still has problems, though. He cannot see out of one eye and walks with a limp. His right arm is also weak. Today I am tending the village sheep and watching the world around me. Just below us on the hillside are the sheep, about thirty of them, peacefully grazing. One of the sheep starts to wander off, and I send my dog to bring him back. Last summer, my father helped me train him to herd the sheep. It is a warm, pleasant day, and I don't feel like doing anything else right now, though not far away is the beginning of a hut that I decided to try to build. I've never built a hut before, but I have watched others build them. Up on the ridge are trees and brush that I have been using for the hut that will protect me while tending sheep when the weather is bad. Today we will take the sheep back down to their pen before the sun sets. Some days I take my friend across the river to the other village because there is a shaman there who can see into the past and the future and knows all kinds of things. The Wanderer is learning from him how to be a shaman and has stories to tell of times before we kept sheep and what it was like to spend more time hunting. The Wanderer will probably go live with the shaman next year. He is not strong enough to poll himself across the river, so I take him across and visit friends I have made there. On those days another boy from our village watches the village sheep in my place. But today I am sitting with the sheep and watching the world around me. I return home before the sun is at its zenith and spend time with the men of the village, learning all sorts of skills . . .

On January 18, 2012, my wife and I arrived at Maho Bay, Saint John, in the Virgin Islands, and the following morning I used the Nyborg Man to enter into a trance, which brought me a death/rebirth experience of great spiritual meaning. As I entered the trance, I could hear the waves breaking on the sand and the vibrant, deep drumming of the Bridgewater Drummers, the CD I sometimes use for inducing ecstatic trance. The drumming quickly took me down to the beach—the beach of the river near Ladby, in Denmark . . .

The drumming is for the funeral of my mother's father, an elder of the village, who has died. His funeral pyre is set. It is lit, and as the smoke rises it drifts down toward the drummers, and the sound waves from the drums can be seen in the rhythmic motion of the smoke. The smoke billows upward and away from the drums in all directions. That is why drumming is used for a funeral—so that the spirit of the deceased can rise in the smoke from the funeral pyre and is sent in all directions, back to the Great Mother, Mother Earth. As the fire burns, the ashes of the body are also returned to Mother Earth. Thus, we keep up the drumming for many hours. I watch the smoke rise and in the distance come back down to settle on the earth again. We drum until the last glow of the fire has gone out, and my grandfather is back in the arms of the Great Mother, from whom he first came . . .

On Friday, January 20, 2012, I returned to the Freyr Diviner and more images of village life in the time of the Great Mother. This time I was again the father . . .

It is morning, and I am walking to the garden just beyond and upstream from the village. In the garden there are turnips and carrots, and now some of the women are trying to grow herbs, but mostly they go out looking for herbs and other things to eat along the river or in some clearings on the hill where there are plenty. At the edge of the garden is a spring where I stop to take a couple scoops of water. I rinse the sleep from my face and take a drink. I will go back to the hut in several hours for our first meal of the day. Work starts early. Beyond the garden and along the river there is a place where wild barley grows thickly. It is fall, and the grains have turned brown, ready for harvest. I am carrying one of my prized possessions, a long flint knife for cutting barley. As I cut and rake it up into sheaves, I am thinking. I am always thinking. This time, I am wondering if there will there be enough grain and hay for the winter, grain for flour for bread, and a little grain and enough hay for the sheep. How many sheep I will be able to keep depends on how much hay I can store. The other ones we will kill to eat. Since my wife's father died, her mother has not been in the best of health and has moved in with us. This means we have seven mouths to feed. The stalks

look full of barley, and as I cut it I feel hopeful that I may also be able
to keep two of the sheep for their milk to make cheese, the other thing
that helps us get through the winter. On the way back to the village
for an early meal, I look over the garden and look to where the vegetables are planted, the turnips and carrots that have not yet been dug
up. While cutting the barley I found a wild turnip that I dug up, and
now I dig a hole and plant it in the garden so it can continue to grow
and get bigger. We have had a good summer. After breakfast we go back
out to the field of barley. My son and the Wanderer gather the sheaves
behind me, setting them upright, leaning them against one another so
that they can better dry. Later we will take them into the storage hut
and beat them to separate the grain from the straw, winnow the grain,
and store it in large pots for my wife to grind and bake.

Since my father-in-law died there are those in the village who are
starting to look to me for answers to their questions, though there are
a couple of other elders who come before me that I feel are wiser. This
evening, when we get together in the men's hut, we will talk about how
prepared we are for winter and to decide if, beside the grains of barley
and oats, we have smoked and dried enough fish and meat and have
enough vegetables stored. But now we are all working in bringing in the
barley. I see the other men farther up the stream, cutting another stand
of barley. I stand to stretch my back and wave to one of them. These
fields stretch up along the river and up along the hillside to a row of
trees that I can see in the distance. Since my father-in-law was one of
the more respected elders, his field, though smaller than some because
he is getting old, is the closest to the village. It is in that field that I am
working today.

Suddenly I remember the traps we have dug and set to catch animals, and so I stop cutting to ask the Wanderer to go check the traps to
see if we caught anything. I would not want a trapped animal to start
to rot or for something else to start eating on it. This is one thing that
has to be done every morning, and I always send one of the boys to do
it, but this morning I had my mind first on the barley. The Wanderer

comes back a little later to report that there is a deer in the pit with a broken leg, tangled in the branches that covered the hole. Thus, we have to stop cutting the barley and drag the deer back to the village for the women to take care of. Then it should be time to eat. So goes another morning . . .

Later that day, January 20, using the Freyr Diviner, I asked if there was more I needed to learn about this time when we valued the Great Mother, and was told that it was time to move on. At first, no clear images formed, but then I found myself in a new place, looking out to the west, toward the broad expanse of the ocean, the North Sea. The sun was behind me, shining on the crowns of the waves breaking on the sand . . .

6

THE TRANSITION

What happened that ended these early times when people acknowledged and appreciated the nurturance of a Mother Goddess? What was the transition like between the era of a feminine deity and the later male-oriented era, with its masculine warrior gods, which has dominated the earth ever since through aggression and violence? The second experience of January 20, 2012 using the Freyr Diviner posture continued . . .

I find myself as a youth accompanying my father as we wander through what had been our village at the edge of the North Sea. Our relatives are lying dead all around us, some burnt in their huts, others with their heads cut off. This is not the proper way to deal with the dead, and so we set the wood for a fire down on the sandy beach. We are on the western coast of Sweden, in a little cove. We start dragging the bodies down to the sand. I feel bad because we have to drag them rather than carry them with dignity. We build a platform and pull the bodies up onto it. The way they are burnt makes it hard to tell who some of them are. As we continue with this work we realize some villagers are missing, and that the ones missing are the younger women. We find a drum, and my father starts drumming as I light the fire and carry more wood. It takes all day, that night, and the next day to send most all of the people of the village back to the Great Mother.

A couple of days earlier, a ship had come in from the sea with men bearing swords, axes, and torches. They set fire to the huts of our village and killed the men, older women, and children. Our hut is up the hill, the farthest from the water's edge and not far from a line of trees. Through the trees is a meadow where I was tending the sheep. Father came running up to me and told me to run. We crossed the meadow and ran into the woods to hide. He then started back. He tells me now that mother had sent him to warn me. When he got back to the edge of the village he saw a man killing her. He knew he could do nothing and so he ran back with one of the children of the village, a young girl, who had just run into the woods crying. That night and the next we slept in a clump of bushes, where we felt safe. After we send the dead back to the Great Mother, we wander inland for a couple of days. We have my dog to help herd a few sheep and a couple of our pigs that we usually just let run in the woods to root for grubs and whatever else they can find to eat. The pigs generally stay close to the pile where we throw our garbage.

When we stop wandering, I help my father build a hut to shelter the three of us. It is fairly early in the summer, and though we have meat to eat we have little else, and so we go looking for what else we can find to eat. Father finds some wild grains, oats, and barley, and some other wild plants he recognizes, mainly wild carrots and other roots. He digs them up, brings them home, and plants them again. He knows that such roots will usually keep growing. When he has planted them before, he would have to thin them so that the remaining ones would grow large. When he has the space he sometimes plants the ones he thinned. But now he is worried about the coming winter. We are not near the sea or close to a large river, so we do not have fish to dry or smoke, and we know it is not safe to live near the water.

One day another young man, a little older than me, wanders into where we have built our hut. He does not know what he wants to do except to continue wandering in search of a new village where he will be welcome. He tells us that his village was also burnt. We wonder who these people are who destroyed our villages and took the young women. They came from the sea. We had heard from a wandering skald of such things happening south of us and up the other side of the land on which we live. His songs tell of ships coming from the land across the sea, from the east. These men pride themselves on being great warriors, and some were made famous by the number of people they killed. They would even kill one another to become more famous, something we don't understand. We have never heard of anyone killing anybody else. Why would anyone want to do that? We need one another to help in hunting and fishing and planting our gardens. These warriors sound crazy—we did not believe it when the skald sang of them . . .

The next day, January 21, 2012, using again the Freyr Diviner, I questioned how this father and son could survive. This time I found myself as the father . . .

We have a few animals and I have built a sufficient hut for the three of us, with a central fire to keep us warm, but we have little else. I have been cooking the meat over the fire. I have to thank the Great Mother that whenever I left our hut in the village I automatically grabbed my belt with my knife and my ax, tools that I so much depend on. I know little about cooking. My wife generally used the cauldron hanging over the fire and would boil the meat with other vegetables, but we don't have a cauldron. I had no thoughts of grabbing what I would need for preparing meals or spinning and weaving as I fled—something my wife was constantly doing when she was not cooking or foraging for herbs. I am worried about the approaching winter. We do not have the woolen clothing and blankets we need. It would not have been respectful to take any of the clothing from those whom we cremated.

One day, a few days after my son and I had finished building the hut, killed a sheep, and hung the meat from the roof to dry, I find myself wandering in the area, but what I am really doing is looking for other people. I am feeling very alone and responsible for our small and incomplete family. My son, the young girl who lives with us, and I go north up along the coast and come to what had been another village that too was burnt and not long ago. Again, bodies are lying here and there. I send my son home to get the one possession I greatly value, my drum. When someone dies, the person's possessions, including food, are also burnt for this person's final journey. I hesitate, but my fear of winter overcomes me and I start taking some of the clothing from the bodies. I feel very guilty in what I am doing, but we will need them for winter to survive. While waiting for my son to return, I continue digging around and find in the remains of one hut, under a partially burned sleeping bench, a warm skin blanket. It smells of smoke but it is still usable. In another hut I find that the raiders had not taken the cooking cauldron and a few other cooking implements, things I was not thinking about when we were showing respect for those who died in our old village. By the time my son comes back I have a stack of things for us to take home. This brings me some relief from my fear of the coming winter.

At home we have two sheepskins that need to be softened, and I have been spending the evenings chewing on these skins and stretching them to soften them. I saved the wool from our sheep, but I don't know how to start weaving it into cloth, yet I know the wool is valuable. I am concerned about the young girl living with us now because there is no one to teach her what she needs to know about life. She is another reason I have been looking for other human beings . . .

A few days later, on January 23, 2012, using the Freyr Diviner, I returned to the scene of desolation to experience more of the life of my ancestors . . .

I find myself again as the father, searching for turnips and other vegetables we can eat, but really searching for other human beings. This time the three of us are walking south, with my son and the young girl carrying the wild turnips. We are in a wooded area. Much of the land is wooded, with an occasional small clearing, so we cannot see too far ahead of us, but I smell smoke. At first I fear another burnt village, but I know there is no village in the area, and the smoke smells not as vile as that of a burnt village. We go in the direction of the breeze carrying the smell of smoke and come to a hut. Other people!

As we approach, we see a woman sitting near a tree on which her loom is tied, weaving. I call out a greeting and she jumps in fright, but when she sees us there is a great smile. She is young and no one else seems to be around. She reports that her husband is out hunting and checking his traps, but she expects him back for their late-morning meal, hopefully with something to eat. I see her look at the children and the turnips. I tell them to give them to her, and she is very grateful. Her husband returns with a rabbit. He skins and cleans it, and she puts it in her steaming cooking pot with the turnips. We are all so happy to have someone else to eat with.

As we talk and share stories of what happened, I learn that the raiders destroyed their village a day or two before ours, so they must have come up the coast. Their story is not a whole lot different from ours, but they have no children and only themselves to look out for, so they were able to run into the woods together to flee the invaders. It had been early morning when the raiders attacked, and they were still together before the day's work had begun. After the attack, like us they had gone back to their village and burned the bodies of all the others, and they too took nothing except their own cooking cauldron and a few other implements that had survived the fire, items the raiders were not interested in taking. I tell them of my worry about the young girl with us, that she has no mother to teach her what she needs to know about life. It makes a lot of sense to all of us that this young couple could provide her with what she needs. We talk of moving our little homesteads closer together, but realize that there is now danger in having a village, which would more easily attract the raiders. It is safer to live alone, separate from others. We realize that our homesteads are not a great distance from each other, so we can still visit and do things together. In walking a straight line, we are maybe twenty minutes apart. Knowing this, we both feel great relief. They do not have sheep, and the wool that the wife was weaving smelled strongly of smoke. She had a good supply of herbs, most of which I could not identify. I offer to trade her wool for herbs that she thinks would be best for flavoring mutton. I have no use for wool since I know nothing about spinning, weaving, and sewing, though by paying attention and learning I could learn to find the herbs for myself. She shows me some wild parsley that is growing nearby.

Both of our families know that we are about to become great friends and important to each other. One thing I feel too embarrassed to tell my new friends about is the way I raided the burnt village to the north for the clothing and bedding we will need for winter. As we leave to return to our homestead, we together thank the Great Mother for this day, though I still feel guilty and know that she is disappointed in me for what I did . . .

On January 24, I again asked the Freyr Diviner how the little family is going to survive the winter. I found myself once again the father. It is late summer, going into fall . . .

We have not wanted to go back to our devastated village, but this morning I decide that we must make the trip. The walk takes us only about thirty minutes. The village is greener than I expected, with new vegetation sprouting everywhere. I start thinking about what the raiders must have wanted from our simple village. Gold or silver is rare, and therefore so is jewelry. My wife had one broach that she used that the smithy in our village made for her, but his work was mostly for valued tools. The raiders did not seem to take these tools—they were not farmers and had no need for them, though I can't find any of the knives we used. They must have taken them. I look in the place that my wife kept her broach and it is gone. She may have been wearing it.

The raiders had smashed all the jars in which we stored grain, or maybe they broke because of the fire, but where they are smashed all that is left are the husks, the rest eaten by rodents, deer, and other animals. As we continue to scavenge through the remains of the village my son finds one small jar of barley that had escaped being smashed, something that we dearly need for spring planting at our new homestead. I look toward our fields of grain and other vegetables and see that the raiders had tried to set fire to them, but because they were still green the fire had not gone far. It is apparent that deer have been foraging in the grains and pigs have been digging at our turnips, but we are pleased to see that a lot has survived and is not quite ready for harvest. With some hard work, maybe we will have enough for the winter. The root vegetables are not in the greatest shape because we had not thinned them, but we dig a few and return home.

The next day we visit our neighbor to report on what we had found. Though we may have enough oats and barley for the winter, I know nothing about baking bread, but the woman says that she can bake for both families in exchange for the grain. In the course of our conversation I tell them that I did not feel bad about taking the jar of grain because there was no one else to use it, but I now talk about how bad I have been feeling about taking the clothing and bedding from the destroyed village to the north. They understand, but as we talk we realize how different the raiders are from us—to them, there is no value to life and they hold no love for their ancestors. All they value is what they can take from others and their own personal survival. We wonder how they can be this way. They do no farming and raise no animals. Then I remember the remains of a fire and the bones of a cow or two in the village, and that we had not had such a feast before the raid. That is how they must eat—raiding village after village. But they cannot do that forever. Soon there will be no more villages. What a frightening world . . .

On January 25, the Freyr Diviner took me back to visit our neighbors again . . .

It is now fall. The husband of the other family excitedly tells me that there are two other families in the area, families from his village. They tell us that when the raiders attacked, some of the men of the village tried to fight them with their knives and hoes, but it was obvious that they did not have a chance. When these men came out of their huts, they knew they had no chance and knew they had to do what they could to save their families. They grabbed the others and ran into the woods while the raiders were busy fighting. That was the same scenario first reported by our neighbor, but these two families ran in different directions. They did not feel guilty in not fighting, they said, but felt like heroes in saving their families—one man saved his wife, two daughters, and a son, and the other man rescued his wife, a son, and a daughter. The two newly discovered families stayed together and were living close to each other. They understood our fear in living close together, but so far they had had no problems and needed one another's support. During the raid on our village, when I ran into the woods with my son, I did feel guilty, and my indecision that caused me to wait those few minutes likely meant the death of my wife. I feel some responsibility for the whole village since my wife's parents had been the village elders.

As we talk, one of the newly discovered neighbors comes out of the woods with a man we know to be a wandering skald by the manner in which he is dressed. After introductions, our new neighbor reports that we must hear one of the skald's stories, because our lives might depend on it. The skald begins:

"The land some distance to the south is being settled by a warrior chieftain and his 'retainers,' as he calls them. The chieftain has built a great hall where he and his men spend their nights. The women have their own hall where they do the cooking, spinning, weaving, and sewing for their men, but they may spend some nights in the great hall with their men, or, if their men have some authority, they may spend the night in a hut that he built for them near the great hall. These warriors and the chieftain grow nothing, or very little. The women may have an herb garden to spice their foods or to use in healing. Otherwise they get their food from farmers like you who live in the area, in exchange for protection from the warriors of other chieftains who might try to get their land. Chieftains use their warriors to get more land and thus more food from the farmers of that land in order to support more and more warriors. They spend all their time trying to become stronger and stronger, with more and more land, and more and more farmers to support more and more warriors to gain more and more land. Many people are dying, even some farmers, because one way to conquer a neighboring chieftain is to weaken him by preventing him from getting enough food for his retinue. A farmer's or serf's chieftain tries to protect him, and needs to allow the farmer to keep enough food to survive, but the chieftain needs a lot and is always trying to get more from his serfs. As little sense as this makes, the farmers need to support their chieftain in order to survive."

In hearing this story I realize with dread what is ahead for us . . .

Again using the Freyr Diviner the next day, the 26th, I decided to go back to our first spring after the village had been destroyed. This time I experienced a role shift, becoming the son . . .

The four families that survived the destruction of the two villages continue to live in three places, more distant from one another than when they lived in larger villages. We work together when needed, especially when the men go hunting. We also get together for different celebrations such as the winter and summer solstices and the spring and fall equinoxes. We share freely and have become trusted and close friends. The first winter was difficult, but we survived. We had harvested what we could from the fields and gardens of our old village, and also from the smaller village to our north. The other families had returned to their village to harvest their fields and gardens, too. This first spring equinox is especially special, because we have worked hard to establish our new households and have made it through the winter with all of us in good health. We have saved enough seed and are preparing our fields and gardens for planting. We killed a pig for the celebration and come together on what is closest to the middle homestead, our neighbor to the south.

At this time I am old enough to get married. I have had my eye on the daughter of the family that escaped with two children. She is about a year younger than I am and close to being ready to marry too. At this equinox celebration we spend much of our time together and feel love for each other. We talk of getting married and decide we need to wait until the following spring. That will give me time to start our own homestead. Though it has been traditional for the man to move to live in the village of his wife's family, times have changed, and I think it would be better for us to live on our own. That summer I go scouting and find land to the northeast of my fiancée's family and southeast of our neighbor, about a twenty-minute walk from either homestead and about forty minutes from my father's. I am very concerned about him, though, since he will be alone. We talk about it a lot. I think he should move to be closer to the other families, to somewhere between the two other homesteads. After all of the work he has put into our homestead, he does not want to move.

Then time moves ahead, to the next spring equinox. It is the time of my marriage, the first marriage since the raids. We are all together at my wife's and my new homestead. We feel it will be safer because we are farther east from the sea from where the raiders came. We have heard that a group of raiders are settling a couple of hours down the coast, building a village with a great hall for their chieftain, but they have not bothered us, and we believe that they will not wander too far from the coast. I have spent time over this last year building our new home, and my father has given us a cow. It is a sunny spring day for this celebration of both the equinox and our marriage. During our feasting we hear noises coming from the woods to the west. We all jump up, and the men step forward in front of the women with their hands on their knives. Three men with swords appear in the clearing, large men who stand tall and strong, but their swords remain on their belt and they wave at us, saying that they come in peace. We invite them to join us in our meal. We learn they are retainers for the chieftain who has recently settled to the south at the edge of the sea, and they want to be our friends. When they hear that my wife and I were just married, one of the men takes off an arm ring and gives it to me as a gift, and he takes from his pouch a broach for my wife's dress. He says that his chieftain had given him these gifts to give to the families he meets in the chieftain's domain. This is the first time we hear that we are living in someone else's domain.

As the conversation continues, these warriors tell of another chieftain in the area who wants this land, and that it is their intent to protect us from this other chieftain or any other chieftain who might threaten us. In exchange for this protection they know we would want to help them by providing them with the necessary food to sustain them and their chieftain. My father explains to them that this is only the beginning of the second full year of our homesteads, fields, and gardens, and that we barely have enough to get us through this last winter and do not have much to share. The warriors continue to smile and say that they know this and do not expect much, but that since it is spring we should plant extra for the chieftain and his men. They report that the chieftain is a fair man, knows our life is difficult, and wants us to remain healthy and strong to produce what we and the chieftain together need.

Though the three warriors are friendly and have gifts for each of us, I know that my father and everyone else is worried and afraid of what might happen. Later that afternoon the warriors leave and this worry is expressed. At the same time we talk about needing to expand our fields and gardens for the chieftain as the best way to protect ourselves. We realize that if we pick up and move the same thing will happen all over again wherever we go. I am even more worried about my father living alone and what he can do for the chieftain. The others join in, and all think he should move and that they will help him start his new homestead. They know the exact place where he should move to, between their homesteads, and the one friend leads the way to take us there. By that evening my father feels that he has no choice but to move. They assure him that the field he has already planted will survive and grow like the fields did in the burnt villages, and that they will help him harvest them for the chieftain in the fall. Between them they have enough seed for him to plant a new field near his new hut, and they will help him build the hut so it should only take a couple of days. Thus my father moves, and we are all a little closer together . . .

I continued my exploration of this time of transition on January 27, using the Freyr Diviner, who took me back to the west coast of Sweden, about a month after my wedding . . .

It is late in the afternoon when two warriors with an ox cart come to our homestead. The cart is mostly full of vegetables, a couple of loaves of bread, and meat. It is obvious that they have already been to the other homesteads, as ours is the farthest from the coast. The two men walk over to the garden and I run over to them. They see our beans, turnips, and other vegetables and say they will take half as they start pulling up the turnips. I ask them to not pull them up all in one place but to take every other one so the others would have space to grow bigger. Then I say we will need to save some for seed for next year. They answer that there are only two of us, that there are over a hundred of them, and so we will have enough. They then go to the hut and first look in a couple of jars, which are empty. They ask, "Where is your grain?" My wife answers, "We have none. We are newly married and have not been together long enough for a grain harvest." "Then where did you get those loaves of bread?" She answers, "I baked them with my mother who shared her grain with us." "Then you have two loaves. We will take one. There are over a hundred of us and only two of you." Looking at the meat hanging in the eves, again they take half. My wife feebly protests, saying that there will not be enough for us and we will not survive. They again answer that there are over a hundred of them and that they are here to protect us. "You will find a way to survive," they tell us. Then they leave with their ox cart laden down . . .

On January 28, Freyr took me to the fall equinox and the gathering of the five families . . .

The ox cart and warriors have returned twice since their first visit, and each time they take half of what they find in our homesteads, telling us that we have enough left to survive the winter. On their last visit just a couple of days ago, we had just completed the harvest of grain and they took half. All of us are worried, but two things have happened that give us some hope. Since my father moved to live closer to the other four families, he returned to his old homestead every two or three weeks to check his fields and garden there and discovered that both are growing quite well, though he has not had the time to harvest them. Each time he has gone there he has done some weeding and thinning, but has not given them much attention other than that. Though we do not know for sure, we think that we will not see the warriors and their ox cart until next summer. The men of each family tell my father that they will go with him next time to help him in the harvest and that the extra vegetables and the grain will be a big help in getting us through the winter. The other thing that gives us hope is a discovery I made while journeying farther east while hunting. I found a large lake where I will be able to ice fish during the winter. There are others living along the lake who have not yet had a visit from the warriors and their ox cart. I report this to the others, and we are all excited about becoming acquainted with our new but more distant neighbors. The fish, too, will be a big help. On their last trip to our homesteads the warriors had taken half our sheep and a couple of pigs that they were able to catch. Among the five families we have seven cows and a bull, and they took two of the cows. The warriors know that we are close friends, will share the bull, and hopefully have a good number of calves next spring. Thus, we are prepared for our third winter . . .

On the morning of January 29th I awoke knowing that it was time to return to the initiation posture that would reveal how this new way of living changed my distant Nordic ancestors' lives at the time when a life of nurturance and mutual support died and a life of anger, aggression, and conflict was born. I used the Nyborg Man, and a death/rebirth experience was revealed to me as I once again became the father . . .

I am sitting alone as I have been since my son moved out to be with his new wife. I am sitting by the fire and have feelings that I had never felt before. It is a few days after the warriors with their ox cart have paid their last visit, and I am feeling angry. When we lived in the village there was so much love and support from everyone we lived close to. Now I am alone. I still have friends who I see every few days, but we have all lost the life we had before. I am angry enough to think of killing the warriors who have taken so much from us, but I know that would only make things much worse. I still have the Great Mother, who provides for us, though it now takes so much more work to grow what I need and for the chieftain and his men. These feelings are strange to me and they frighten me. At this point I become the son. I am having the same feelings of anger as my father, but also much fear. I look up from our fire and see my wife standing nearby. She is pregnant, and I fear for the new baby who will not know the way life was when we lived in the village, will not know a life where other people would know and all help care for our child. Our child will be alone, with only two of us close by. My wife is standing in the Freyja posture, the initiation posture of birth, and I know she is thanking Freyja for the baby inside her. I am glad that she can still feel the support of Freyja and the Great Mother.

I had heard another story from the skald who visited us a few months ago, a story of another god, called Odin, a god of violence who collects warriors who have died in battle. He must be the god of those warriors who come and take our food. I feel hatred for this dreadful god. I don't like these new feelings I am having. After I had returned from the lake to the east and had visited a village there, I mentioned to one of our neighbors that maybe it would be safe to live as a village there, but he said that one of the warriors with the ox cart had said that would not be permitted. They do not want us to live together because then it might not be safe for the two warriors with the ox cart to visit us. My anger keeps growing, but I know it would scare my wife if I told her about it . . .

I now backtrack a bit, as the following series of ecstatic journeys took place during the first nine days of December 2011—over a month earlier than the previously described experiences, but about five generations later in the timeline of the experiences just described. With the time-free quality of ecstatic journeying, the experiences do not always linearly follow one another. These experiences were of some of the ancestors who remembered the older era and did not understand the new era, such as the father and son above, as well as experiences of those who sought the prestige and fame of being a great warrior in the new era.

On December 1, using the Freyr Diviner, I asked what posture I should use in going back to early Nordic times. I have on occasion changed postures when the diviner told me to do so but not this time, though a new Realm of the Dead posture was revealed to me, as you will see, by my wife in this experience. Then I asked what life was like between husband and wife in terms of values and beliefs in the gods of violence. I quickly entered into a trance . . .

I am walking in out of the fields in the evening, carrying a hoe over my shoulder. As I go into my hut, I see my wife sitting in the dim light at the table, her elbows resting close together on the tabletop with her forearms upright and forming a *V*, with her hands about shoulder-width apart, palms facing each other and fingers pointing upward. She is facing forward, as if looking out between her two hands, though her eyes are closed. Her chin is behind her hands, not resting on them. I have the feeling I have seen her sitting in this manner before. I ask her what she is doing and she answers that she is just getting back from the Realm of the Dead and had a talk with her great-grandmother. I knew that she had never met her grandmother who had died some years before my wife was born, though she had heard stories about her, and knew nothing or very little about her great-grandmother. My wife had taken her concern about our young son, now eleven years old, who now wants to become a berserker and was out somewhere with his cousin playing berserker. She was not happy with him valuing and leading such a violent life. She says, "Why can't he be happy with farming, like you?" My son knows that I am not very happy because I am always tired from all the hard work . . .

I interject here to explain why my wife, in this trance, seemed so upset about her son's desire to become a berserker. Back in 2008, I had a trance experience with the Bear Spirit that gave me a visceral understanding of not only the strength of the bear, but more to the point here, a suggeston of the violent energy of the warrior known as a *berserker*. Until then, for me, the bear, as represented by the posture known as the Bear Spirit, has always represented nurturance and healing. On this occasion I was using the Bear Spirit with the intention of finding comfort and healing for myself. As I went into the trance, I at first felt the familiar soft, comforting warmth of the nurturing she-bear holding me. Then, my vision abruptly changed and I found myself as a berserker in Lejra, Denmark, at the remains of King Hrothgar's great hall, lying naked on the floor of the great hall with my hands on my abdomen, feeling it rise and fall with each breath, focusing my attention on increasing my strength to fight Grendel, the monster in the Beowulf story. Then I arose, dancing, wearing a bear skin with the bear's head over my own head, moving in the Native American style of toe-heel dancing but in the more frenzied manner of a berserker. I stood up and felt the sinewy power of the bear, and I understood then the violence of the berserker, as I stood there with my muscles bulging, showing their sinew, knees slightly bent and planted, as I worked myself up into a fighting frenzy.

On December 2, while using the Tanum Lower World posture, I found myself as a dead warrior, the same son from the previous day's trance journey, but this time a few years older . . .

A ship takes me to the Realm of the Dead. There I meet my mother's great-grandmother and great-grandfather, who are sitting next to each other. My great-great-grandmother tells me that I have forgotten the ways of the past, the powerful ways of magic of a vǫlva in her practice of seiðr, and that she could have protected me and given me direction in life. A vǫlva could have told me about the dangers of mixing love with the role of a warrior. If I wanted love, a berserker's life was not for me, she says . . .

On December 5, I returned to the Freyr Diviner and went back to the same farm in Sweden . . .

As I go back to my hut in the evening, I hear talking inside and know we have a visitor. It takes a while for my eyes to adjust to the darkness. I first see the light from the ends of the roof, the smoke holes, and see smoke rising and going out the holes. I see the glow of the embers in the central fire from which the smoke rises. To my left is a fence, and behind it is a cow chewing its cud. My wife had milked her earlier. As I enter I see that our visitor is a tattered old lady, a wanderer in ragged clothes, but I recognize her as a seeress, a vǫlva. My wife wants her to give us her visions before we eat, as it is better for her to have her visions when her stomach is not full. Against the wall at the left hangs a platform that I lift that is supported by legs. I lash the diagonal braces to hold it steady and place a stool on it. The old lady climbs the ladder and sits on the stool. Her eyes close and she holds one knee with her left hand while she shakes a rattle with her right hand. After a while, the rattling stops and she opens her eyes. She reports that she saw our son sitting with my wife's great-grandparent. He had left a couple of weeks before with our chieftain, and now he is dead. I ask why he is not in Valhalla, and she says that he was killed without knowing what hit him. He was with a woman, at a distance from where the fighting was taking place, when he was hit with an ax. He did not die fighting. Though my wife is crying, she mentions that it is good he is with family, with someone who knows him, though he had never met them. I have confused feelings because he was not a hero in death . . .

Using the Tanum Lower World posture on December 9, I felt myself being slowly pulled along by my right heel . . .

I am standing outside of a small hut with my wife. We are both old and feeling very sad. Other huts downhill in front of us are burning, and people are running around. Several men from a boat had come ashore and started ransacking the place. We turn and slowly walk into the woods behind the hut. No one seems especially interested in us and we walk uphill to where I know there is a cave, and there we sit just inside the entrance, feeling confused and sad. My wife is chanting over and over, "Great Mother, why? What's happening?" I start to chant with her quietly under my breath. We are the great-great-grandparents of the youth who will visit us in the Realm of the Dead.

In this new time, women continue to value the nurturance of the Great Mother and Freyja in caring for their families, but new pressures on the men to protect and provide for their families make their lives considerably more difficult, fearful, and vengeful. They begin to find strength in the warrior gods Odin and Thor. The women are understanding and support the men, realizing that their anger and fear is warranted as a means of self-protection, and that there is little else they can do in their struggle to survive. The old nurturing life of mutual support and appreciation and respect for the Great Mother is forgotten after only a few generations, and this crazy new way of living has replaced it . . .

7

THE WARRIOR AND
HIS FAMILY

What was life like for the Nordic warrior? With this question in mind, on December 24, 2011 I used the Freyr Diviner to enter an ecstatic trance to learn more of the beginning of this age . . .

I am in the great hall sitting at a table below the chieftain, who is sitting in his high seat. We are eating and drinking, and our women are serving us. My wife is one of the women, and when she comes to me I grab her roughly, pull her to my lap for a few minutes, and fondle her. I'm a bit drunk. This drinking and eating continues as we talk about the last battle. I have a couple of arm rings on my left arm. The hall smells strongly of male bodies, sweat, and mead. Later that evening I pass out on the floor and my wife comes to lie next to me. Otherwise she spends much of her time with the other women, the wives of the other warriors. Our closeness is mostly sexual. We are generally well fed and warm. Not much else is expected of us because I am gone frequently and who knows how long I will live? I have made for us a small hut that we call ours, but we are rarely if ever there, though I check it out every so often to keep it in repair and put fresh straw on the bed pallet. When I am away with the other warriors my wife stays in the women's hall off to one side of the great hall, where much of the cooking is done and where the women take care of the children. It is warm in there. When I come home I know where to find her . . .

I awakened the morning after this trance experience struck with a new realization of how the warrior society functioned—that a woman's identity was essentially that of a servant, and she was used sexually by her husband, with little identity beyond this basic function. In the warrior-oriented society, particularly in the hall of a chieftain, a woman thought very little about the Great Mother; the focus of her life was to serve her husband and the other warriors. Not until around two millennia later would women begin to exert their own identities through the feminist movement. After only a few generations from the time of transition, women had lost their relationship with the Great Mother, and life became very fragile as the survival of a woman's husband could not be expected. During this time there were still, however, peasant farmers who likely had more of a family life in which the wife was more respected and had responsibility for the household. If a warrior lived beyond the age of being an effective warrior, he might leave the king's retinue with his wife to become a farmer. The wife of a warrior or farmer may have continued to worship Freyja or the other fertility gods and goddesses; however, her husband, in his need to protect others and in his fear for survival, likely turned to Odin for strength, though Freyr was still his aide in farming. The son, even of a farmer's family, might have sought to be a warrior because the warrior was not a peasant and likely lived at a higher standard, as fragile as that life might be.

With this realization in mind, on December 25, I used the Freyja Initiation posture. As I held my belly in this posture, I immediately connected with a sense of anxiety. This time I was a woman . . .

I find my husband in the great hall with a severe arm wound. He tries to laugh it off, but I am worried. I go out to my medicinal herb garden with a couple of the women and we talk about the herbs to be used for such a wound and about what incantations can be used. I feel that he is not going to want to put anything on the wound because he is tough and to do so would look weak. Incantations can be used without him hearing them. I wait, but when his wound starts getting hot and turning red and he is in bed because of it he is willing to use the herbs. I call to Freyja and Idunn for help, for knowledge to use the right herbs and incantations, and call on the spirits and gods for health and prosperity . . .

From these experiences I learned that in the warrior era a woman's role is to care for her husband; more importantly, her survival depended on it. If he and the other warriors died in battle she could be taken as a slave by some other chieftain and abused. If she had a husband, however, she had some protection from the other men who otherwise might take advantage of her. She prayed to the Goddess, primarily to be attractive to her husband and for the knowledge of healing and food preparation to keep him healthy. She could not imagine life being any different.

With these fresh insights, on December 26, 2011, I was eager to use the same Freyr Diviner posture to journey back to those times . . .

The spirits appear from the four directions and take on human forms: a farmer's wife, the farmer, a daughter about ten years old, and an eleven-year-old son who is small in size and still at home. Another son, fifteen, is big and strong and off being trained by the chieftain's retainers. I am the farmer's wife and in charge of almost everything for the family. We have close neighbors and are not too far from the chieftain's hall. My husband is usually not around, but instead out hunting with our neighbors or hoe-ing weeds around the turnips. As I sit here in my herb garden, I am pull-ing weeds, picking herbs to dry, and thinking. My husband is out with the other men hunting, and last night he spent the evening with the men checking their hunting weapons and planning for the hunt. It is a warm summer morning and the air is fresh. We give most of what we grow and hunt to the chieftain. We do not object because it feeds our son, who is living in the chieftain's hall. Because of this, we hear that the chieftain seems to like us and looks after us. We are lucky to have a cow that is bred to a neighbor's bull. Most of our neighbors are also doing alright because of the protection they receive from the chieftain.

I am proud of our son but also worried because I know how dangerous his life will be in fighting for the chieftain, how easily he could be wounded or killed, but that is life. I have my daughter to teach, and I call on Freyja to make her beautiful so she can marry a warrior. I am happy with our younger son because we need his help with everything. I pray to Freyja for our crops and our health. My husband sometimes calls to Freyr for help when he goes hunting. What he gets on the hunt is shared with the other families, and half goes to the chieftain. I spend some time tending the garden. The herb garden is used to keep us healthy. The rye, oats, and barley I grind into flour for bread. I set aside half of the flour for the chieftain. I am concerned about the coming long winter, and so our prayers are for enough to get us through—enough flour for bread and a good supply of turnips and other vegetables, along with the dried meat and the milk from the cow, which will dry up by spring, but I have made some cheese to help get us through. With these thoughts I go back inside our hut and hang the herbs from the post that supports the roof. I then go down with our daughter to the swampy edge of the water to pick reeds to make a new basket and to help her make one, too. Our son is out in the turnip garden, hoeing around the turnips, parsnips, carrots, and other roots. It is a pleasant day . . .

These last two experiences answered one of my major questions, "How could a woman, with her nurturing nature, think anything other than that men are crazy in their need to fight?" It seemed apparent from these experiences that they knew no different life than this one and had to appreciate the men for what they did. Both the farmer's wife and the warrior's wife worried about their families, and both spent a lot of time apart from their husbands.

On December 28, I used the Freyr Diviner to show me where I needed to go next. He quickly took me to the chieftain's hall, to the warriors' training grounds . . .

I am the chieftain's first retainer, in charge of keeping the warriors in shape and prepared for battle. I have been very fortunate to achieve this position because my parents are just farmers. I am quick to call on Thor for strength, and my concern is for protecting my chieftain's warriors from being injured in their practice, yet I also want them to push themselves. In sword-fighting drills I want them to fight with restraint, but in wrestling practice I encourage them to go to their limits. In sword-fighting their goal is to get inside, to get close to the warrior they are fighting, and then they wrestle, imagining that in their right hand is their long sword, which they drop to their side, but in the left a short sword with which they use to kill their opponent. Each man calls on Thor, and each wears Thor's hammer, Mjölnir, which the men reach for and touch to focus in preparation for the fight. Standing erect, with shoulders back, chest out, and hands resting on the lower abdomen in the Bear Spirit posture, each warrior feels his abdomen rising and falling with each breath and his chest expanding. In this posture, with each breath a warrior feels greater and greater strength, so that when he grabs onto his fighting partner he feels maximum strength. And with this feeling of maximum strength he feels invulnerable. I pair each of the warriors with a warrior whom I believe to be of equal strength and skill. In this fighting practice our vision is often of the fighting in Valhalla, of the great warriors who have died in battle but continue to fight each day, who inspire us. Each chieftain has a fighting field where the warriors practice, and off to one side of the field the young sons of the warriors play at fighting, copying their fathers with the dream of becoming great warriors themselves . . .

On January 29, 2012, while using the Freyr Diviner, I found myself as the young son of the chieftain's first retaining, a boy of four or maybe five years old, living among the warrior families . . .

Mother has just given me my breakfast and tells me to go out to play with the other young boys and watch my father. I don't think Father knows who I am among the other boys. He is always with the other men and does not seem to care about we children. Mother is always busy, too, and so I spend most of my time with the other boys. We all sleep at the end of the hall near where the women cook the food, and some of the other younger women sometimes watch us, but we are generally by ourselves.

We go out to the edge of the field where my father is showing the other men how to fight. Today is a little different because one of the older boys for the first time has been taken out onto the field by his father, and his father is showing him how to hold and swing a sword. We watch him, and with our sticks and wooden swords try to do just what he is doing. I have never seen this boy with his father and did not know until now who his father was. In our play of sword-fighting and wrestling I am hurt and run back to where the women are cooking, spinning, weaving, and sewing. One of the younger women comes to me as I run in, and she washes and puts something on me where I was hurt.

As I sit there holding the poultice on the spot where I was hurt, I watch a young girl learning to spin wool or flax and roll it into a ball. I see Mother on the other side of the hall. She is weaving, and she waves and smiles at me. After a few minutes I feel better and run back out to be with the other boys my age. After supper at night and before we go to bed, one of the women sits down with us and tells us stories about the gods and goddesses, about Odin, Thor, and Freyr. I especially like the stories about Thor. He sometimes does silly things, and the stories are funny . . .

On January 31, the Freyr Diviner again took me back to the chieftain's great hall and the hall of the women. This time my question concerned how the young women lived, and I quickly found myself as the first retainer's young, fifteen-year-old daughter . . .

I am in the hall practicing the woman's craft of weaving when I see a young boy run in, a friend of my brother's. He has been hit hard on the arm with a wooden sword and has a red bruise. It is my turn to show that I know how to make the healing poultice that we use on such injuries, so I go over to him, check his arm, go get the herbs used in the poultice, and bind them to his arm with a strand of the linen I was using in my weaving. I look up to see my mother watching me. She nods her approval and smiles.

Later she comes over to me and I take her out toward the practice field. I want to point out to her the young man who has been taking an interest in me. He is one of the stronger and bigger young men learning how to fight. Again she smiles at me and puts her arm around me. I know what she is thinking. Even though she has a husband, and an important husband among the other men, she does not see much of him. He spends all his time on the practice field when he is not out on a raid or fighting against the warriors of other chieftains. It is always important for chieftains to become more powerful and take over the land of other chieftains in order to gain more wealth, and he has to lead our chieftain's warriors in these battles. Sometimes I wake up at night and see that my mother is not in the woman's hall and know that she has gone in with the men to lie with her husband, but that is not very often. She is always worried that he might not return alive from a battle.

I think of my best friend, another girl whose father did not come home alive, and I have watched to see what has happened to her mother. Her mother now is no more than a servant to the chieftain and all the men. She has no one to call her own, and when she goes into the chieftain's hall the other men grab her, take advantage of her, and show her no respect. I have noticed that without a husband a woman has no standing, and if her husband is killed she generally does not find another husband unless she is really special in some way. I know my mother is thinking about me, what is ahead for me, knowing how hard life can be for a woman. She has told me about such things. She and all the women spend a lot of time praying to the goddesses Freyja and Frigg for strength and protection, asking them to protect their husbands. She wants me to be happy and knows how badly I could be hurt. But if I learn to be the best at all the women's skills—spinning wool and flax, weaving, sewing, knowing the herbs and when to use them, and cooking—I might be lucky enough to find a man as strong as my father who can protect me. The young man who has shown an interest in me just might be that man . . .

For a deeper understanding of a woman's relationship with her husband, on February 1, 2012, I decided to use the Freyr Diviner. I found myself again as the first retainer's daughter from the previous session, but about twenty years later . . .

I am in our small hut, a hut built by my husband, sitting by myself, thinking *I am alone because my husband is dead.* I am recalling my experience of a few days ago while I was in the women's hall, when I had a frightening vision of my husband being killed in battle, being hit with an ax from behind. In my vision my brother arrives on the scene and kills the man who killed my husband. A couple of days later, when the warriors returned from battle, the story they told was exactly as I had seen it in my vision.

My brother now is the first retainer to the chieftain. Our father, the former first retainer, was wounded several years before and now remains at home as an elder and protector of the village while the other warriors are off in battle. My husband was a respected warrior under the leadership of my father. We buried the body of my husband and encircled his grave with large stones, but we know he is now in Valhala.

As I sit in the hut, my older son, who is now seventeen, comes with food for us. We sit and eat, though I am not greatly hungry. He is the one person who understands me at this time. I feel confused and frightened, but I feel a strange power growing within me. The vision I had comes from that power, but it also frightens me. I realize how much I can see with my power of seeing. I saw my son preparing the platter of food for us and leaving to bring it up the hill to my hut. I now understand my son, who has the same power. I am confused and frightened by this power. I feel I am on a new path in life and don't know where it is leading. My son, smaller and weaker than most of the other boys in the village, had dreams or visions when he was very young, seeing things that were happening at a distance, such as this battle that killed my husband, seeing the location of lost sheep, and knowing ahead of time when visitors were coming. I had a hard time accepting this power in my son for a long time. For this reason he spent a lot of time alone, and his favorite activity was to be alone in his hut that he built while watching the sheep of our village. There he had many visions, and now he has become respected in advising the chieftain and my brother as the second in command among the warriors. With my vision of my husband's death, we now understand each other. So he sits with me quietly as we eat. My younger son is a new warrior and I worry about him like I worried about my husband, but so far I have had no frightening visions about him. He seems happy in his practice of fighting and striving to be a great warrior for our chieftain. Because of my visions, my path is different from the other women, who are servants to the warriors. I know this path is a much lonelier path, but it is also a path where I will not be taken advantage of by the men of the village. I feel comforted by my son, who has been on this path and understands it better than me. I am glad he brought us some food. I remember that he used to come down to the woman's hall and take a platter of food with him back to his hut with the sheep. I am thankful for him and thank Freyja . . .

The next day, February 2, I used the Freyr Diviner again, asking the question, "Is there anything else I need to learn about the life of the warrior and his family . . . ?"

I am a young boy, maybe eight years old. I think I may be another son of the chieftain's first retainer. I go out to the practice field with the other boys like we do nearly every day, but after a while I am bored and look around in the other direction. I notice a cloud of smoke and run in that direction to see what is going on. The smoke is coming from several different fires. The first one I come to is the blacksmith shed. It is more open on the sides than the other huts, and there is a rock fireplace inside. I see inside the fireplace a hot bed of coals. A large, sweaty man is in there with his back bare and his arms and front covered. His left arm appears larger than his right arm, and in his left hand he is holding a hammer. In his right hand are tongs holding a piece of red-hot iron that he is pounding with the hammer. I watch him awhile, and he does not see me at first. He then turns and sees me. He tells me that when I am big enough to swing that hammer he could teach me how to make swords, axes, and other such things. He smiles and is friendly. The scene changes and I then see a cup in a fire with a long handle and some shiny molten metal in the cup. I think it may be a different fire, but the furnaces are similar. A man lifts the cup by the handle and pours the metal, silver or gold, into a mold, making some piece of jewelry in the mold.

I wander on to another hut and another fire and there I see an oven. The door is open and someone is taking out pieces of pottery that have been fired. Next to it is a table, and on the table are a bunch of pots that the man has taken out. I have seen women in the women's hall using a wheel to form clay into pots and decorating them. I think that the women make the pots and bring them over to the kiln, and the man takes care of firing them. I then look out into the woods and see more smoke. I wander out there and see a large hill or mound covered with mud with smoke coming out of the top. There are several men dirty with black charcoal working in there. I know that inside the mound is a stack of wood burning. The men are making charcoal for the furnace of the blacksmith. There are a lot of other things going on around the chieftain's village that are important jobs for others who do not want to be or are not strong enough to be warriors. Something inside me tells me I don't want to be a warrior but want to do something else in my life. Thinking of being a warrior frightens me, though that is something I should not admit. I feel more excited about making things like the blacksmith, things that others can use. My brother knows he wants to be a warrior like our father, who died a hero, and another brother, who is not as strong, is always having strange dreams of things that are going to happen. But I feel different from them. I saw how sad mother felt when father died, and she has not been the same since. I want to make things instead of fight . . .

On February 3, before calling on the Freyr Diviner, I called on the spirits of the six directions as I always do, and in calling them I felt, in the words of Gregg Braden, the divine matrix. The source of information, the universal mind, has been described in many ways, including *holographic energy field,* but Braden calls it by this name. He describes it as being three basic things: the container for the universe to exist within; the bridge between our inner and outer worlds; and the mirror that reflects our everday thoughts, feelings, emotions, and beliefs. Three major attributes set it apart from any other energy of its kind. The divine matrix is everywhere all the time, it originatred at the beginning of creation and it responds to the power of human emotions, i.e., it has intelligence.[1] This feeling of connection with the divine matrix brought everything ever known close to me, especially the life of the ancient Nordic people, who felt very close, surrounding me, in fact. I felt that I was among them as I assumed the posture and found myself as the same young boy I experienced during the previous day's journey . . .

I am sitting on a driftwood log on the beach by the sea. Behind me, up a hill, is our village. If I turn my head I can see the thatched roof of our chieftain's great hall, but I am looking at the waves coming in and going out.

I feel a deep and thoughtful quietness within me. Yesterday I ran out to the practice field with all of the other boys who dream of becoming warriors, but I left them and wandered around the sheds and huts of the craftsmen of the village. Today I did not follow the other boys but ran down here to the water's edge. Not far from me are men building a new ship, hewing logs into planks, and behind them is the skeleton of the ship. Farther up the coast are two other ships for when the warriors go on their raids and then return with all kinds of interesting things from faraway places. There are a number of smaller boats, several in the water with men in them, and another just being pushed out into the water by the fishermen of our village. Each day they go out to fish and bring home the fish we eat, a big part of our diet.

Some of the food we eat comes from the farms of the peasants who live more inland in the domain of our chieftain. Other food, and much of the wool the women use in their spinning and weaving, comes from our large herd of sheep, but we usually do not start eating any of the sheep until winter. We also have a large garden that is tended mostly by the women. But a lot of our food comes from the sea.

Sitting there by the sea I recall the days I have sat on the hillside far above our village watching the sheep, something all young boys must do. Now I am looking over the village and see smaller huts out at a distance around the edge of the village. I know that these huts belong to the families of the blacksmith, the shipbuilders, and the other craftsmen of the village. Their wives have their gardens to tend along with all of the other wifely activities. Their lives are more like the lives of the peasant farmers who live farther out from the village. These craftsmen and their wives do not spend time in the great hall, because that is only for the warriors.

My quiet and deep thoughts are about who we are, what we do, and what I want to do. I now know I don't want to be a warrior. I want to make things, and I think I want to become a blacksmith . . .

Later that same day, February 3, I went on another ecstatic journey, this time using a "launching pad" to travel into the upper or Sky World. During the previous few days I put together five such launching pads, as described by Felicitas Goodman,[2] to use with my posture group that meets on Sunday afternoons. Images of the Tanum Sky World posture have been found in several places, including Egypt and France, in the Lascaux Caves, and several were found in the petroglyphs around Tanum, Sweden. The figure is depicted lying on his back, rising at a 37-degree angle. This was my first experience with this posture. This time I found myself again the Viking boy, but, curiously, also myself. I realized how this experience deeply describes how I myself felt as a young boy in my current life, a feeling and philosophy that I have carried with me all my life . . .

I am journeying to Valhalla. We arrive at the fighting field and are greeted by my father, who was recently killed in battle, and as a hero was taken to Valhalla by the Valkyries. He does not seem surprised to see me, and he puts his arm around me and we sit on the grass. I am surprised he that puts his arm around me. I was never sure that he even knew I was his son. I ask my father why he wanted to be a warrior. He answers that it was exciting and he felt important as a hero to the chieftain. He wears several arm rings given him by the chieftain for his valor, showing that he was a respected hero . . .

Being in a trance journey as myself adds an additional evaluative dimension to the trance experience. Psychologist Ernest Hilgard, famous in the 1950s for his research on hypnosis, refers to this observer part within a hypnotic experience as the *hidden observer*.[3] In the previous experience I realized that the warrior's whole life was that of the warrior. When he was not fighting or practicing he was in the hall of the chieftain drinking mead and getting drunk. Only then would he interact with his wife, and only for casual sexual contact. Combat, and even just practicing for combat, produced an adrenalin rush that felt exciting to him, and nothing else was as important. That is the way it had to be for him to be the best warrior he could be. He couldn't allow anything else to interfere with his role as a warrior; there could be no other worries, no concerns. This was evident in the petroglyph story of the Tanum Lower World posture.

When as the Viking boy I saw how my mother suffered, I knew something was missing in that life. As that young boy I experienced so much more of life all around the village and did not want to miss all that by becoming a warrior, not even to be a hero respected by the chieftain. As myself while simultaneously being that young boy, I did not fight and could not understand fighting. In my present life, on five different occasions I have found myself in fights that I did not start; I remember each incident vividly. I recalled only a few years ago, now in my older years, watching two adolescent boys wrestling on the lawn across the street from my office, realizing that this kind of fighting as a way of bonding that the two boys were actually enjoying was actually a very strange idea to me. So in this way I greatly identified with the young Viking boy, my distant ancestor.

One important question I had regarding the warrior era concerned what role, if any, magic played during this harsher era that had replaced the magical era of the Vanir gods. On December 27, 2011, while using the Freyr Diviner, I had an experience in which I was in service to my chieftain as his shaman. This journey described how magic, in the form of seiðr, still functioned in the warrior society. On this day, without having any expectations, I asked Freyr where I needed to go next, and he quickly took me to the hut of the seiðrman . . .

As seiðrman, I already know that the chieftain has returned from a battle and now wants to know of the future, so I go to his private hall with my student, a young warrior who was blinded in his first battle. My chieftain's domain is on the shore of the great sea with the land of two other chieftains surrounding him, one who carries the banner of a falcon and is considerably stronger, to whom my chieftain pays tribute, and the other equal to or weaker in strength to my chieftain. The last battle with this weaker chieftain resulted in both sides losing men, but with less of a loss for my chieftain.

The chieftain wants to know from me of the future, particularly when he should launch his next battle. I sit on my high platform in the style of the Nordic shamans and call on the wisdom of Odin, the far-sighted god. I see a battlefield with a lot of bodies, mostly of the weaker chieftain's men, but my chieftain also has considerable losses. I tell my chieftain he will win, but his losses will weaken him considerably. It will take time for him to rebuild his strength. He will gain the remnants of the other chieftain's domain and will be able to collect needed supplies from his neighbor's peasants, but he will be vulnerable to his more distant and stronger new neighbor . . .

About a month after this experience, I awoke on the morning of January 12, 2012, feeling very agitated. I lay in bed trying to bring back a very strong dream. I recalled two images from the dream; both suggested that I was again the chieftain's shaman from the earlier experience, and that the dream I had just had was related to the previous trance experience. The first image was the same as earlier, when as a shaman I reported to the chieftain a battle scene with many dead warriors on both sides. The second image was of a battle scene in which a line of warriors faced me, carrying a banner with a raven on it. Behind them was a battlefield, again with many dead warriors. As I thought about this dream and my life as the shaman as experienced in the previous journey, I realized that the dead were the warriors of my chieftain's neighbor to the north, and that the raven banner was that of the chieftain even farther to the north, the chieftain whose domain was north of our neighbor's. It came to me that after the last battle our neighbor had lost a lot of strength, such that he was unable to pay tribute to the raven chieftain, causing the raven chieftain to attack and take tribute. Now facing us, was he thinking of attacking us? I had to take this to my chieftain. I quickly took the Freyr Diviner posture and immediately went back in time, where through the magic of ecstatic trance posture work I found myself standing before my chieftain as before . . .

I tell him my dream—the dream I, as myself, had just had. He understands and asks that I wait outside while he thinks this over. Though I understand many of the issues involved, it is the chieftain himself who has to make the final decision. We are not strong enough to attack the raven chieftain, and if he attacks us or captures us, then what? Do we pay tribute to the chieftains on both sides of us? Do we relinquish our chiefdom to the stronger chieftain? The falcon chieftain to whom we now pay tribute is responsible for protecting us. We need to send an emissary to him, asking for help. In this way we hope to be safe. Yet I cannot see how it would work to have a weak chieftain residing between two strong chieftains. For the protection of our people and retainers, our chieftain may need to swear loyalty to the one to whom he pays tribute now and give up his title—a better alternative than dying. But chieftains do not easily give up their titles. . . . Soon the chieftain calls me back into the hall. He has decided to call on the falcon chieftain to help him in protecting his domain. He expects that this battle will be a stalemate, and that the two chieftains will call a truce, exchange some gifts, and become allies. My chieftain's men will still be in the middle but will be considered by the raven chieftain as retainers of the falcon chieftain and will be respected as such. We will still be in debt to the falcon chieftain, but this is the best we can expect. The falcon chieftain's protection is worth the tribute . . .

Thus, went the struggle for survival in the warrior society. Besides seeking victory over his neighbor, a chieftain had to protect his retainers in order to maintain his strength. If he decided to go into battle too quickly, the outcome would be as the seiðrman had predicted; if he waited too long, the other chieftain would have time to increase his strength, though it was generally difficult for chieftains to find new warriors without going into battle and gaining them through victory. Good warriors sought to be with the stronger chieftain, and though they swore loyalty to their chieftain, if they were defeated in battle and survived they were free to then swear loyalty to the winning chieftain.

Now, in the warrior society we live in, we are in a world of constant fighting, a world that has forgotten the Great Mother, a world that worships Odin, the warrior god of gods, where each day the life of the warrior may end. We live no longer in the Garden of Idunn. The garden has been relegated to our distant memory, to a small area of the Sky World, no longer available to us. We have been thrown out of the garden because of our relationship with good and evil, a relationship that was discovered and reflected to us by Odin, who is also the god of wisdom. From where does this god of gods gain his wisdom. As the ancient story goes, two ravens—Hugin and Munin—sit one on each of his shoulders and bring him the news of the world. These black ravens bring him the dark and hidden knowledge of the minds of man, the knowledge that paradise and the beauty of the earth have been forgotten, lost in world strife. Michaela Macha beautifully tells of this transition. These ravens used to be white and would visit the world of beauty, carrying with them what they saw in paradise, the Garden of Idunn.

How Ravens Came to Be Black
by Michaela Macha

Once upon a time and long ago, Odin was walking under the branches of Yggdrasil when two ravens swooped down and settled on his shoulders. The raven on his left was white as the mists of Niflheim (for back then, all ravens were white), and his eyes mirrored the clouds. The raven on his right glistened in the sun as the snows of Jötunheimr and looked at him with bright, clear eyes. And Odin called the raven to his right Hugin, which means Thought, and the other one he named Munin, which means Memory.

As the days passed, Hugin and Munin matched the Allfather's curiosity for everything in the Nine Worlds, flying around and watching and listening to whatever they could, and in the evenings, they returned to him to tell him all they had seen and heard in the long hours of the day. They told him about the slow thoughts of the mountains, the colorful and ever-changing memories of men, and the sound of the song in the heart of everything that lives. And though Odin delighted in the knowledge they brought, he always felt they had missed something, and he said, "That was much, but not yet enough. Tomorrow you must fly again. Try to rest now." And the ravens slept uneasily, not knowing what they had missed, and every morning they flew out again.

There came one of many evenings after another long day when they had once again seen all that Sunna's* shine could show, had listened to all men's bright thoughts in Midgard and read their waking memories, when Hugin said to Munin, "We cannot return yet. It is not enough. We must go farther." And they flew on into the night.

And Hugin flew through the dark dreams of mankind and heard their thoughts, which they dared not think during the daytime, not even before

---

*Sunna is Michaela Macha's poetic word for the sun.

themselves. He winged through the black void between the stars, where there was nothing at all, and on to the twilight world of the future, where there is equally nothing and everything at once. And when he returned, his feathers, from tip to tip, were black as the night.

And Munin flew through the minds of men into the shady corners and cellars where they had hidden all the things they did not like and locked them away, saying, "I do not remember." He soared through the sightless void of Ginnungagap, and on and on until he arrived at the ashes of Ragnarǫk, which obscured this age from the next. And when he returned, his feathers, from beak to tail, were as black as soot.

The ravens returned to Odin just before the break of morning, when the night is at its darkest, and when they settled back on his shoulders he knew all that they had seen, and they did not need to tell him. And he understood what had been missing, and nodded, and said, "It is much, and it is enough. For tonight, you may rest." And the ravens blinked drowsily into the first rays of the rising sun, which glinted on their now-black feathers, tucked their beaks under their wings, and slept very well.

Since that time, all ravens have been seen to be as black as a shadow on a starless night. Very rarely does it happen that somebody catches a glimpse of a white raven, and should you ever be lucky enough to see one you'll know that you have wandered far off and back into the land of memory, before ravens came to be black.

The blackness of these ravens comes from the ashes of Ragnarǫk, the final battle over power and greed, over good and evil. The survivor of this battle, the new king of kings, is the god Baldr, the most beautiful and gentle of the gods, a god that remembers the Garden of Idunn and can bring us back to this garden. In the warrior era the ancient stories and the power available from the earliest times have not been forgotten. In the stories above, the women through their knowledge of herbs remember them; the seiðrman remembers them, though he uses them to assist the chieftain in war.

8

BALDR'S REBIRTH

The rebirth of Baldr happens daily with each sunrise, annually with the rebirth of spring, and personally with those death and rebirth experiences that provide us with personal growth throughout our lifetime. Thus, the rebirth of Baldr is very much alive and dynamically present in our lives.

The rebirth of Baldr is also arriving collectively with the awakening of Nydagan, the New Age or New Dawn, which is happening now, in the twenty-first century. This represents an awakening to Jean Gebser's era of time-free transparency—a return to valuing the magical and mythical paradigms of earlier eras of consciousness, which still exist within us. It is an awakening to Barbara Hand Clow's vision of the human being evolving from *Homo aggressus* to *Homo pacem*. It is the awakening, predicted by Richard Tarnas, of our connection to the world soul or *anima mundi,* ushering in an era in which we will no longer be separate from the world but part of it. It is Riane Eisler's description of what it is like to value the nurturing Great Mother. And it is Carl Calleman's foretelling of a great awakening into clarity and the dissolution of the dualities of life with the emergence of unity consciousness. The descriptions of my ecstatic experiences in this chapter bring alive the nature of this awakening, this rebirth of Baldr.

As we will see in the next few experiences Baldr is not dead but remains alive in the minds of those who maintain their connection to nature and the Mother Goddess. On December 20, 2011, the Nyborg Man provided me with a new, rich insight into the nature of death and rebirth. This time I found myself as a black panther, same as in five previous experiences, but this time I was a female just returning from a journey into the Realm of the Dead . . .

I sit down in a jungle clearing and become human: I am an ancient farmer whose son was killed,* and also the son's maternal great-great-grandfather. Yet I am also still the jaguar. I am sitting as all three in a farm field in the early morning, and there I watch a blue chicory flower open to the sunrise, watching its rebirth. The experience becomes intensely spiritual—an experience of feeling not only the rebirth of the day, but also the rebirth of the year at spring, and the rebirth of my own understanding of life . . .

The rebirth of Baldr is any and all of these rebirths: the death of violence and the dependence on muscular and technological strength, and the rebirth of the magic and power of intuition, compassion, and gentleness—a rebirth of the beautiful and gentle Baldr as he existed millennia ago, but happening now, in a world that has become too violent to be sustainable. This insight into the meaning of rebirth seemed to be very powerful and significant at the time. It offers a clear alternative to the apocalyptic view of a Second Coming of Christ. The rebirth of Baldr, as well as the Second Coming of Christ, when seen as a rebirth of gentleness, love, and nurturance—characteristics represented by both Baldr and Christ—is what brings us great hope for the way life can be in the New Age. The next few ecstatic experiences, in which I learn from the panther, continue to feel exceptionally powerful in defining the awakening of this new age.

My wife and I had decided to spend New Year's Eve of 2012 with my daughter's family in California. On the last night of 2011, using the Freyr Diviner, I asked Baldr what he had to teach or show me . . .

---

*This is the same farmer as in the Scandanavian experiences described earlier.

I go quickly to the story of all the gods of the Æsir throwing everything imaginable at Baldr, with nothing harming him. A deeper meaning to this story then comes to me: that no matter what is thrown at me, it does not have to hurt me, yet it could kill me, depending on my response. If I let what hits me kill me without fighting back, I will be reborn in innocence. I am able to feel the real and deeper power of not responding in kind, in retaliation, by fighting back against aggression. Frigg, Baldr's nurturing mother, who I believe was originally one of the Vanir gods, nurtures Baldr and teaches him this peaceful and gentle attitude, which is demonstrated when she seeks the assurance from every substance and everything that could harm a person that it will not harm Baldr. Thus, she is doing what she can to protect her son from his death, the death that he saw in a dream . . .

The next morning, New Year's Day, I again used the Freyr Diviner, first thanking Baldr for what he had taught me the previous night, then asking him what more he could teach me . . .

I am surprised that Freyr takes me back to times of the *Prose Edda*, this time to Loki and Loki's response to the hypocrisy of the gods in valuing strength and violence, but at the same time loving and appreciating the gentle, peace-loving Baldr. Whereas Loki confronts this duality in the thinking of the gods by arranging the death of Baldr, Baldr shows no resentment toward the gods as they throw everything imaginable at him—actions that I suspect Baldr thinks are crazy. The world does not change by the reconciliation, repentance, or redemption of the gods, but rather with their death at Ragnarǫk and with the rebirth of the gentle, forgiving, innocent Baldr. Their death does not lead them back to Valhalla, where they fight every day, but to their final demise, the situation that brings about Baldr's rebirth . . .

All this came to me in a rush of thoughts, along with the powerful realization of the relevance of this ancient story in today's violent world. Though Christ preached peace and forgiveness and showed it through his own death, the Christian story does not appear to have convinced most of its adherents that violence and revenge are a totally hopeless and senseless response to life situations. Christians show a kind of hypocrisy—something that Loki is fond of pointing out—in their seeming appreciation of the love of Christ, all the while relying on extreme violence to push the levers of society. In our current world, I identify many, if not most of the world leaders with the warrior gods Odin and Thor. Even with Odin's foreknowledge of the gods' demise, he was unable to repent and reconcile. Yet there are also many in our world today who *do* understand the senselessness of violence and war, who are leading us to a New Dawn and the time of the rebirth of Baldr. Violence and war do not change the way people think. The power of compassion, empathy, and nonviolence has been proven to be the most effective way to bring about actual change in the way people think and act, as demonstrated by such leaders as Martin Luther King Jr., Mahatma Gandhi, Cesar Chavez, Danilo Dolci, and many others.

As this New Year's Day continued, the rest of the family went out for the afternoon, and I found myself alone in the house, so I decided to use this time of solitude to return to the time-space continuum I had experienced earlier. This time I used the Freyja Initiation posture . . .

I am in the Realm of the Dead, where Baldr resides before the final battle and his rebirth. The *Prose Edda* tells us that Baldr's brother, Hermöðr, is sent to the Realm of the Dead to attempt to bring him back, but Hermöðr is told that Hel will release Baldr only if every living creature will shed a tear for him. Baldr gives his brother gifts to take back to their father, Odin, including the golden arm ring, Draupnir, that Odin had placed on his funeral pyre. Upon the brother's return, all living creatures are asked to shed a tear, but the giant Thok* is unable to do as requested.

On this trip to the Realm of the Dead, I wait at the gate until Garmr, the bloodstained dog that guards the gates of Hel, is asleep. I

---

*It is believed that Thok is Loki in disguise.

sit outside the iron fence that separates me from Baldr. Baldr comes to where I am sitting and tells me of his love for his family and his need to reassure them that he is okay, but also that he is not ready or it is not time for him to return since they still value their strength as powerful warriors. He explains that only when they die can there be peace and a world of love, nurturance, and cooperation. He knows that they are otherwise incapable of changing, and only through their death can he be reborn . . .

On the second day of 2012, using the Nyborg Man, a death/rebirth posture, I quickly reviewed what Baldr had taught me earlier: first, that he cannot be hurt and is not afraid of death; second, that Loki's antics in confronting the hypocrisy of the gods is senseless and leads to their death; and third, that Baldr does not resent the warrior gods, nor is he ready to rescue them. I then thought about the various events, both on the national landscape and in my own personal life, that seemed to value the use of violence, retaliation, and aggression, and as I did so I went deeper into a trance . . .

I am me, but then I become the stalking panther. I do not understand why I am a panther, and so I decide to instead seek the identity of the animal that best embodies the characteristics of Baldr. The panther's strength at first seems to make it an unlikely animal to represent these characteristics, but the vision does not go away. The panther is indeed beautiful and sleek, like Baldr. Then I let myself fully experience the panther, and the more I experience it, the more I think that maybe it represents what I need to express—alertness, awareness of everything around me, and having total confidence, the confidence of not fearing or feeling threatened. I realize that my initial concern about identifying Baldr with a panther comes from a place of resentment of others who do not hold my values. Resentment does not seem to be a characteristic of a panther. I realize that in some ways resentment is like jealousy or the feeling of being threatened, and in his strength and self-confidence a panther has no need to fear. In this context, being a panther begins to make complete sense: becoming a panther is becoming one with the characteristics of Baldr, incorporating Baldr within me . . .

Afterward, as I reflected on this experience, I realized that a stalking panther is not separate from the world of rationality but is part of it: as a panther I can listen to and learn from the world and the cosmos. And I can learn more about the nature of cooperation as a panther as well. In cooperation, I can use my strength to sustain myself but not to control others. The loss of duality and competition brings us to a world of peace, the world of Barbara Clow's *Homo pacem*. With this realization, I decided I needed to review my previous experiences of being a panther, all of which occurred during the previous year.

While using the Olmec Prince, a metamorphosis posture, on January 23, 2011, I sat before the prince in a jungle clearing in Mexico, and a black panther sat next to the prince in the same posture. The panther stretched with his hind end up and his head down and then came over to sniff around me before wandering off into the jungle. I followed him on all fours. We came to a pond of water and he drank with his lapping tongue, and so did I. While looking into the pond I saw my reflection—black face with green eyes. When I looked up the other panther was gone. I wandered off, saw a rabbit, and playfully batted at it with little interest. I then wandered back to the Olmec prince. Throughout this experience I had an attitude of being above it all, of not letting myself resent the irritations of life—that as a strong panther, nothing could harm me.

Several months later, on May 15, while using the Nyborg Man, I listened to the deep, growling sound of a drum. For a few moments I found myself in Tibet, with the monks doing their growling overtone chanting. Then I found myself in a jungle clearing in Mexico. An Aztec or Mayan priest was sitting in a high-backed chair with a black panther sitting at his side, growling contently. The panther got up and wandered into a nearby cave. I followed. There was a carcass of some large animal. The panther lay down and started gnawing on the carcass. As myself, I picked up a bone and started gnawing on it. I could feel the grease running down my chin. The panther growled softly. I then left the cave and found the sunlight shining through the jungle leaves. I went into the cave before dusk, where I could see the dust particles suspended in a beam of light. I remembered this feeling from my childhood and then became my childhood self, sitting innocently in a beam of light as it came through the window, again with dust suspended in it. The sunbeam felt so warm and I felt so relaxed that I fell asleep on the floor in the beam of sunlight.

As I thought about this experience I realized that once again the panther had been showing me the power of being above it all, of not letting the little hassles of life bother me. Then I reviewed my experience of October 30, 2011, in which I used the Tennessee Diviner.* I found myself in the jungle in a village clearing. I could see two yellow eyes shining in the darkness. We were sitting around a fire and someone was drumming and someone else rattling. I focused on the yellow eyes, and on all fours I crawled toward them. It was a panther, and I followed it as a panther. I felt myself to be female and the other panther a male. He led the way to a spot deep in the bush where some sort of deerlike animal was lying asleep. As it sprang to run, the male panther leapt on it and brought it down. We started tearing at it. I was surprised at how hard it was to tear off a piece of meat. Even with my sharp teeth, I pulled and tugged against his pulling and tugging in the opposite direction. Then a piece of meat eventually ripped off, and I tried to chew it. I could taste the juicy, bloody meat, but I couldn't chew it into smaller pieces to swallow. I chewed and chewed, and finally I swallowed a fairly large piece whole. After eating this way I felt greasy and messy. I sat and licked my face and my paws and used my paws to wash my face. After a while I felt content and lay down next to the other panther and fell asleep.

The fourth experience with the panther occurred on November 13, 2011. Using the Olmec Prince, I found myself in the jungle brush, just

---

*This is not one of the Nordic postures. It is based on an artifact found at a grave site in Wilson County, Tennessee and is dated from about 700 CE. See Belinda Gore's *Ecstatic Body Postures* (page 116–22).

waking up. I stretched, lengthening my back, with my rear end raised and my forelegs stretched in front of me. I then started to walk through the night jungle, stalking. I could see something and crouched, feeling the vibrating energy in my hind legs, ready to spring, but I changed my mind, since I was not especially hungry. I continued to walk through the jungle and came to the edge of a village clearing, to a pyramid. There was a fire and probably more than one person, but I watched only one—a man who was dancing around the fire wearing a panther-skin robe. He moved on his hind legs as if he was stalking, and in his dance he jumped or sprang—not quite with the energy that I felt when I sprang, as he was standing on his hind legs and not pushing off from his front. Yet I felt he had something to say. He was expressing appreciation for me and reaching out to me as a panther. I was fascinated and crept closer to him, to where he could see me. When he saw me he made a roaring sound that came from his throat. I watched a while longer and then wandered off, feeling no fear of him.

Each of these experiences of the strength and self-confidence of the panther reflect the real power of Baldr and the weakness in the other gods' needs for retaliation and confrontation. I then reviewed my fifth experience with the panther, which occurred on November 27, 2011, in which I used the Nordic Halstatt Warrior posture while pursuing my Nordic roots. On this occasion, as a panther, I went into the underworld to visit with my ancestor—an experience I described in chapter 4. I stalked or walked cautiously along a path, first to the east, then down to the west, to the underworld, to the Realm of the Dead, to the place of those who died of illness and old age, in search of an ancestor. I felt safe going to the underworld as a panther because as a human I would not have been allowed to return. I sniffed among the dead until I found the right person sitting under dripping water from the ceiling, looking almost like a skeleton, but with a nose with water dripping off its end. I asked this person what he had to teach me. He answered that I needed to trust my intuition, not my muscular strength—that my intuition is my strength. He recognized me as his descendant, even though I was in the form of a panther. I then began my journey back up out of the underworld and returned home realizing how the message ran contrary to so much of life, although there are many who can understand and accept this message. This ancestor was old; I knew that he lived life not as a warrior, but maybe as a farmer.

Following my review of these previous experiences with the panther I decided to use the Freyr Diviner on January 5, 2012, with the intent of gaining further understanding into how to set aside the duality of the old world that promotes conflict and aggression, to open the way to the newly awakened world of cooperation. After a brief journey to the *Prose Edda,* in which I experienced the way the gods worked together to try to save Baldr and bring him back from the dead, with only Loki causing failure in this pursuit, I started having brief flashes of various things going on in my own personal life and in our times . . .

I feel like I am in a considerably deeper ecstatic trance than previously. I have brief flashes of the serious medical problems of my friend Bob; of the pedophile at nearby Penn State University who was arrested; of some situation in which I am pouring split pea soup; and a number of other brief flashes that I do not remember, issues of concern within my own community for which I offer help. I realize that though it may take just one person's wrong action to cause total failure, as with Loki or the Penn State pedophile, I realize we need to begin to work together in cooperation within our communities. Even though we may fail, we still need to move forward to help others. A community can stand behind the victims of the pedophile, but what happens to the pedophile himself is not in our hands. Yet we do not need to feel resentment or great disdain for him; those feelings only diminish our strength. Instead, we need to cultivate compassion for him. The traits of Baldr would have us working in cooperation in support of the victims, to prevent this from happening in the future. As I write this, this ecstatic experience makes sense to me in a new and important way . . .

Saturday morning, January 7, 2012, I returned to the Freyr Diviner and asked Freyr, "What of magic does Baldr have to teach me?" I went into this experience with no expectations, which is contrary to my nature, which is to have expectations; in this way, without expectations, the message I received was most revealing . . .

Sitting with Freyr I first go to his magical weapon, his ship Skiðblaðir, built by the dark elves, a ship that always has a fair wind for its sail and can be folded into a small packet, such that it can fit into Freyr's pocket. Then I go to the other magical weapons of the gods, including Thor's hammer Mjölnir and his magical belt, but I realize that all of these weapons are for aggressive actions and not for the magic of Baldr. I recall from the story of Baldr that the most powerful nurturing magic is that of Frigg's ability to talk with each substance and to receive reassurance from each substance that it would not harm Baldr. Also, there is the magic of Idunn's golden apples that are able to keep the gods young and healthy. Other stories I have heard over the years of this magic are of holding plants to one's chest or abdomen to receive from them an understanding of their healing properties. The magic of Baldr is the magic of listening to the enchantment of the world around us. I realize that over the last few centuries, with our focus on objectifying the world through our scientific, rational mind, the world has become disenchanted. This new awakening, this reawakening, brings us back to the natural magic of our enchanted world. I thank Frigg and Baldr for bringing us/me back from the desolation of the disenchanted world. As this experience ends, I feet relaxed and at peace . . .

As a result of these experiences, I now firmly believe in the rebirth of Baldr, whether with each sunrise or with the renewed warmth of spring; whether it is those personal rebirths I experience periodically or the New Dawn of peace and the rebirth of magic and enchantment.

The dynamic nature of this rebirth makes Baldr more relevant to our world today than the fundamentalist belief in a Second Coming, as held by some Christians, a belief whose foundation could be challenged as being too narrow if the translation from the original Greek of the three verses in Revelations (3:11, 22:12, and 22:20) that mentions the return of Christ is considered. According to the New International Version of the New Testament, the phrase ερχομάι ταχυ (*erchomai tachi*), used in all three verses of Revelations, translates as "I am coming soon." The first word, ερχομάι, is the first person imperfect form of the verb *to come,* thus it is correctly translated as "I am coming" or "I am continuously coming," since it is in the imperfect tense. The second word, ταχυ, is more correctly translated as "swiftly" or "quickly," not "soon." Thus, what has been considered a second coming or rebirth of Christ is instead a continuous action that happens quickly, as in the rebirth of each new day or the annual birth of each spring, and especially in the many deaths and rebirths that each of us experiences throughout our lives with those sudden insights or inspirations that periodically shake us to the core.

Yet beyond these personal reflections on rebirth, the many writers mentioned in the first part of this book also predict a significant cultural change or rebirth that moves us collectively into a New Dawn, an era of peace (*Homo pacem*), a dissolution of conflictual dualities that will bring us into unity, as well as a new and deeper understanding and reclamation of the magic and myths of past eras, the reenchantment of the earth, and the return of our appreciation of the nurturing Great Mother. The predictions of Calleman and Clow, based on their research and understanding of the Mayan calendar, are unstoppable, and they are unfolding now. Similarly, Tarnas's predictions are based on in-depth research and understanding of the cosmos and the alignment of the planets—predictions that are again inevitable and are happening *now.* Nydagan, this New Dawn, is bringing us to a new heaven on earth—the return of Baldr, or the true meaning of the event often called the Second Coming of Christ.

PART THREE

The Myths and Beliefs of the Ancient Ones

Learning from the Nordic Gods through Hypnotic Trance

There are repeated references to a time of plenty and peace, a time before a great flood, when women and men lived in an idyllic garden. These are the stories from which biblical scholars now believe the Old Testament myth of the Garden of Eden in part derives.

Viewed in light of the archaeological evidence . . . , the story of the Garden of Eden is also clearly based on folk memories. The Garden is an allegorical description of the Neolithic, of when women and men first cultivated the soil, thus creating the first "garden." . . . Likewise, the Garden of Eden and Fall from Paradise myths in part draw from actual historical events.

RIANE EISLER, *THE CHALICE AND THE BLADE: OUR HISTORY, OUR FUTURE*

Vanir

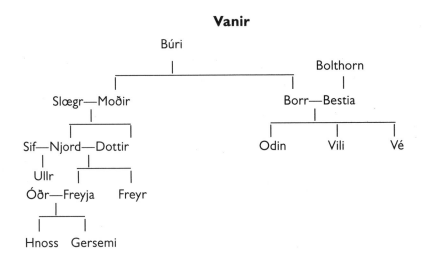

Æsir

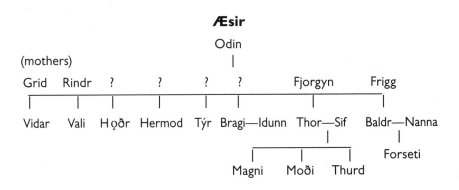

Family trees of the Vanir and Æsir

9

THE ORIGINS OF THE GODS

Before I discovered the power of ecstatic trance, I used hypnosis as one modality of psychotherapy. As described in chapter 2, a basic, defining aspect of hypnosis is the concept of the *yes-set,* i.e., that everything said to the client/patient is said with the expectation that he or she will answer "yes" or recognize that what is said is true. Once a therapist becomes skilled in using hypnosis, the yes-set becomes automatic and is the way the therapist relates to every client/patient throughout each therapy session, whether the therapy being used at the moment is cognitive-behavioral or marital-family. Hypnosis, therefore, quickly becomes part of any modality used.

Another aspect of hypnosis is that the therapist is in as deep a trance as the client. Trance is a learned altered state and can be self-induced. I use trance regularly in my preparation for a therapy session. I sit it my special trance chair, automatically go into a trance, mentally review my notes of the client, and through trance gain deeper insights and direction for the coming therapy session. This is exactly the process I followed in writing each the next forty-two stories that comprise chapter 10, which I have titled "The Lost Edda of the Vanir." This series of stories came about because in reading the ancient myths the *Prose Edda* and the *Poetic Edda,* I had many questions. As I sat in my trance chair and asked these questions, answers would come to me while in trance. In this way, these stories flowed forth, just as the stories of the ancient people of Denmark and Sweden flowed while using ecstatic trance postures, as recounted in the first part of this book. The stories seemed to come to me from nowhere specifically, but in asking while in trance, "From where did you come?" the vision of an attractive woman in a flowing white gown sitting on the ground across from me appeared. She is, I believe, Vanadisdottir, a priestess of Freyja, "daughter of the Vanir" and another name used in the ancient edda for Freyja. In my vision of her we would usually be sitting on opposite sides of a warming fire. Sometimes the fire was in the mouth of a cave, other times it was in an ancient thatched hut. These forty-two lays—a *lay* being a short lyric or narrative storytelling poem, a form characteristic of the *Poetic Edda*—came from her. As these lays came to me while in hypnotic trance, it was enjoyable to hear them as if being sung in the Danish singer Gunrun Gotved's beautiful voice.*

For you to more deeply understand the gods and goddesses of the Vanir and thus what I call the "Lost Edda of the Vanir"—*edda* being a collection of Old Norse poems, or lays—it will be useful for you to know what is already known of the gods and goddesses of the Æsir as recorded in Norse mythology. You have heard some of these stories already in the first part of this book; they have been told repeatedly for more than 1,500 years, and they never seem to get old. I have read and re-read them many times. Many of the stories, though, you may find to be new.

You probably have heard of the names of two of the gods: the high god of the Æsir is Odin, and his son is Thor. You may even know some of the stories of these two gods of the North, of Denmark, Norway, Sweden, and later Iceland. In the second half of the first millennium, as Christianity spread northward through Europe, the belief in these ancient gods was unfortunately displaced by the belief in Christ in a manner that attempted to destroy this rich ancient heritage of the

---

*Gunrun Gotved was the singer at the 2004 Midsummer Blot I attended. Interestingly she uses the name Vanadisdottir in her e-mail address.

Nordic people. Eventually, the last outpost for the belief in the gods of the Æsir was Iceland, and it was in Iceland that the stories of these gods were put into writing by Snorri Sturlson, an Icelandic historian, mythologist, poet, and politician who lived from 1179 to 1241. He wrote the two books that are now known as the *Prose Edda* and the *Heimskringla,* "The Lives of the Norse Kings," a history of the Norwegian kings that begins with legendary material in the Ynglinga saga, which significantly adds to our knowledge of the Æsir, and moves through to early medieval Scandinavian history.

A third book dealing with the mythology of the Old Norse was written at about the same time as these two books, but by an unknown author, is the *Poetic Edda.* The stories of this third book are written in a more poetic form, and again tell of the gods and goddesses of the Æsir. But it is the first book, the *Prose Edda,* that offers us a core understanding of the Æsir, from their creation to their demise. In times past, the ability to record these stories depended on the ability to write and therefore the invention of the alphabet, the earliest being the runic alphabet for Northern Europe. Only during the era of myth did such recording become possible, as related in the *Poetic Edda* in the story of Odin hanging on the world tree, where he gained the wisdom of the runes. Before that, no means existed for recording the older era of magic. During the transition between the eras of magic and myth, there were those who had some memory of the old ways. It was in this time of transition that the old magical ways of the Vanir began to evolve into the newer stories of the Æsir, a mixing of the old with the new. For those of you who have not read the newer stories of the *Prose Edda* and the *Poetic Edda,* as old as they are, having been written in the thirteenth century, the many footnotes will keep you abreast of how this restoration of the lost edda of the Vanir is related to the edda of the Æsir during this time of transition.

CAST OF CHARACTERS

From these eddas, recorded in the thirteenth century by Snorri Sturlson, we learn of the twelve gods of the Æsir, the most powerful being Odin, the god of gods, or Allfather. Odin is the god of poetry, battle, and death. He watches and protects the world from his high seat in Asgard, the dwelling place of the Æsir. From this high seat, called Hliðskjálf, he can see all corners of the world. He is wise and understanding as well as punitive. We will soon hear about Ymir, from whose body Odin and his brothers made the world as we know it, creating the sky, the earth, and everything within. The greatest of Odin's works is that he made man and gave him the spirit of life.

You may ask, from where did Odin come? The creation story of the Æsir says that before Odin was the ice and cold of the North. The South is called Muspell; it is bright and hot, a land of fire. The one called Surtr, an important figure in the demise of the gods of the Æsir, defends Muspell with his flaming sword. The land between the North and the South is called Ginnungagap; it is mild, with soft air that thaws the ice of the North. From this thawing ice, life appeared as Ymir, the first frost giant. As Ymir slept, from under his left arm came a man and a woman, and from his foot, a son. This is the beginning of the race of frost giants. Formed from the melting ice also was a cow whose milk fed these frost giants. The cow lived by licking the salt stones, and as the cow licked a stone, the first human, named Búri, was uncovered. He had a son, Borr, who married a giantess called Bestla, who was the daughter of the giant Bolthorn. Borr and Bestla's first and greatest son was Odin. The three sons of Borr, Odin, Vili, and Vé, killed Ymir, and when he fell, different parts of his body formed the mountains, ocean, sky, trees, and rocks.

Odin married Frigg, and it is from her name that we get the name for the sixth day of the week, Friday. But before his marriage to Frigg, Odin had several other children from other women he met in his wanderings. The strongest of these children was Thor. Thor carries a powerful hammer named Mjölnir that, when swung, causes lightning, just as the wheels of his goat cart cause thunder. Thor has two sons, Magni and Moði, and with his goddess-wife Sif, a daughter, Thurd. Thor gives us the name of the fifth day of the week, Thursday.

Another son of Odin is Týr, a god who sacrifices his hand in order to bind the monstrous wolf Fenrir. Týr is the god of war and the bravest of the warriors. It is from his name that we get the third day of the week, Tuesday. Odin's son by Frigg is Baldr, the most gentle and best-loved of the gods.

Another of the Æsir is the giant Loki, the trickster god. He repeatedly gets into trouble by challenging the gods but is smart enough to get out of the scrapes until near the end. As the story goes, Loki is happily married and has two sons with his wife Sigyn, but he has an extra-marital affair with an evil giantess who lives in the land of the giants, Jötunheimr, and with her he has three monster children: Jörmungandr, a sea serpent; Fenrir, a gigantic wolf; and Hel, whose body is half beautiful but the other half rotten with decay. When Odin sees these three monsters from his high seat, he knows they do not bode well for the future and sends someone to Jötunheimr to bring them back to Asgard. From there the gods throw Jörmungandr into the sea, where he grows and grows until he surrounds the earth so that he is able to hold his tail in his mouth. From that day on, Jörmungandr becomes the terror of seamen. Hel is thrown into the underworld, where she cares for those who die without the honor of dying in battle, but rather from illness and old age. The third child, Fenrir, is the wolf whom the gods let wander the fields around Asgard, until they realize that this wolf is no ordinary wolf: he does not stop growing. Only Týr is brave enough to venture into the fields to feed him. The gods decide they must restrain the wolf and first try to bind him in heavy chains, but with each attempt Fenrir breaks the chains. Only the dwarfs found in the cave of the dark elves have a magical binding that will hold the wolf. The wolf will not let the gods bind him in what appears to be a very flimsy binding unless one of the gods agrees to put his hand in Fenrir's mouth. Týr accepts this challenge and puts his hand into the wolf's mouth. As the wolf struggles to get out of the binding, he bites down, severing Týr's hand. In the end, in the final battle, these three monsters return to face the gods of the Æsir.

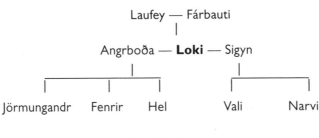

Loki's lineage

We will learn of several more gods, including Njord, the god who puts the wind in the sails of ships, and his twin children, Freyr and Freyja. Freyr brings us the rain and sun so crops will grow, and his sister, the goddess Freyja, is the goddess of love. She brings together couples in love and helps in pregnancy and childbirth. Then there is Heimdallr, who is the watchman and protector of the gods of the Æsir. These last four gods, Njord, Freyr, Freyja, and Heimdallr, are all gods of the Vanir who, for various reasons, became gods and goddesses of the Æsir. We will learn of these stories in subsequent chapters of this book.

THE NORSE UNIVERSE

The Norse universe consists of three levels. Asgard, the home of the Æsir, and Vanaheim, the home of the Vanir, are in the Sky World. Also in the upper world is Alfheim, "elf home," the land of the light elves. In Asgard is a place about which you have already heard, Valhalla, the home of the slain Viking warriors. These warriors fight all day, and those who are injured or who die in combat are brought back to health to fight again the next day.

Midgard, "middle enclosure," the Middle World, is the home of humans. Located in this middle region is Jötunheimr, the home of the giants, and Svartafheim, the land of the dark elves. The gods are able to travel from Asgard to this Middle World by crossing the flaming and trembling bridge called Bifröst. One pastime of the gods and goddesses is to disguise themselves as humans and travel throughout Midgard to learn what humans think of them.

Niflheim, "mist home" or "abode of mist," the lower earth ruled by Hel, is the home of those who did not die a heroic death (i.e., in combat), but from illness or old age. It is a primordial realm of ice and cold.

Yggdrasil, the world tree, has roots in each of these worlds. One root is in the Sky World ending at Urðarbrunnr, the "well of Urðr." The root of Midgard finds the spring of Mímir, and the Niflheim root is at the spring of Hvergelmir. An eagle sits high in the branches of this great ash tree, and gnawing at the root in Niflheim is the dragon Niðhogg. The squirrel Ratatosk runs up and down the tree carrying rumors between the eagle and dragon.

Vanaheim, in the Sky World, is the home of the gods and goddesses of the Vanir; it preexisted the Æsir. In the story of the Æsir as found in the *Prose Edda,* the warriors of the Æsir attack and lay siege to Vanaheim. With "The Lost Edda of the Vanir," chapter 10 of this book, we will hear why the Æsir could not win this war and will hear of the magic and compassion of the gods and goddesses of the Vanir and the fall of the Æsir. We will learn of the real power of magic and how the quarrelsome nature of the Æsir prevents them from standing up to this magic and eventually causes their death.

Now, for the lost, but now recovered edda of the Vanir.

10

THE LOST EDDA OF
THE VANIR

I cannot let the people of the world forget the stories of the Vanir, thus I spend the cold long nights of winter by the light of my fire with a stylus in my hand, remembering all that I can.

VANADISDOTTIR, PRIESTESS OF FREYJA

As mentioned earlier, I visualized in trance the following stories being told to me by a priestess of Freyja, Vanadisdottir. I often met her sitting across a fire from me as I listened to her stories. I do not recall the first time I met her, or maybe I should say, created her, for she came from within me. She was likely there from the beginning of these stories. I always went to her with a question about the ancient Nordic myths and she filled in for me what was missing from ancient edda.

The Lay of Freyja's Audience with Odin

As we know from the edda, the Æsir went to war against the Vanir.* The two armies fought and were found to be of equal strength. The battle went first one way, and then the other. First one side gained the advantage, then the other. After some time, both sides decided that it was impossible to win, so they had a meeting, declared a truce, and exchanged hostages in order to ensure the peace. The Vanir sent to the Æsir their highest gods, Njord and his son, Freyr. The Æsir offered the god Hœnir, whom they thought well-fitted to be a leader because of his leadership qualities, and the wisest of giants, Mímir. In turn, the Vanir sent their wisest man, Kvasir. Freyja joined her brother, Freyr, and her father on the journey to Asgard.

The question I asked as I entered into trance was, "Why could Odin's army not win?" His army, the Einherjar,† were the greatest and most courageous warriors of the North, selected by the Valkyries, the emissaries of Odin, for their valor. These warriors practiced every day in the fields of Valhalla. The ones who fell during the day rose again, fully healed, to join the others at the evening meal.

Why, too, did Odin's army attack the Vanir? Since the Einherjar were known to be the strongest, and the Vanir had no known army and seemed no threat, such a war seems senseless. Yet an army without an adversary cannot call itself an army. Being omniscient,‡ Odin knew this war would be a challenge and decided that in order to keep his army in top shape, the Einherjar should go to war with the Vanir.

---

*The story of the war between the Æsir and the Vanir is found in Snorri Sturluson's *Heimskringla,* or *The Lives of the Norse Kings,* in chapter 1, "The Ynglinga Saga."
†Einherjar, the army of Odin, is comprised of the dead warriors of Valhalla, who fight each day and if wounded or killed are brought back to health to spend the evening drinking and feasting and to again fight the next day. This is found in verse 41 of "The Lay of Vafthruthnir" of the *Poetic Edda.* At Ragnarǫk they take the side of the gods in fighting against Fenrir, Loki, and the other foes of the Æsir.
‡Odin is described as all-knowing in the Gylfaginning of the *Prose Edda.*

But from where did the Vanir's army come? How could it be an equal match to the Einherjar? The answers to these questions will soon be evident but cannot be answered until we first learn something about the gods and goddesses of the panetheon of the Vanir.

First, as a result of the truce between the gods, Freyja went to live with the Æsir, and what she saw and learned was a shock to her. The Æsir had neither an understanding of the power of her magic nor of the power of the magic of the Vanir, who were skilled in the use of seiðr, herbs, spells, and all sorts of wizardry. The Æsir held no respect for the Vanir and had no knowledge of how their own lives depended on the Vanir. If they had known, they would never have been so foolish as to attack Vanaheim.

If you recall, the warriors of Valhalla who fell during the day came back to life again in the evening so they all could eat and drink together and return to fight the next day. Yet no one ever questioned how the wounded and slain could rise again. None noticed or thought to question why the quiet Idunn, a goddess of the Vanir, administered slices of her golden apples to the fallen.* Now you know another reason why this war was foolish.

Additionally, no one among the Æsir appreciated Freyr's famous sword that fought battles by itself, or his famous ship, Skíðblaðnir, made by the dark elves, and how the wind always filled its sails.† Others were impressed by the size of Skíðblaðnir and how Freyr could fold it down into such a small packet that it would fit in his pocket, but they had no appreciation for the Vanir's spells that made the sword fight or the

---

*The story of Idunn and her use of her golden apples to heal and keep the gods young is told in the Gylfaginning of the *Prose Edda*.

†The story of Freyr's sword and his ship, Skíðblaðnir, is found in the second part of the *Prose Edda* called the Skáldskaparmál ("language of poetry"). This story tells of how the treasures of the gods are made in the cave of the dark elves, and how they were brought to the gods by Loki. This is an example of the time-free nature of mythology. You may think that rationally Freyr must have received these treasures from Loki after he became part of the Æsir, but when actions are free of time, what happens afterward may, at the same time, happen beforehand.

sails billow by themselves. The Æsir had no conception of such spells or magic, and thus paid no attention to this strength of the Vanir, a strength that would be used against them. Thus, when the Æsir went to battle with the Vanir, they thought victory would be easy.

What army and what gods could be stronger than the army and strength of the Æsir? They quickly learned that the strength of magic and the strength of spells was a good match to their physical, muscular strength, the strength of the sinew of a bear and the strength of the roots of a mountain. They had no appreciation for the strength of the sound a cat makes when it walks, the spittle of a bird, the breath of a fish, or the beard of a woman, strengths greatly appreciated by the Vanir.* The nature of these six strengths will soon be revealed.

Freyja was shocked by the ignorance she discovered, but after she was told by Odin that she was to be a priestess and teacher to the Æsir, she took her place among the Æsir in good faith and began teaching them these powers. She thought the gods were foolish in their incessant interest in fighting and in their sole reliance on physical strength. She thought that if they learned the other, more subtle strengths of her spells and magic, they would lead much less violent and much more loving lives. She did not understand the insidious power that their belief in physical strength held over them, nor did she anticipate how they might use her magic in a poisonous way.

When Freyja first arrived at Asgard, Odin called her into an audience. When she entered his great hall, Valaskjálf, she saw Odin sitting in his high seat, Hliðskjálf. At his feet sat two wolves, Geri and Freki, and on his shoulders Munin and Hugin,† the two ravens who whispered

---

*The six substances—the sound a cat makes when it walks, the sinew of a bear, the roots of a mountain, the spittle of a bird, the breath of a fish, and the beard of a woman—are the magical strengths used by the dark elves in making the binding that will hold Fenrir the wolf, the second child of Loki. The story of this binding is found in the Gylfaginning of the *Prose Edda*.

†Odin's great hall, Valaskjálf; his high seat, Hliðskjálf; his two wolves, Geri and Freki; and his ravens, Munin and Hugin are described in the *Poetic Edda* in the poem "Grimnismal."

in his ears the news of the day. When Freyja came before him, Odin boomed, "What do you have to offer the Æsir?"

Freyja said nothing. Her countenance changed. She became calm and moved her attention to her center of harmony, or *hvildgardr*, just a couple of inches below her umbilicus. No one in the hall noticed what was happening at first, their eyes on the silent Freyja. But something truly amazing began to happen. The two wolves, Geri and Freki, crept away from Odin's feet and moved toward Freyja. When they were about half the distance to her they rose up with their tails wagging and trotted to her feet. At the same time, the ravens left Odin's shoulders and swooped down to Freyja's knees. Sitting on her knees, they peered up into her beautiful face. Odin, his jaw hanging in true amazement, watched what had never happened before. The wolves had never before left the hand that fed them, and neither had the ravens. Never before had these animals and birds shown such affection for someone else. Indeed, when Thor approached the throne of Odin, the wolves crouched back with a rumble coming from deep in their throats. When Baldr approached his father, they lay comfortably at their master's feet but did not move away.

Odin's voice boomed, "How does this happen?"

With a smile, Freyja answered, "It is something we of the Vanir learned long before you were born—to be in harmony with all living creatures, with all substances. Hopefully, we can teach you and, if you can learn, the world will be at peace."

Odin grumped, "Why do we want peace?" But then he added, "You will be a priestess and teach us your magic and wizardry."

Freyja left with a cryptic comment: "The way your pets came to me, the trees and rocks and every substance come to the Vanir to protect them against any enemy that might approach. Frigg used the same power to gain the assurance that no substance would harm Baldr after he had his dream of death."*

---

*Baldr's dream and his mother Frigg's journey to gain the assurance from all substances that none would harm him is found in the Gylfaginning of the *Prose Edda*.

That night Freyja had a dream. She was before her beloved grand-mother, Moðir. Moðir was sitting in her familiar chair in her hall, Moðirasalr, in Vanaheim. In the dream, Moðir looked at Freyja with her beautiful look of love and compassion. Though she said nothing, Freyja knew Moðir was telling her that it was up to her to carry on this love and compassion. Then Moðir spoke cryptically: "It is up to you to carry us through the wolf's belly to Nydagan, to the New Dawn." We will soon learn about the importance of the wolf's belly.

The Lay of Freyja's Cats

When the gods sought to restrain Fenrir the wolf, they went to the cave of the dark elves, where the elves made them the magical binding made of six unusual substances. These substances were the sound a cat makes when it walks, the breath of a fish, the spittle of a bird, the roots of a mountain, the sinew of a bear, and the beard of a woman. I wanted to know more about why this bizarre collection of substances would make a binding to hold Fenrir. This and the next five stories answer this question, beginning with the sound a cat makes when it walks. Learning of these substances also introduces us to the leaders among the Vanir . . .

Moði,* a son of Thor, was watching Freyja in her chariot pulled by her cats. He knew from his own cats that ran free in his hall that cats have minds of their own. His cats came to him if they were hungry or wanted to be stroked. At other times they would have nothing to do with him. He especially enjoyed watching them stalk rodents. He was impressed with how Freyja, with her magic and use of her center of harmony, could control her cats.

With these thoughts, he watched her cats pull the chariot through the air and then land not far from him, silently, without a noise. As they flew, their bodies were outstretched and sleek. Their ears were flat and their front paws stretched in front of them. As they came in to land, they pulled their front legs back with their claws out, their ears became erect, and their bodies caught the wind to slow them down. They each landed silently on all four feet. It was beautiful to watch.

Freyja emerged from her chariot and ran over to Moði. She had something to tell him: "Where have you been? You missed all the excitement. Again your father got into trouble while fighting giants."

---

*Moði is the son of Thor and his name means "the wrathful." As told in the Gylfaginning the first part of the *Prose Edda*, he survives Ragnarǫk, and along with his brother, Magni, becomes the owner of Thor's hammer.

"Slow down and start from the beginning. Sit down and catch your breath," he said.

"I was flying back to Sessrúmnir* when we heard a loud noise. It was loud—it was actually a roar. The cats instantly landed with their ears up and without a sound. We hid in some tall grass. They stood, but close to the ground, their backsides trembling, ready for anything.

"What we saw was strange. The giant Hrungnir† was standing on his shield and holding his whetstone in front of him. All of a sudden he threw the stone into the air, where it hit something above our heads and split in two. Part of it fell to the ground not far from us, and then we saw Thor's hammer smash into the giant's head. We heard groans from both behind and in front of us. Then we saw your father fall to the ground and Hrungnir fell too, on top of him. Thor was trapped under

---

*Sessrúmnir, "seat room," is Freyja's hall at Fólkvangr, the "field of folk," in Asgard, as told in the Gylfaginning of the *Prose Edda.*

†The story of Thor's duel with Hrungnir ("brawler") is told in the second part of the *Prose Edda,* the Skáldskaparmál. In this story, Odin, while seeking excitement, rides his eight-legged horse to the hall of the strongest giant, Hrungnir. The giant challenges Odin to a horserace. In this race back to Asgard, Odin beats Hrungnir. There he invites Hrungnir in for a drink, where they continue in their challenges. Eventually, Thor arrives back at Asgard and is horrified to find Hrungnir drinking with Odin. He threatens the unarmed giant with his hammer but stops when the giant points out to Thor that killing an unarmed giant would not add to his honor. They then agree to meet at the borders of Jötunheimr, the giants' land, and Asgard on an appointed day for a fair fight. Hrungnir returns to Jötunheimr to prepare for the battle. There he builds a huge giant with clay and gives it a heart from a mare. On the appointed day, Hrungnir goes to meet Thor. Hrungnir's own heart was made of hard stone with three sharp-pointed corners. His head was also made of stone, as was his shield. He holds his shield in front of him, and his weapon is a whetstone resting on his shoulder. There he stands next to the clay giant. Meanwhile, Thjalfi, Thor's companion, runs ahead to meet Hrungnir. He tells the giant that he is unprepared because Thor is traveling underground and will come at him from below. Hrungnir stands on his shield to protect himself from that direction and grasps the whetstone in both hands, and thus Thor finds Hrungnir standing on his shield. The story of the battle then proceeds just as it is told by Freyja to Moði: Hrungnir throws the whetstone when he sees Thor flying toward him from above, and Thor throws his hammer. The hammer shatters the whetstone in mid-air and then proceeds until it smashes into Hrungnir's head. Though Hrungnir dies in this battle, Thor carries the piece of Hrungnir's whetstone-imbedded head from that day on.

the giant's leg. Swift Thjalfi,* Thor's servant, tried to lift the giant's leg but couldn't budge it.

"I returned quickly to the chariot and we flew back to Asgard to get help. When the gods arrived at the battle scene, only your brother, Magni, was strong enough to move the giant's leg. Your father is fine, but he has a wound on his head where he was hit by Hrungnir's whetstone. I came to find you. Your father is always in some sort of trouble because of his impetuous ways."

Moði just shook his head. He was very familiar with his father's behavior and could not get excited or show great concern. He had something else on his mind: "Your cats are truly amazing. How silently and powerfully they move and what control you have over them."

When Freyja heard Moði describe what he saw, she knew that he was experiencing the power of a cat stalking. At that moment she saw an image of the future, of the final battle, the battle that Moðir had predicted. Moðir could clearly see the final battle. Freyja saw a glimpse of it, and what she now saw was Moði after the battle, standing and looking bewildered.† She knew he would survive the battle and realized how much she needed to teach him. He needed to know the magical powers of the Vanir for the new world to be a compassionate world. She was pleased that he had experienced the power of a cat stalking. That was a good beginning.

---

*The story of Thjalfi, Thor's swift servant and the son of a farmer, is told in the *Prose Edda* in the story of Thor's journey to Utgard. On this journey, Thor stays overnight at Thjalfi's father's farmstead. This farmer and his family do not have food to feed Thor and Loki, who travels with him, so Thor butchers his own goats and instructs the farmer to lay the the bones on the animal skins so that the next day the goats will again have flesh and live. But Thjalfi, the farmer's son, has split one of the leg bones in order to eat the marrow, and thus one goat is found lame the next morning. In payment Thor takes the farmer's son and a daughter as his servants. When Thor, Loki, and Thjalfi, and his sister arrive at the hall of Útgarða-Loki, the competition with the giant begins. In this competition Thjalfi has the chance to demonstrate how fast he can run in his race with the giant Hugi, thus gaining the title "swift servant."

†The story of those who survive the final battle, Ragnarǫk, is found in the Gylfaginning of the *Prose Edda*.

Freyja continued, "I know. The dark elves have been the most impressed. They too have watched the cats and wanted their power for a long time, the sound a cat makes when it walks. They made me this chariot in exchange for this power. The elves somehow slipped up behind the cats when I took them into the elves' cave at Svartalfaheim,* and they caught the cat's silence in a jar. They now have that magic to use, to give that power of silent stalking to some of the things they make.

"I am pleased that you were watching and are aware of that power. That is some of the magic I want to teach you and the rest of the Æsir, which I learned when I was young and living in Vanaheim. I have used it many times. Just watch the cat. Put yourself in the cat. As Moðir might say, 'Dream the cat.' Feel the power of carefully watching, carefully listening, observing; know exactly what is happening, being ready to spring into action. As you watched my cats you were doing pretty much what the cat does in stalking: watching, listening, and being ready to spring into action. You will also want to learn about the power of the breath of a fish. Freyr can teach you about the roots of a mountain and the spittle of a bird, those magical substances used by the dwarfs in making Gleipnir, the binding used to tie Fenrir. You can learn of those powers, too."

---

*Svartalfheim, the cave of the dark elves, is found in Midgard, the Middle World of humans. The gods visit this cave to attain the powerful and magical items the elves make in their forge. These stories are told in both the Gylfaginning and the Skáldskaparmál of the *Prose Edda*. Psychologically, journeying into the cave of the dark elves means journeying into the unconscious mind. Such therapeutic techniques as dreamwork, hypnosis, and ecstatic trance facilitate access to the unconscious and can be useful but also terrifying to a person in uncovering information useful for healing and change. We will see how the Vanir's and Æsir's relationship to the unconscious differ. The Æsir go into the cave, or unconscious, to find weapons of defense, offense, or strength, such as Fenrir's binding. They threaten and connive to gain such items. On the other hand, the Vanir have more open access to and are friendlier with the elves because they share their knowledge and provide the dwarfs with materials of strength and creativity. Thus using the magic, compassion, and creativity of the Vanir is a healthier way to live. See my article "Loki's Children: A Mythical Understanding of Hypnosis in the Process of Change."

With these suggestions, Moði used the power of dreaming that night and dreamed of a cat stalking, ready to pounce. He dreamed of a dark elf or dwarf coming out at night. Moði watched it sneak around Asgard. He watched him and listened with intense curiosity. The dwarf was looking in windows and cracks of doors. He went to almost all the doors and windows of Asgard, snooping, looking, but then before daylight he slipped out of Asgard and back to his cave, taking nothing of importance with him except for what he saw. Moði had no need to pounce, but he knew that the dwarfs were smart and always seemed to know what was going on. Now he knew why. The dwarfs knew how to stalk silently, like a cat.

What he learned he would use, especially after Nydagen, the New Dawn that will shine after the final battle, Ragnarǫk. Moði would be one of the few gods to survive and would be sorely needed to build the new world.

The Lay of the Fish's Breath

Sitting in my trance chair, I asked about the meaning and source of the second substance used in making the magical binding, the breath of a fish. While sitting there, the story flowed and grew . . .

In her teaching, Freyja had many stories to tell. Another was when she learned of the power of the breath of a fish. When Freyja was young, she was stomping around in frustration and anger because of an argument she was having with her brother, Freyr, when her father, Njord, stopped her and suggested that she let Freyr's comments roll off her back. That only made her more angry, being told what to do by her father. She didn't understand the power she lost when she allowed such things to anger her until Njord took her to one of his favorite places at the bottom of the sea. Njord, the Vanir god of the sea, spent a lot of his time wandering the ocean bottom.

When they arrived, Njord asked Freyja to take a seat on a piece of coral and watch the fish to learn of their magic and power. "Use your power of stalking, of focusing your attention on what you are watching, the power of the sound a cat makes when it walks. You will learn the power of the breath of a fish."

As Freyja watched, she at first didn't understand, but she knew how to stalk. She asked herself *How does a fish breathe?* The fish were swimming back and forth, the tail fins moving to let them change direction. She noticed their breasts expanding and contracting, just as her own chest expanded and contracted as she breathed. She noticed the gills on the sides of the fish open as their breasts expanded and then close as their chests contracted. *They must be breathing when water goes over their gills,* she thought, but she was most fascinated in watching the graceful way the fish moved through the water.

As Freyja watched the gills open and close and the fishs' chests expand and contract, the fish moved silently through the water with a graceful rhythm, the rhythm of its breath. She was now beginning to feel the rhythm of the fish's breath. This rhythm took the fish around all obstacles as they swam in and out of the plants and coral and through the holes of a boat's wreckage lying on the bottom of the sea. The more she watched the fish, the more she felt their movement, rolling gracefully with this rhythm of breath. She reached her hand out, and as she did she felt the resistance of the water and its current as it flowed around her hand. When she reached for a fish, she felt it flow and roll around her hand in the current, flowing with the rhythm of its breath. Freyja felt the dance of this movement, and she wanted to dance, but the water inhibited her movement. Only when she moved slowly with the rhythm of her breath could she feel the rhythm of the dance.

After watching for some time, Freyja knew the two lessons she was supposed to learn. She learned the patience needed to move slowly with her breath, and she learned the feeling of going with the flow of the current, rolling with the current while moving rhythmically with her breath. As her father said, she could let Freyr's comments roll off her back, like the fish flowing in the current around her hand. If you roll with the current, nothing can stop you. Rolling and flowing with the current was the feeling of a dance.

One day, when she was in the cave of the dark elves where the dwarfs lived, she told Ivaldi, one of the dark elves who helped make the treasures of the gods, about the strength of the breath of a fish. The elves had never been under water and had no concept of what the underwater world was like, but they appreciated the story of another kind of strength. One night, several of them crept to the water's edge and saw the flow of the current around the grasses as a fish swam by. They were able to capture this current in a jar as it rolled by. They took this strength with them back to their cave and stored it for future use in their creations.

In partial payment for her necklace Brísingamen,* Freyja gave the

---

*Brísingamen, Freyja's beautiful necklace, is found in the *Poetic Edda* poem "Lokasenna." Loki's accusations of Freyja suggest that she may have slept with the dark elves in order to possess this beautiful necklace. This same necklace is also mentioned in the Old English poem *Beowulf*.

dwarfs this story. Loki's story that Freyja was given the necklace for sleeping with the dark elves was thus not totally true.

With time, Freyja learned well the strength of the breath of a fish. She learned to let things roll off her back. One time, in playfulness, Freyr threw something at her. She was not quick enough to catch it, and she was not sure she wanted to catch it, not knowing what it was. She was quick enough to roll or flow to one side for it to fly past her without it hitting her. When she saw that it was a frog, she went over and picked it up with care, not wanting it to be hurt. Again she showed her power and even took power from her brother by not showing fear or anger. She stayed focused in her center of harmony. The frog sensed her care and felt protected. When she put it down, it hopped off, appearing unharmed.

On another occasion, when her two beautiful daughters, Hnoss and Gersemi,* were young and of an age to feel the urge to roam, they wanted to venture away from Sessrúmnir, Freyja's hall. Their mother had a dream of their being assaulted by trolls and was concerned about their well-being. When she stopped them and told them they could not leave, they were angry and yelled at their mother, "We hate you." They were still quite young, at an age of pushing limits. Staying with her feelings of centeredness and compassion, Freyja just let these words flow past her. Catching the words would have hurt her, but she remained strong. Her daughters were testing her limits, and rolling to let the words pass her only added to her strength.

The use of this strength was sometimes very difficult for Freyja. On one occasion she lost her composure, but her father was there again to rescue her. They were invited to a feast by the god Ægir,† who wanted to show off his new ale kettle. Loki was also there, and it was at this

---

*Hnoss and Gersemi, the beautiful daughters of Freyja and Óðr, are mentioned in both the Gylfaginning and Skáldskaparmál of the *Prose Edda*. Hnoss means "treasure" or "jewel," and Gersemi means "treasure" or "precious object."

†The story of the feast of the sea god Ægir and the rantings of Loki is told in the poem "Lokasenna" in the *Poetic Edda*.

feast that he went around the table insulting all present. In confronting Frigg, he admitted that he was the cause of Baldr's death and prevented his return from Hel. Freyja could not let his admission pass and accused him of being insane for admitting his evil acts. In his cunning way he set her up to lose her personal power. He turned on her, accusing her of sleeping with every god and elf. That was too much for Freyja, and she accused him of being slanderous. Thus, Loki got the best of her with his own ability to roll with the punches. He had nothing to hide, since he and everyone else knew he was slanderous and evil. He relished in this attack. Only then did Njord enter the fray by telling all that who Freyja slept with didn't matter. When a father accepts such in his daughter, who can argue with him? Loki then turned on Njord, but his accusations flowed off Njord's back like the breath of a fish. He allowed nothing to hurt him.

Freyja again learned a lesson. And when she went to visit Hyndla,* a wise giantess, to learn of the ancestry of Óttar, her human lover, Hyndla's accusations of Freyja cavorting with a herd of he-goats flowed off her back; she again used the strength of the breath of a fish.

---

*The story of Freyja seeking to learn the ancestry of her human lover, Óttar, from the giant Hyndla is told in the *Poetic Edda* poem "Hyndluljóð."

The Lay of the Spittle of a Bird

The next magical substance for which I sought an answer while sitting in my trance chair concerned the spittle of a bird, and this was revealed . . .

We haven't talked of Freyr's adjustment to living among the Æsir. He had mixed feelings. Being a god who carried a sword, he could somewhat understand men whose only desire was to fight all day. Yet part of him did not want to fight. He was a handsome god, compassionate about the feelings of others and concerned about his own appearance. That was why he enchanted his sword to fight by itself. Because of his vanity, opening himself to the chance of getting injured was not appealing to him. Yet he would go out to the fields of Valhalla to watch the warriors practice whenever he had a chance.

One day, while he was watching, he found one particular warrior's style fascinating. This warrior used a short sword, little more than a long knife. He would move in very close to his opponent, so close that the opponent had no room to swing his sword, and he would move with his fighting partner as if they were glued together until he found the spot in the other man's armor through which to thrust his dagger. This warrior was quite effective with this style of fighting and that day won several battles. This started Freyr to thinking. He was well-trained in the power of the silence of a cat when it stalks and was able to easily put himself mentally in that warrior's place to experience how he experienced each battle. As he thought about it, the phrase that best described this style of fighting was that he "stuck to him like glue." He thus came to appreciate the power of glue and became sensitive to watching for that power or strength in other situations.

The next day, Freyr was sitting outside his own great hall, watching a swallow coming and going from under the eaves. The swallow would dip down to the water's edge of a nearby stream and scoop up some mud in its beak. It would then fly back to the eave and dab the mud on its nest. Freyr went over to the stream and took a handful of mud and took it back to his hall. There the mud sat for a couple of days and dried out. When Freyr again looked at the ball of mud, it had become very crumbly, almost like sand. But in looking up into the eaves of his hall, he could see the nest was not crumbling. He remembered finding such a nest on the ground where it had fallen when in disuse. It was very hard and had not broken when it fell. He then realized that the only reason the mud the bird used was still hard and not crumbly was that it was mixed with bird spittle, the glue that held together the nest. Freyr then appreciated the strength of the spittle of a bird.

One day, Freyr ventured into the cave of the dark elves, where the dwarfs lived. He knew that they did not come out of their cave in the daylight because if they did they would turn to stone.* Nevertheless, they were always very curious about what was going on in the outside world. On this particular day, Freyr told them about watching the warriors fight and how the one particular warrior would move in so close as to appear glued to his opponent, and he also told them of the strength of the spittle of a bird. With this, Ivaldi, one of the dwarfs, knew he had to have some bird spittle to use to enhance his crafts-manship in working with metal. The next night he wandered out of the cave and started searching in the eaves of the great halls in the area to find mud bird nests. He collected several and took them back to the cave for later use.

In exchange for this story, Ivaldi put his sons to work to make for Freyr his famous sword. When Freyr sang the song to enchant his sword to fight battles by itself, he taught it the strength of the spittle of a bird. In the war between the Vanir and the Æsir, Freyr hovered above the battle lines to see where he was needed most. Then he would send his enchanted sword in to fight where needed. His sword would swing back and forth, following the movements of its opponent, just waiting for an

---

*The dwarf Alvis was promised a bride, Thrud, the daughter of Thor, in payment for weapons he had made. When Alvis went to Thor's hall to claim his bride, Thor spent the night testing Alvis's wisdom by asking him questions. When the morning arrived and the first rays of sunlight struck Alvis, he turned to stone. This poem was recorded in "Alvissmal," in the *Poetic Edda*.

opening in its opponent's armor in which to thrust itself. It knew the strength of the spittle of a bird.

One night, Freyr had a dream of the final battle, a battle in which he did not have his sword that was now carried by Skírnir, Freyr's messenger. Freyr had given Skírnir the sword for carrying a message of love to Gerðr, the beautiful daughter of the giant Gymir.* In the final battle, he saw Surtr, the flaming guardian of the gates of the South, swinging his fiery sword, looking for a vulnerable spot in his own armor. Freyr knew that his best defense would be to move in so close on the sword that it could not move or pull back to strike such a vulnerable spot. This is what he did, and he was effective for a while, but Surtr's sword was so hot that he was unable to stay close for more than a few moments. Freyr had to step back, and when he did, he met his end.

It was the practice of the Vanir to take their dreams to Moðir. This Freyr did. As she listened to his dream, she knew that this was the way his life would end at Ragnarǫk, but she did not want to burden him for the rest of his life with this knowledge. She told him that the most effective strength in fighting is stalking like a cat. If he watched with centered attention, he would be an effective and valiant warrior. Freyr felt effective in stalking and felt reassured that he could protect himself, especially with his enchanted sword. Adding to his feeling of effectiveness was his skill in flowing like the breath of a fish.

---

*The story of Skírnir's journey, from the "Skírnismál," ("sayings of Skírnir") in the *Poetic Edda,* tells of how Freyr's love for the giantess Gerðr incapacitated him such that he had to send his messenger, Skírnir, to tell her of his love. In payment for carrying this message, Skírnir asked for Freyr's sword that fights by itself, and Freyr was obliged to give it to him.

The Lay of the Roots of a Mountain

My next question concerned the roots of a mountain . . .

Njord was probably the god most skilled in the use of magic, being the oldest and the leader of the Vanir. He was wise and exceptionally skilled in watching and learning from the world around him. He looked at the world like a cat stalking its prey.

Now, living with the Æsir, he had little time for all the fighting and activities of the warriors and the warrior gods. He preferred to spend his time in or at the edge of the great seas. But on one of his ventures to visit Odin, he spent some time watching the Einherjar fighting. In watching them, he was quick to see something in their style of fighting that even the warriors did not understand or appreciate, even though it was very natural and automatic for most of them. When fighting, their center—what the Vanir called the *hvildgarðr,* their "center of harmony," just an inch or so below the navel—would drop. With their feet spaced apart about shoulder-width and their center dropped, they could not be moved when they wrestled or were hit or pushed by their opponent.

Focusing on this center of harmony for the Vanir was a very healthy and peaceful experience. This experience in no way was considered a threat to anyone or anything. Thus, using the center of harmony in order to fight disturbed Njord a great deal. He was disgusted that something so harmonious could be used so destructively. He did not want to think of warriors using the center of harmony in conflict, and he knew in fact that they did not understand or respect this center. They only used it to plant themselves so as to not be moved or knocked over. He at first thought of them as trees with deep roots, but trees would not use this kind of strength destructively, either. The trees' planted roots were used for protection and nourishment, and he appreciated their strength in protecting the Vanir as their army. The trees knew how to stand and take up arms against the Æsir as the army of the Vanir, to effectively protect them, but without destructive intent. In fighting in this way, the Vanir could not lose, but neither could they win. The Vanir loved their trees and planted more and more of them. Vanaheim was deep in the woods, and each year around Vanaheim the woods became deeper and deeper.

What a difference! Asgard was on the open plains, with much sunlight, with much room for an army to move and practice, and room for the final battle. The final battle could never happen near Vanaheim because there was no room there for it.

Njord did not want to liken the Einherjar to trees. From his ventures into the caves deep in the sea and the caves on earth, he knew that mountains rested on deep roots of rock. That was his answer: the warriors knew how to plant themselves so as to not be moved, like the roots of a mountain. His wife, Skaði, lived in the mountains in her storm-home, Thrymheim ("power house").* They lived together for nine nights in the mountains, and the next nine nights by the sea. Skaði hated the sea as much as Njord hated the mountains, so they took turns where they lived. To Njord, likening the warriors to a stormy mountain made sense, though he did not want to tell them of his observation because they might start valuing it.

Yet, on one occasion, while visiting the cave of the dark elves, Njord told Dvalinn, the dwarf, about the discovery. Dvalinn became excited by the story. He knew well about the roots of a mountain, as he lived among those roots. He wanted to give Njord something for his story and made him a beautiful and strong sword, something for which Njord had no need, so he gave it to his young son, Freyr, to play with. His son wanted to be like the other boys in playing at sword-fighting. But as Freyr grew older, he, too, didn't like to fight, so he used another of the

*The story of Skaði finding a husband and her married life with Njord are found in the Gylfaginning of the *Prose Edda*. She is sometimes called the snowshoe goddess. When her father died by flying as an eagle into the fire set inside the wall of Asgard, Skaði was given her choice of gods to marry, but she had to choose only by looking at their legs. She selected the whitest pair of legs, thinking she was going to marry Baldr, but as it was, Njord's legs were whiter. As is told in this story, she did not like living by the sea, and Njord did not like living in the mountains.

Vanir's spells, the same spell they used on trees to teach them to take up arms, in order to give his sword the power to fight by itself.

Njord continued to dwell on the use of the hvilðgarðr, the center of harmony. He discovered how the center was used in different ways. The most familiar was to focus on the center in relaxation. It was then that he felt most harmonious and that unexpected things would happen, like Odin's wolves going to Freyja. On the other hand when the center dropped, roots were sent down and a person could not be moved. When stalking like a cat, he observed that the center would vibrate, enabling the person to act quickly. When the center rose he would feel agitated.

Like Freyja, when Njord first arrived at Asgard he was called into audience with Odin. With his booming voice Odin asked him what he had to offer the Æsir. Njord was tempted to let his center drop in a stance of self-protection, but he did not want to appear a threat to Odin. He thus let his center continue to vibrate while considering all possible actions. When he decided what he was going to say, he moved his focus on relaxing his center so it would become a center of harmony. He told Odin that he was not a warrior and did not feel he would be of benefit to his army. He went on to explain that he most loved the sea and that he caused the wind to fill the sails to move ships. He could benefit the Æsir by assuring them that he would fill the sails of their ships with wind to take them wherever they wanted to go. This pleased Odin, and he gave Njord that commission.

Njord returned to his hall on the shore of the great ocean. In standing on the bluff above the ocean and blowing into the sails of ships, he realized that he needed to use the roots of a mountain. He needed to plant himself so as not to be thrown backward when he blew. Dropping his center to plant his roots made his blowing into sails much more efficient. He knew that his wind was important for the safety of sea travelers, and he could appreciate the roots of a mountain, knowing that rooting thus could be used for positive things and not just the fighting so valued by the Æsir.

While experimenting with the movement of his center of harmony,

Njord made another discovery. When Loki attacked Freyja, telling everyone that she slept with every god and elf, Njord felt his center drop in his need to protect his daughter. As his center dropped, a feeling of stubbornness flowed through him, and when he told Loki that it did not matter to him who Freyja slept with and that spreading love was her job, he thus disarmed Loki and felt his center rolling and flowing with the pleasant sense of harmony.

Focusing on and staying with the movement of his center of harmony taught Njord a great deal about the power and strength of that center. What he and the rest of the Vanir learned from such observations gave them the magic of harmony and the compassion so much needed for the world to survive.

The Lay of the Sinew of a Bear

The fifth substance, bear sinew, was the concern of my next question as I sat in my trance chair . . .

It was very hard to get away from the activities of warriors and fighting while living among the Æsir. For everyone, from Odin on down to all the Einherjar, fighting was their life. Only Baldr seemed to disdain fighting. Among the goddesses, Frigg seemed to have no great love for fighting, either. As for Sif,* the wife of Thor, as sensuous as she was, she still had to support her impulsive husband in his warlike demeanor.

The one strength that the warriors appreciated was that of the sinew of a bear. They even named themselves after the bear in calling themselves berserkers, which means "bear shirt," and many of them wore only bear skins when fighting. The warriors would go into such a fighting frenzy that they felt they were impervious to wounds and to danger. They would bite their shields and were as strong as bears and as frantic as dogs or wolves when fighting.

Odin would watch them with a gleam in his eyes, smiling and cheering them on. The brief time that Njord watched them, he considered their antics a waste of energy that could be used for more productive ventures. Besides fighting against the Vanir, and occasionally against a wandering giant when one would threaten Asgard, their only real battle was in the end, Ragnarǫk, and there they lost. Njord believed that this final battle was really unnecessary and that the Æsir brought it on themselves because of their high value of the warrior's power.

What more is there to say about the sinew of a bear? Njord was the one who, when venturing into their cave, told the dark elves about the strength of the sinew of a bear. The elves were happy to add this strength to their storeroom of materials to be used in their crafts. Njord

---

*Sif, the wife of Thor, was famous for her beautiful golden hair, as told in the Skáldskaparmál of the *Prose Edda*.

wanted nothing in return for this story and in some ways wished he had not mentioned it.

Yet Njord and his son, Freyr, enjoyed boar hunting, and in so doing they learned to appreciate the sinew of a bear. Boars are known for sometimes flying into a blind rage when attacked and injured. On one occasion, father and son cornered a boar in a thicket, and Freyr's spear entered the boar's left shoulder, but the giant boar had the strength to overcome its pain and charged. Freyr held onto the spear and was thrown into the air by the charging boar. Letting go of the spear, he fell onto the boar's back and hung on with his arms around the animal's neck. Freyr luckily missed being gored by the boar's huge tusks and knew he was safer behind its head than in front. The boar threw its head back trying to reach Freyr, while Freyr with his hands had the strength to dig his fingers into its neck to crush the boar's windpipe. The boar began to slow down and finally collapsed.

Njord saw the power of the sinew of a bear both in the raging boar and in the strength of his son in an emergency. He stood watching and felt helpless to do anything to protect his son. He was proud of Freyr's strength in overcoming the boar. When the boar fell, Freyr bellowed in triumph—the bellow of a berserker. He felt the contagion of victory, and this contagion worried Njord, though his worry was unnecessary. Freyr quickly recovered, becoming his compassionate self because of his faith in the magic of compassion, a faith he had learned from Moðir.

On another occasion, Njord happened to be in Odin's great hall when Odin was drinking with the giant Hrungnir. There he watched Thor enter the hall, and when Odin's son's eyes fell on Hrungnir, Njord saw steam snorting from Thor's nose. He saw him threaten the giant. He saw him lose control in his rage. He saw him lose the power of the stalking cat. Thor did not understand Odin's willingness to befriend this giant, nor did he care to know the reason for it. His mind was closed to asking the question, "Why?" His anger blinded him to any other possibility. Njord saw him lose the power of the breath of a fish. Nothing was going to roll off Thor's back. His body was tense from top to bottom, ready to explode. He was so rigid that he would be unable to flow with his adversary's energy, to stick to him like the spittle of a bird. He was the sinew of a bear only. His center did drop. He planted the roots of a mountain, but only in one direction. If Hrungnir would have charged straight on, Thor would not have moved.

Even though Hrungnir had been drinking and probably too much, he was quick to see Thor's vulnerability and came at him from another side, saying, "If you kill me unarmed it would be dishonorable and not add to your fame." Thor was thrown off-balance and was quick to back down with his threats.

Njord understood these six strengths and could see Thor's weakness. Njord recognized these strengths as the source of real magic, magic held by the Vanir, magic to which the Æsir turned a blind eye.

The Lay of the Beard of a Woman

If each of the first five substances is a different kind of strength, what does the beard of a woman have to do with strength . . . ?

Maybe the greatest strength is the beard of a woman. Freyja and the Vanir highly valued this particular strength. It captured very much the way they looked at life—with a sense of humor and a sense of freedom without fear of death or reprisal. In her younger years, a woman generally seeks to please others, but in old age, the time when she starts to grow chin hairs, she can express herself with nothing to lose.

One time this strength became apparent was when the sea god, Ægir, invited all the gods to a feast to try out the ale brewed in his new giant cauldron. During this feast, Loki proceeded to go around the room and insult each god and goddess. When he came to Skaði, the giant wife of Njord, she took the initiative. Skaði, who became one of the Vanir through her marriage to Njord, was a practitioner of seiðr, as was Freyja. As a vǫlva, she was able to foretell the future. "You are so quick with your tongue, but you won't be able to twirl your tail much longer. The gods will bind you to three boulders, bound with the entrails of your soon-to-die son."

Loki retorted, "Even so, I led your father, Thiazi, back to Asgard through the flames that burnt his wings, to the gods who killed him."

With this reminder, Skaði added, "Your name will always be cursed in our hallowed halls."*

Loki could not help but implicate himself as his mother Laufey's son in escalating the harangue: "When you beckoned Laufey's son to your bed, your words were so much sweeter then, though in saying this I admit my own weakness."

With laughter, Loki went on next to attack Sif, the wife of Thor, and did not hear the rest of what Skaði had to say. Only Njord, who was

---

*Again we return to "Lokasenna," in the *Poetic Edda*, a poem that describes Loki attacking each of the gods and goddesses, and their retorts.

sitting near his wife, could hear her and was able to tell the rest of the story with a grin on his face:

"Her comment was priceless: 'Even with the hairs growing from my chin you found me attractive. At my age I am happy with all that I can get. Everyone should cheer me for it. I know that Njord cheers me. He is proud of me.'"

Njord had a good time telling this story to the dark elves, though they already had a good supply, having heard similar stories before. The beard of a woman is one of the oldest strengths, especially of women. It is just the lack of this strength, of one's ability to laugh at oneself, that was the demise of the Æsir.

On one of his visits to Moðir, Njord told her of Thor's confrontation with the giant Hrungnir, of how Thor lost his powers of the stalking cat, the breath of a fish, and the spittle of a bird. He told her of how Thor planted his roots in such a way that he was still vulnerable. His only strength was the sinew of a bear. All she could do was shake her head and talk of Thor's self-importance. It was his self-importance that caused him to lose his strength. "As strong as he is, for some reason he is insecure and needs to prove to himself that he is strong. This motivation is a sure way to fail. Letting go of self-importance, letting go of his need to prove himself, is the real strength of the beard of a woman."

On another occasion, Njord again showed the power of the beard of a woman. He really did not fit in with the other gods of the Æsir. He spent most of his time down by the edge of the sea or up in the mountain with his wife. On his journeys between the sea and the mountains, which occurred every nine days, he would stop at Asgard for a short visit. Some of the gods, especially Týr, felt resentment toward him. Týr felt that Njord was not committed and would be least likely of any of the gods to sacrifice any of his own pleasures for the Æsir, even though now he was one of them. To this point, on one of Njord's stops at Asgard, Týr confronted him on his commitment.

Njord had been around a lot longer than Týr and had seen disagreements come and go. He answered, "You have sacrificed your hand to protect the rest of the Æsir, and they appreciate your sacrifice. I too value your heroic act. You believe I would not have made such a sacrifice to Fenrir. You are likely right. You believed that Fenrir was a danger to all. You may have been right. You fed the wolf and knew it better than any of us, but I have seen the Vanir befriend most all animals, and even the giants, and the Vanir can call the animals and giants their allies. You saw how Odin's wolves went to Freyja. I think Fenrir could have become your ally and come to you to protect you. We all know about the final battle, and that Odin will be swallowed by Fenrir. I tend to believe that the final battle is unnecessary, that those you consider a danger to you could become your allies."

In this way, Njord showed compassion for Týr's way of thinking, yet he expressed his own beliefs. He did not feel the need to prove that what he had to say was right. He was acting with the power of the beard of a woman.

We will learn much more about the goddess Moðir, who is the daughter of Búri and the mother of Njord and the aunt of Odin. This matriarch of the gods and goddesses of the Vanir showed the strength of the beard of a woman above anyone else. She saw her brother, Borr, and his son, Odin, only value physical strength in the form of the sinew of a bear, and knew it was a weakness. In her confidence in old age she was able to sit in her hall to hear the stories of her children, grandchildren, and all those of the Vanir. She heard the stories of her nephew, the high-god of the Æsir, and cared for him. She was the one with the exceptional strength of patience and love. She was proud of her family and pained by their mistakes, but her countenance was always of a calm strength. It was this strength that gave power to the Vanir, a power not dependent on the sinew of a bear, but much deeper—the power of all the strengths and much more, the power of true magic.

The Origin of the Vanir and the Power of Naming

These stories of the true and powerful magic of the Vanir must not be forgotten as they were forgotten by the Æsir, but before I go on, you likely ask, as I did: where did the Vanir come from . . . ?

Where they came from also must not be forgotten. In the beginning was the icy rime in the northern regions, north of Ginnungagap, the vast, primordial void that existed prior to the creation of the manifest universe. Where the icy rime met the warm winds of the southern region, Muspell, life sprang up. The likeness of man appeared first as the frost giant Ymir. He was evil, as were all his frost giant descendants. Next from the thawing of the icy rime came Auðumla, a cow with milk flowing from her udders to nourish Ymir and the race of frost giants.* The cow was nourished by licking salt from the blocks of ice. As she licked, she uncovered the first man-god, Búri. On the first day, Auðumla uncovered his hair; on the second day she uncovered his head; and on the third day the remainder of his body. He was big and strong.

Búri had a son, Borr, about whom we have already heard a little. He also had a daughter, Moðir. Her disposition was very different from her brother's. While Borr was out trying to take charge of the world around him, gaining in power and strength, Moðir was honing her powers of observation. She was curious and wanted to understand everything in nature as she saw it at the time. She watched the cow licking the ice and tried licking it herself, finding that it was salty. She called this animal a cow and named it Auðumla. She drank from the rivers of the milk that flowed from its udder. She felt the warm air from the South and that give this region its name, Muspell. She felt the cold from the North. The green land in between the North and the South she called Ginnungagap.

---

*The creation story of Ginnungagap, the frost giant Ymir, and the cow Auðumla is recorded in the Gylfaginning of the *Prose Edda*.

Before this time nothing had names. Moðir even first named her father Búri and her brother Borr. Borr was too busy running around to think up names for things. In his wanderings he found his wife among the giants, and he brought her to meet Moðir, but he didn't know what to call her or how to introduce her. It was Moðir who gave her the name Bestla. Borr and Bestla had three sons, Odin, Vili, and Vé. Borr taught them to fight. All three sons were very strong, but there was not much around to fight. The first being they came to that offered them any challenge was Ymir, so to practice their skills they attacked and killed him. When he fell, everything around them changed. His blood made the sea and lakes, his flesh became the earth, and his bones the mountains' cliffs. His teeth became stones and gravel, his skull formed the sky, and burning embers from Muspell became the stars. The clouds are from Ymir's brain and the trees from his hair. Thus, the world as we know it was formed.*

Moðir also found a giant as a husband, and she named him Slœgr, which means "creative," because he was very creative in making things with his hands. Moðir and Slœgr had a son whom she named Njord.† He took after his mother in disposition, was curious about everything, and enjoyed giving names to what he saw, heard, smelled, tasted, or felt. Since Ymir fell and the earth was formed, Njord had a lot to name. He also had a sister named Dottir and they were very close, such that they had a daughter and a son together, Freyja and Freyr.

It was Njord who discovered the power that he named hvilðgarðr. When he was traveling to do things, whether in the ocean depths or on the land, he would try to get close to the sea and land creatures, but they would run away. He felt a need to touch what he named. He had a sense that naming gave him some power over whatever he named, and in fact, it did: it gave him a way to tell others about each creature. But one day

---

*The story of Búri and Bestla and their children and the outcome of the death of Ymir is also recorded in the Gylfaginning of the *Prose Edda,* but here for the first time we learn that Búri also had a daughter, Moðir, who had the power of naming.
†Though much is known about Njord from both the *Prose Edda* and the *Poetic Edda,* for the first time here we learn about his mother and father and how Njord discovered the center of harmony.

he was just sitting and breathing, wondering about the way his stomach would rise as he inhaled and drop when he exhaled. At that time he did not understand air. Later, when he discovered the strength of the breath of a fish, he realized that there was some sort of substance that he could not see or feel that must enter his body to make his stomach rise. He felt very peaceful, and he also felt a real quietness in his belly, especially just below his navel. He was thinking about his own body and giving names to different parts of it when a deer wandered up and nuzzled him with its nose, something that had never happened before. Over the next few days he practiced quieting his abdomen and found that when he did so, animals would come to him. However, when he became excited about the animals, they would run off. He found such quietness truly amazing. He had found a way to really get to know the animals. He taught this skill to his son and daughter, and they all found great harmony in the world. Moðir watched and was proud.

I will soon tell you about the healing powers of the goddess Idunn and her knowledge about plants. Her naming of the healing plants is a large part of her power of healing. Only by naming them was she able to remember and identify each plant important to her. The names she gave them often had something to do with the way they looked. One day Vár,* the goddess of oaths of marriage, came to Idunn because her throat was sore and she was losing her voice. What Idunn said was that she needed some tea made from *rejnfang,* or tansy. Vár asked, "What's that?"

"It's a tall plant with tight yellow flowers. Its leaves are fernlike. Here, I'll show you, there is some over there."

"How do you remember all these plants?"

"I gave them names like *rejnfang,* meaning tansy, and those names help me remember them. I've sometimes thought if I didn't name them I would become very confused, because there are so many different plants."

---

*The little we know about the goddess Vár is told in the Gylfaginning of the *Prose Edda.*

Vár was impressed and asked if there was a plant that would make love last. Idunn turned but only gave her a smile.

One name that had great power was Mjölnir, the name of the hammer of Thor. This hammer, made in the cave of the dark elves, was brought out of the cave and given to Thor by Loki.* When swung, this hammer caused lightning, thus it was given the name that means "lightning" or "white lightning." When Thor threw this hammer it would always hit its mark and then return to his hands. Its power was such that Thor had to wear special gloves to catch it, and men throughout the ages wore replicas of it on chains around their necks to give them power. The word *hammer* does not carry much power, but the name Mjölnir, which means "crusher," does.†

Many of the warriors and warrior gods gave their weapons names. They recognized the power of naming, but a few of the Vanir thought this was wrong. They felt that names should be reserved only for those things that are sacred, and that life is a sacred thing. They reasoned that those things that take away life should not be named. Idunn, whose life was spent healing others, was especially appalled at the value the Æsir gave to their weapons by naming them.

---

*The story of the making of Mjölnir is told in the Skáldskaparmál of the *Prose Edda*.
†Odin learned the power of the runes, found in the poem "Havamal" in the *Poetic Edda*. Whereas the Vanir found power in naming things, Odin found power in writing with the Old Norse alphabet, the runes. It was this power of writing that allowed for the evolution from the era of magic to the era of mythology.

The Attack on the Vanir and
the Power of Seiðr

We finally arrive at the answer to my first question concerning the nature of Vanir strength. How could the Vanir defend themselves against the powerful and well-trained army of Odin? The answer to this question slowly revealed itself, as the story of the first battle unfolded . . .

Skaði was sitting on her *seiðhjallr,* the high platform on which a vǫlva or seeress sits to go into a trance for making predictions of the future. It just so happened that Freyja was sitting on her seiðhjallr, too. Both goddesses saw the same vision: a large horde of armed men moving toward Vanaheim with none other than Odin leading them. They both raced to tell Njord what they saw and reached him at almost the same time. Though Odin could see everything from his high seat, Hliðskjålf, and Heimdallr could hear everything in the present, it was Skaði and Freyja who could see and hear into the future. These experts in the practice of seiðr had something, too, for reassuring Njord: they told him that the Vanir would not lose this war.

Idunn awakened from a dream and also ran to Njord. She said that in her dream she was hunting in the woods collecting plants for healing and looking especially for a *hvidtjørn* [hawthorn tree]. "It was a pleasant morning until the branch of an *ask* [ash] swung down in front of me, blocking my way. When I looked around, all the trees were thrashing about, looking very frightened. I heard one saying, 'The warriors are coming, I fear being cut down.' To get back here I had to crawl to get under the swinging branches. Something is wrong."

Even though Njord had no idea why the army of the Æsir would want to attack Vanaheim, he could not discount the information provided by his two greatest and most trusted vǫlvas. He quickly called the gods of the Vanir together to begin singing spells to alert and arm the woods of Vanaheim. Peering out into the woods, they could see that the trees had heard the spells and were beginning to flex their lower branches, branches that could strike at the incoming army, branches that could become intertwined and not let the army through, branches that could take up stones to hurl at the enemy. The Vanir also sang a spell to the rocks and stones, a spell that led them to roll and fly to be near the base of each tree. Soon big piles of stones were seen throughout the woods. This army of the Vanir could not march nor move. That meant that they could not advance, but neither could they retreat. To the army of Odin, the trees would appear as an army: an army of giants, an army as strong as their own, and it was Odin's army that would have to retreat, after an extended fight, to regroup and replenish their strength. Odin's army would need to spend time foraging for food, while the army of the Vanir would be able to stand their ground and find nourishment where they stood. As often as the Einherjar would attack, they would gain no ground.*

The warriors of Odin did attack, and they attacked again and again, but each time they had to retreat. The Vanir were prepared, and the war went as they expected, until a truce was reached, and Njord and several others of the Vanir went to live among the Æsir.

After the war was over, Bragi, the skaldic god of poetry, composed this song. We will soon learn more about Bragi and the power of his poetry.

Swords and shields approach	*Shimmering in the sun*
Arms of trees do thrash	*Shimmering as Njord's warriors*
Branches strike the shields	*And swords strike their foe*
Branches hold the strikes	*Not letting go of swords*
The warriors do withdraw	*A tree wall does expel*
Swords again attack	*The weapons again repelled*

---

*The strength of Odin's army is well known from both the *Prose Edda* and the *Poetic Edda* as well as other sources, but this is the first time that we learn why the army of the Vanir was an equal match.

Woods fling high the shields	*Swords are left behind*
Again, again they try	*Again, again repelled*
Both sides call for talks	*See futility of war*
Vanir's high one leaves	*With him leave his twins*
Hœnir takes his place	*Mímir at his side*
Hœnir knows not how to lead	*To the loss of Mímir's head**

When Skaði and Freyja had their visions of the troops marching, they were lying on their seiðhjallrs. A vǫlva would lie on her seiðhjallr, her high platform, to leave her body and travel where she pleased. She would either lie on her back, left arm resting across her forehead, or on her stomach, arms outstretched in front of her. It was Freyja who discovered the power of the platform. She was up in a tree one day, stretched out along a branch, relaxing and watching birds fly to and from their nests, when she experienced leaving her body and flying through the air. She tried this at other times and enjoyed the experience of exploring the world, seeing things she had not seen before. In this way she could travel faster than when pulled in her chariot by her cats, and she would not be seen. But the tree branch was not comfortable for very long. She then had the idea of building a high platform that would be flat and more comfortable. She found that this new platform worked just as well. The experience of quieting the mind and going into a trance to travel in this way she named *seiðr,* which means "sorcery," and she named the platform *seiðhjallr.* Freyja found that if she simply sat on the platform with her hands wrapped around her knees, quieted herself, and relaxed in the same way, she could see visions of the future.† She enjoyed spending time on the platform because it was generally quite restful, except when she received such a vision as an army approaching. It was in this posi-

---

*The story of Mímir losing his head is told in the Ynglinga saga, chapter 4 of Snorri Sturlason's *Heimskringla* or *The Lives of the Norse Kings.*

†Sitting with your hands wrapped around your knees has been determined by Felicitas Goodman to be a divination posture.

tion that she happened to be sitting on the day she saw the army. Freyja greatly valued this power of seiðr and shared it with many of the Vanir. As she sat on the platform, she began to think of all the different powers that were available to her if she was quiet and listened and observed: the power of dreaming, the power of naming, the power of her center of harmony, the power of the sound a cat makes when it walks, of the spittle of a bird, of the breath of a fish, of the beard of a woman, and even of the roots of a mountain and the sinew of a bear. She would soon learn of the power of plants from Idunn and of singing from Bragi.

Though the Æsir forgot the magic of living in harmony, these stories will not be forgotten, but will be carried on to future generations, to a time of rebirth, when the harmony and compassion of the great Moðir will return.*

---

*Jean Gebser, in his book *The Ever-Present Origin,* believes we are on the verge of this new era, an era of transparency that will allow us to see, understand, and value the earlier eras of magic and myth, the true magic of our origin.

The Power of Idunn's Plants

Another daughter of the Vanir was Idunn. We know of her and her husband, Bragi, as a goddess and god of the Æsir, but in her early years Idunn was of the Vanir. We will later learn about how she became one of the Æsir, but first I asked about and learned of her powers . . .

Idunn, too, knew the powers of observation and naming. She had learned these powers while living among the Vanir. By naming what she saw, she brought it close to her, and in one sense, it became hers. Idunn closely watched plants and trees, especially those the animals ate. She noticed that deer liked to eat apples, so she tried eating an apple. She found the fruit delightful and shared what she learned with others. She sampled apples from different trees, some red, others yellow or even gold in color. She felt especially good after eating a golden apple.

One day her grandmother, Moðir, who was getting quite old and wrinkled, complained of feeling tired and sick. Following Idunn's suggestion, she ate a golden apple and quickly felt better. But a couple of days later, Moðir stopped breathing and nothing would rouse her. She never breathed or moved again. This scared Idunn, and she worried about the way Njord also was getting old and wrinkled. She had him eat an apple and she thought he looked a little younger. She had him eat an apple every day, and soon he was looking quite young again. She had Skaði also eat an apple every day, and soon Skaði also started looking younger, though she still had hair growing from her chin. Idunn was excited about the power of eating the golden apples. After this discovery, she started experimenting with other plants to learn of their powers, and this experimenting became her life.

One day Idunn was lying on the ground on her back, relaxing in the sun. She had just picked a plant and was holding it in her hands, which were resting together on her belly. She happened to fall asleep, and in a dream she saw what the plant could do. In her dream she put the leaves from this plant in a bowl of boiling water for just a minute or two, then rolled it up and tied it over a warrior's wound, and the wound healed quickly. She named this plant *kulsukker;* we know it as comfrey. Idunn was good with the power of dreaming. If you recall, she dreamed of the trees coming alive to protect the Vanir.

When Idunn woke and returned to where the others were, she saw them standing around the young Freyr. He was lying on the ground with a cut on his leg. He had been playing with the sword his father gave him, swinging it like a great warrior, when it hit his own leg and he received a cut. Everyone knew how such cuts often become red and inflamed, and how sometimes the wounded person becomes feverish and can even die. Idunn was quick to get some kulsukker, boil it, and put it on his leg. After a couple of days, everyone was pleased because the cut, instead of growing inflamed, seemed to be healing nicely.

In the same way, by holding plants against her belly and dreaming them, Idunn quickly learned what many other plants could do. She learned that some plants would help to keep people healthy, such as *purpur-solhat* (echinacea), and others could quiet one's stomach when drunk in a tea, like *kamille* (chamomile), or calm one's nerves like *cikorie* (chicory). *Isop* (hyssop) tea could be used to sooth one's throat, cool a fever, and give relief for a stuffy nose or cough. *Hvidtjørn* (hawthorn) berries could reduce chest pain or discomfort. Another plant that helped keep people healthy and helped the heart beat regularly was *hvidløg* (garlic).

One day Freyja was walking in the fields and brushed her arm against a plant that caused her arm to become red and burn. This plant Freyja named *nælde* (nettles). Because she prided herself on her beautiful skin, she was upset and went to Idunn for help. Idunn rubbed the place on her arm with *burre,* burdock, and Freyja found relief.

But what was most important to Idunn was when she met Bragi. Bragi was one of the Æsir, but he seemed different. In many ways he was more like the Vanir. He knew some of the magic of words and singing spells. When he saw Idunn, he sang a love song, and the spell worked. The two were then in love, but soon Bragi became very agitated. Although he was one of the Æsir, he knew that something was wrong because while the Æsir were always fighting and proud of their strength, Bragi saw even greater power in words and songs. He loved Idunn and loved the magic of the Vanir, but he didn't know what to do because he was loyal to the Æsir. Idunn loved him, took pity on his dilemma, and did what she knew best. She mixed a drink of *perikon* (St. John's Wort) and *baldrian* (valerian) root with *mynte* (mint) to make it taste better, and gave it to Bragi to drink. Bragi wondered about the name she gave the root baldrian. She explained that she had named it after his brother, Baldr, because of his gentle and calming ways. This did calm him so that they could discuss their future productively

As we shall see, Idunn and Bragi decided to go together to live with the Æsir, with the hope of teaching them to live more peacefully. Thus the Vanir, especially Idunn, learned more and more about the flora, finding another source of power and strength.

The Power of Bragi's Songs

Very little has been said about Bragi's poetry and songs. I asked, "What more can I learn about Bragi, the god of poetry?"

Bragi liked to go out into the fields away from Asgard to sit and think. Sometimes his brother Baldr would join him. Both gods enjoyed time alone and away from all the activity of Valhalla. On this day, Bragi was humming to himself. When he really listened to and felt the humming inside of him, he noticed that as he changed the pitch he also changed where inside himself he could feel the vibrations. He felt them first in his chest, but he played with trying to move the vibrations down deeper into his abdomen and to spread them throughout his body. With his mouth rounded and with a deep *hum,* he could feel the sound vibrating in much of his body. As he did this he felt an inner quietness and comfort.

Bragi then tried making sounds of words while he hummed in this way. He used the word for peace, *friðr,* and as he trilled it deeply he felt a deeper peace within him. He knew that some words sounded like others in some ways, and when he put such words together they rhymed and had a rhythm that was playful. When he expressed himself to others in this way they would stop what they were doing and listen intently, with interested expressions on their faces. Bragi soon had people gathering around him to listen, enjoying the poetry he made in his deep-throated voice that would vibrate throughout his body. He would sometimes make his voice go up and down, and he called this *singing.* People stopped and listened to him as if it was magic.

Bragi enjoyed spending time with the Vanir because they appreciated his poetry and singing more than the Æsir, who valued their physical strength above all else. He told his story of poetry and singing to Idunn, and she was very interested. She too tried talking, making her voice go up and down and putting words together that rhymed and were sung with a rhythm. There were many different ways this could be done, and they spent the afternoon at Idunn's hall laughing together while trying out these different ways. Idunn's voice was much higher than Bragi's, and when they sang together in different ways they could make even more beautiful sounds.

They found that there was one way they could sing that would make them sleepy. When they sat outside singing in quiet and harmonious voices, sometimes animals would come up to them, just as when they focused their attention on their center of harmony. They discovered a real power to singing and the spell it cast on others. Sometimes when out walking by herself, Idunn would become nervous about the dangers of being a woman alone in the woods. But when she sang she would feel self-confident. At those times she would sing a rousing and strong song that would keep the animals away. Just as Idunn found that eating some plants helped kept her healthy, she found that some songs would also help in keeping her in good spirits, and she knew that when she felt content and happy, she would also be healthy.

In this way Idunn and Bragi spent much of their time together. When they sang in the woods they could see the trees swaying and moving with the rhythm of their songs. They made up some special songs just for the trees, praising the trees and their strength, and they sang these songs in a very majestic way. It became obvious to them that the trees listened and responded to their singing. One day, as they were going back to their hall, one tree put down its branch to block their path, and they could hear the deep rumbling sound of the tree saying, "Just one more song." With a big smile for each other and the tree, they sang one more song. On another occasion when they were in the woods singing together, a bear came up, stood on his hind legs, and roared. A tree near him threw back its branch to knock the bear for a loop, and off he ran.

Idunn and Bragi were very excited about the power their singing had over the trees. The other gods and goddesses recognized this power, and some tried to sing songs like Bragi and Idunn, but they were not as good at it. Through learning and appreciating the power singing had in their lives, Bragi and Idunn learned how to communicate with the trees, and they knew that the trees would protect them when their protection was needed.

Bragi composed a love song especially for Idunn:

Beautiful Idunn with golden hair   *Flowing with the golden apples*
Loving Idunn, goddess of youth   *Feeds all her golden apples*
Lovely Idunn with golden hair   *Feed me from your golden tree*
I sing you this love song   *To keep our love young**

But Bragi was beginning to feel a need to return home. Idunn and Bragi talked a lot about this. They went to talk with Njord about it, too. Njord was disappointed that Bragi felt he needed to go back to the Æsir, but he was also concerned about the warlike disposition of the Æsir and wished there was a way of convincing them of the power of living in peace and harmony with the world around them. He gave Idunn and Bragi the challenge of teaching the Æsir that there are other ways to live, but before they left, Njord called for the goddess Vár† to witness the oath of love made between Idunn and Bragi. Bragi offered his oath in the form of a poem:

My eternal love is for Idunn   *My love for her will last*
I will take her to my home   *The goddess of our hall*
My father, Odin will love her   *All Æsir will praise her too*
There we shall raise our family   *There I will provide and protect her*

Then Njord wished them well on their new life's journey.

Bragi offered a farewell song to Njord:

---

*Ancient Nordic poetry is of a specific style or form. This style or form, with its extensive use of kennings, or figures of speech, is well described in Lee Hollander's translation of the *Poetic Edda*.

†Vár is the goddess who listens to oaths of marriage and punishes those who do not maintain their oaths, as recorded in the Gylfaginning of the *Prose Edda*.

My love is for the Vanir   *Their magic harmonious ways*
My father is a warrior   *To him I'll take your greetings*
My song can quiet warriors   *My poems can melt their swords*
I'll take the lovely Idunn   *Her love will heal their warrior ways*

Idunn Is Accepted

Bragi returned to the Æsir and took Idunn with him. But how was the magic of Idunn accepted by the Æsir, I asked?

Soon after they arrived, Odin called Idunn into audience. When she entered the high god's great hall she heard his booming voice demanding, "What do you have to offer the Æsir?"

Coming from where the gods are less assertive and much more gentle, Idunn sputtered and stammered for a few moments. Then she found her center of harmony and was able to speak.

"Among the Vanir I am known for my knowledge of plants and trees, how they can keep you healthy, how they can heal your wounds and illnesses, and how they can keep you young."

"Oh, really? Your plants can keep me young?" replied Odin. Though not as old as Njord, Odin was feeling his age.

Idunn said, "Not a plant, but the apples from the golden apple tree."

Odin then ordered Idunn to bring him some apples. As she left, Odin shook his head and said under his breath, "I don't know if I believe her. The Vanir have such strange ideas and ways. All Bragi likes to do is make poetry and sing songs. I don't know about his wife."

Later, when she returned with her apples, Idunn instructed Odin to eat just one a day for the next few days, and that she would bring him more. When she returned several days later, Odin was looking less wrinkled and feeling more spry. "Your apples may be helping. I want you to give them to all of the Æsir. I want to see what it does for them."

After this trial, Odin called all the gods to council. They were very enthusiastic. Thus, Odin assigned Idunn to be the goddess of the golden apple trees. He did not show much interest in the other plants, but in her new role Idunn became familiar with all of the strange activities of Asgard. Though all the aggression and violence made her uncomfortable, she started using her plants, especially the poultice of kulsukker, comfrey, for the wounds of the Einherjar.

The goddesses, especially Sif,* were very interested in Idunn and what she might have to help them keep their skin soft and beautiful. Idunn offered them several different lotions, and they were very pleased, welcoming her into their confidence.

After she gained some confidence with the other goddesses, Idunn complained to them about how the violence of the Æsir upset her so that she had to take some of her own medicines, including baldrian and perikon (valerian and St. John's wort), to stay calm. Frigg was sympathetic, as she felt somewhat the same way herself, and she too had roots among the Vanir. Sif became a little defensive because she felt a need to support her husband, Thor, especially since he was always getting in trouble because of his impulsiveness. Sigyn† was also supportive because she understood the hypocrisy of the gods, hearing of it constantly from her outspoken husband, Loki.

One thing that Idunn and Bragi had learned while living among the Vanir that was never talked about concerned the effect their singing together had on the trees. Bragi did sing while in Asgard, and sometimes he and Idunn sang together, especially for the enjoyment of the Æsir. He taught the Æsir and Einherjar some chants that raised their spirits in fighting and gave them a feeling of greater strength, but they did not show great appreciation for his use of words because he was not a warrior like the rest of them. So Bragi spent his time with the goddesses and with his brother Baldr, who did appreciate him. Baldr also appreciated some of the lotions that Idunn gave him to help him keep his skin white, though this would probably have disappointed his father if his father had known.

---

*Sif, the wife of Thor and a goddess associated with the earth, was known for her beautiful golden hair made of strands of gold by the dwarfs in the cave of the dark elves. From chapter 5 of the Skáldskaparmál of the *Prose Edda*, we know that Loki shape-shifted into a fly and slipped into Sif's bedroom when she was asleep and cut off her hair. Thor, angered, sent Loki to the cave of the dark elves, where the elves made her new hair of strands of gold.

†Sigyn ("victorious girlfriend") is the faithful wife of Loki. After he is bound with a poisonous viper hanging above him dripping poison, Sigyn spends all her time at his side catching the poison in a bowl. When she leaves the cave where he is bound in order to empty the bowl, the poison causes Loki to tremble, causing what we know as earthquakes. This story is found in the Gylfaginning of the *Prose Edda*.

Kvasir's Mead

Since my first visit to Scandinavia I have developed a taste for mead, or *mjoðr*, the ancestor of all fermented, alcoholic drinks, and I now successfully brew my own. I know that it is the drink of the gods, but I was interested in knowing the rest of the story . . .

The Vanir knew a lot about bees. Njord had named them when he got stung, but when he learned about his center of harmony he found that if he stayed centered, he could take some honey from the comb of a hive of bees and not get stung. Honey became very popular among the gods and goddesses because it tasted so good and they enjoyed it in their cooking and drinks. Idunn tried it in some of her lotions and medicines.

Kvasir was considered the wisest of the gods, probably because of this story about him and what he taught the others. Kvasir was a great admirer of Idunn and enjoyed her teas, especially her mynte teas. There were many different kinds of mynte that could be used in tea. When Kvasir brewed a pot of tea he would always put honey in it. One problem, though, was that during the winter the gods could not take honey from the beehives because the bees needed it to survive, and mynte was not available because it died out in the cold. Thus, Kvasir brewed up several large vats of honey-sweetened tea during the autumn so he would have some during the winter. He kept it near the fire in his hall so it would not freeze.

As winter began, he drank from the first vat, and the tea was good. As the winter passed he started drinking from the second vat and found it tasted even better, and near the end of the winter, when he started drinking from the third vat, the drink was really great. It made him feel good all over. When summer came and he had part of the third vat left, Kavsir quickly called the gods together, along with Freyr and Njord, who were still with the Vanir at the time. Freyr brought with him Baldr and Bragi, who were visiting, as well. He offered the gods a drink of his tea and they all could tell it was in some way different. The intoxicating effect of this drink made them all feel good. Kvasir announced that he had given this drink a name: *mjoðr,* which means "mead." He called it the drink of the gods.

That spring, when the bees were making honey and the mynte was up, Kvasir again filled his vats, and he got three more vats to fill so that the gods would always have a good supply of mead. Because of his fore-sightedness, the gods thought of Kvasir as most wise.

When Kvasir went to live with the Æsir along with Njord and Freyr after the war, he did not want to tell the Æsir how to make mead and kept the recipe a secret. So the creative Bragi made up an entertain-ing story about how mead came into being that was quite different. He sang that when the gods of the Æsir and Vanir had the meeting for a truce, all the gods spit into a vat to seal this truce, and from the spit Kvasir, the wisest of the gods, was formed. Kvasir traveled throughout the world teaching others all that he knew until he came to the dwarfs. The dwarfs, wanting the wisdom of Kvasir, killed him, and to his essence honey was added to make the first batch of mead. Thus, mead contains the essence of Kvasir, and whoever drinks it becomes a poet and scholar.* To protect their mead, these same dwarfs were responsible for the death of two giants. But murder always brings with it further despair. Suttung, the son of the murdered giants, came seeking retribu-tion. To save their own lives, the dwarfs offered Suttung their mead in compensation.

Suttung took the mead home and hid it deep in a mountain for safekeeping, setting his daughter to watch over it. As Odin, in dis-guise, traveled through Midgard, he stopped to help the brother of Suttung, for whom he did the work of nine men. In payment, Odin asked Suttung for a drink of mead. Suttung claimed that he had no con-trol over his brother's mead because he wanted it all for himself. After

---

*This story of the first mead made from the essence of Kvasir is told in chapter 2 of the Skáldskaparmál of the *Prose Edda.* It tells of the roundabout way that mead came to the gods: the first vats going to the dwarfs, and then to the giants, before Odin finally gained possession and brought it from Jötunheimr, the home of the giants, to Asgard.

some conniving, Odin produced an auger for the giant to use to bore a hole through the mountain to the hiding place of the mead. Odin changed his shape to that of a snake and slithered through the hole. When he came to the hiding place, he lay with Suttung's daughter for three nights, for which she offered him a drink of the precious mead. In three swallows he drained all three vats. To escape the giant's wrath, he changed his shape to that of a heavily laden eagle, and he flew home as fast as he could. When Suttung saw him flying away, he too changed his shape to an eagle and flew in pursuit.

When the Æsir saw Odin flying toward Asgard, they prepared by placing three ale vats in the courtyard. When Odin flew over the wall and entered the yard, he spat the mead he held in his gullet into the vats. This mead has become known as the drink of the gods. Suttung, though, was right on Odin's tail and so close that in a panic Odin blew some mead out of his rear end. No one showed any interest in the mead that came out of his tail, and so whoever wanted it took it. So from that time on, this mead was called the bad poets' portion.

Over the years, I have listened to the tales of mead with enjoyment and have often thought that with this ending, Bragi must have tasted some of that bad poets' mead, too.

You may ask, if Kvasir was killed by the dwarfs, how is it that he was alive to live among the Æsir. That is part of the magic of these ancient stories.*

I can hear Bragi's beautiful voice ringing out before the gods:

The gods swooned with mead   *What manner of drink is this?*
From the gods' truce-sealing spit   *Wise poet Kvasir rose*

---

*Again, what comes before and what comes after becomes irrelevant in the processes of the unconscious mind and in mythology. The time-free nature of mythology gives it its power. Another example of this power, from the field of art, is Picasso's use of cubism to portray a person in both a frontal and profile view at the same time, freeing his art from a rational, three-dimensional perspective and moving it into a time-free dimension.

Dwarfs killed him for his wisdom
From his essence and honey

The brewer of poetry
They brewed their wisdom brew

This ale brought desire and death
From the death of giants to Odin
For the gods of Asgard
The essence of Kvasir

To those who desired wisdom
Journeyed this golden drink
The drink brought wisdom
The drink of gods and poets

Kvasir continued to live with the Æsir. Because of his wisdom, he was responsible for the eventual capture of Loki.* Loki's capture and restraint led to the three endless winters of suffering and cold and to the final battle of Ragnarǫk. Mead, the essence of Kvasir, is still the drink of choice throughout the North lands.

---

*Loki was experimenting with various ways he thought he might be caught by the gods in search of him. During the day he shape-shifted into a salmon and swam under a nearby waterfall. It occurred to him that he might be caught in a net, so he made such a net to see how it might work. When the gods came to his cabin he threw the net into the fire and left for the waterfall. Kvasir, seeing the ash of the net in the fire, instantly understood Loki's plan. This story is told in the Gylfaginning of the *Prose Edda,* just before the story of Ragnarǫk.

The Lay of Gullveig

Though there were many reasons for the war between the Æsir and the Vanir, one main reason was that the values of each tribe of gods were different enough to be a threat to the values of the other. The magic and compassion of the Vanir was a threat to the Æsir, and the aggressive nature of the Æsir was a threat to the Vanir. This story, however, tells of another reason for this war. It came when, in my trance chair, I posed the question, "Who is Gullveig?"

When the Vanir goddess Gullveig first tasted Kvasir's mead, she fell in love with it, and thus with him. It was because of her love for his mead that she was given the name Gullveig, which means "golden brew." She was rarely seen without a horn of Kvasir's mead in her hand, and it was because of her fondness for him, as ugly as he was, that the goddess Vár was called to hear Gullveig's oath of love sworn to him. In fact, the more mead she drank, the more handsome he became to her, though at times when this couple was with others Gullveig would not know whose arm she was holding. Vár was called because it was her job to hear marriage oaths, but also to punish those who broke them,* which was a concern when Gullveig was seen on someone else's arm.

Once Gullveig was at a feast of the god Ægir along with most of the other gods and goddesses, and as always she was enjoying herself.† Though she was savoring the ale made in Ægir's new kettle, she had also brought a sufficient supply of Kvasir's golden brew. In her state, all Gullveig could do was giggle when Loki began to go around the table insulting each of the gods and goddesses. As his insults escalated, her giggling turned to outright laughter. Soon Loki turned to her. She,

---

*Vár's role as the goddess who hears marriage oaths is found in the Gylfaginning of the *Prose Edda.*

†From this lay we learn more of Loki's ranting, which was not found in the poem "Lokasenna," in the *Poetic Edda.*

in her amusement, was beginning to take away some of the attention given to him. No one ever thought that Loki could be insulted, but apparently her laughter was an insult to him. In his eloquent way he began insulting Gullveig and her dependency on the brew. Addiction was never considered a problem among the gods—drunkenness was accepted as a show of appreciation for the drink and whoever was offering it at the time. But in this situation, Loki decided that Gullveig had a problem. "Ægir's ale is not good enough for you, you had to bring your own. What an insult to our host. You are a drunken sot."

As Loki's words flowed, Gullveig's answer to him was only more and greater laughter. Her laughter was out of control. Finally, Loki just shook his head and went on to the next god at the table.

Njord, with a smile on his face, turned to his daughter and whispered so only those near them could hear, but hear him they did. "With her laughter, Loki's insults just roll off her back. Gullveig is drunk like a fish." From that day on, a person who imbibes excessively into a state of laughter is referred to as "drunk like a fish."

Kvasir was known for his wisdom, not his attractiveness. One time Kvasir wisely advised the Vanir that it would be to their advantage to offer a gift of a vat of mead to the Æsir. This gift would create a bond between the two tribes. Everyone realized that a gift of a vat of mead would be most appropriate because it was very special to the Vanir and something that the Æsir did not have. Yet in deciding on how to present this gift, they did not want to send Kvasir because they were afraid that the the Æsir might kidnap him, holding him until they learned the recipe for mead. Who better to send than the person who loved mead the most: Gullveig.

Thus, Gullveig arrived at the gates of Asgard with a vat of mead on a cart pulled by her two stags. She greatly enjoyed her journey because she spent her time imbibing the drink she carried. When she arrived, and after her stags were pastured, she called on Thor to help her carry the vat before Odin. When Odin peered into the vat, he could nearly see the bottom. Still, when the gods drank what was left of the mead they found it exceptionally appealing. Being of a quarrelsome nature, they were quick to be insulted by the gift of a nearly empty vat of mead. When they found that Gullveig would give them neither more mead nor the recipe, they were furious and threw her into the central fire of Odin's great hall. Yet a few moments later, as they watched, she stood up, brushed off the glowing embers, and walked out of the fire unharmed. The astounded gods grabbed her and again threw her into the fire, but again she walked out without a sign of a burn. After she walked out of the fire a third time they led her to the gates of Asgard to expel her, calling her a *heiðr,* a witch.*

Thus Gullveig returned to Vanaheim with the story of the quarrelsome Æsir's ungratefulness, which was an insult to the Vanir, yet the Vanir likely did not know of Gullveig's part in angering the Æsir. It was because of this insult that Odin prepared to go to war with the Vanir, and it was because of the insult placed on the Vanir that they prepared to defend themselves against the Æsir. They both realized that there was no reconciliation.

---

*We know from the "Vǫluspá," the first and best-known poem of the *Poetic Edda,* only of the Æsir's attempt to kill Gullveig three times in the fire and her rising from the fire three times, to subsequently be called a witch, but this lay teaches us how Gullveig was named and what brought her to the gates of Asgard. Rudolf Simek, in his book *Dictionary of Northern Mythology,* noted that the name Gullveig, besides meaning "golden drink," means "golden power" or "golden intoxication," suggesting that she personified the greed for gold. Instead, it is apparent from this story that her name refers to her fondness for Kvasir's "golden brew."

Ullr and His Inventions

The stories of Ullr, a major god of the prehistoric times, are sparse, thus I asked to learn more about him. We began with what we already know . . .

Sif, wife of Thor, was originally of the Vanir, like Idunn and Frigg. It is recorded that her son, Ullr, was the stepson of Thor.* The beautiful Sif was the most sensuous of the goddesses of the Vanir. She was proud of her long golden hair and spent much of the day in front of a mirror brushing it. Everyone raved about the beauty of her hair. Though Njord was generally faithful to Skaði, on one occasion, when he happened to be alone with his sister Sif, his passions got the best of him. He could not resist her, and Sif was always willing. As a result, Sif gave birth to her son Ullr. Njord had risen to such passion once before with his sister, a union that produced the twins Freyja and Freyr.

Sif's vanity was her flaw, a flaw that greatly irritated Loki and led him to sneak into her bedroom one night when she was asleep and cut off her hair. To appease Thor's anger at this incident, Loki arranged with the dark elves to replace Sif's hair with strands of gold. Sif's new hair was even more beautiful, and from then on gold was often poetically referred to as Sif's hair.

This same flaw had led to Sif's marriage to Thor, for what better husband for such a beautiful but vain goddess than the most powerful son of Odin. Marrying Thor and becoming part of the Æsir required that Sif pledge her allegiance to her husband and the Æsir, a pledge that she didn't mind keeping to be married to this mighty god. Thus, she abandoned the values of the Vanir, the values of peace and compassion, and with her son went to live with the Æsir.

But before Ullr left the Vanir he made a name for himself. Like all the other Vanir, he was very observant of the world around him. One

---

*Though we know that Ullr, Sif's son, was the stepson of Thor from the Gylfaginning of the *Prose Edda,* we now learn that Njord was the real father of this god.

of his observations was that the branch of a yew had great spring and resilience to it. He discovered this when bending a tree to make a snare to catch a rabbit. In playing around with a branch of a yew, he tied a length of sinew to one end of the branch, bent the branch by bracing it against his foot, and tied the other end of the sinew to the other end of the branch. This kind of playful thinking is what made Ullr a very creative god. He was impressed with the spring of the yew when he pulled on the sinew. He followed the idea further by taking another smaller, straight branch and cut a little notch in the end of it to rest on the sinew. Then pulling the sinew and branch back with the other end of the branch lying on the bowed yew and letting go of the sinew, he watched the branch fly through the air. He was impressed with the distance and speed with which it flew. In this way Ullr made the first bow and arrow.* With some experimenting and making some adjustments in the bow and the arrow, he became skilled in shooting the arrow wherever he wanted it to go. This took some practice, but the Vanir are known for being very patient. He soon was hunting rabbits and other animals with the bow and arrow and did not need to use the snare as he had before. Thus, he made a name for himself among the Vanir, and others of the Vanir soon learned how to shoot arrows using a bow.

When Ullr went to live with the Æsir, most of the warriors did not have the patience to learn how to use the bow and arrow. They felt that using a bow and arrow would be unfair and not representative of their strength. They wanted instead to get close to their opponent and use their swords, axes, or spears. That was the best way to demonstrate their strength, they thought. In using a bow and arrow, their opponent would likely not know who shot the arrow, and the archer would not receive the honor for making the kill.

Nevertheless, when he joined the Æsir, Ullr used the bow and arrow in fighting, and since he was the only archer, everyone knew who it was who made the kill. When the Einherjar fought each day, with some

---

*We know that Ullr is an archer from the Gylfaginning of the *Prose Edda*.

dying only to come back to life to fight the next day, some died by Ullr's arrows. Ullr had been commissioned by Odin to teach archery, but at first he found no warriors interested in learning. He soon found that the only way to get the attention of a warrior was to kill him. Upon coming back to life, the warrior would then see Ullr as the ultimate challenge and seek to get the better of him. For some, they had to die a second time, but after only one or two days, the warrior was ready to learn archery. Only when he was able to hit Ullr with an arrow from a distance of the width of the field of Valhalla was he considered sufficiently adept at archery. Even then the warriors considered archery only a hobby and for hunting animals, and the other warriors of the Einherjar were still not sufficiently impressed.

Ullr soon lost interest in turning Odin's army into an army of archers. After a few warriors became adept at hunting with a bow and arrow, they became Ullr's hunting companions, and their interests turned to hiking or skiing through the woods to hunt. He believed that hunting to provide food for the table of the gods was a sufficient contribution.

Ullr was very handsome and was somewhat vain like his mother, so he didn't want to receive wounds that would leave him scarred—another advantage of being an archer. He did carry a shield to deflect arrows if an opponent should happen to be an archer, or if a warrior was attempting to prove his skill by hitting Ullr from across the field of Valhalla. His shield was large enough so that he also used it as a boat to cross water.

Another invention of Ullr's was discovered when he tied bones to his feet, the long rib bones of the great mammoth. These were the first skis, and they enabled him to slide across the snow much faster than others could walk. The other gods had their own ways of traveling, being pulled in chariots by goats, cats, or pigs, changing shape into a bird and flying, or riding a horse that could fly, but the Einherjar did not have such an advantage, so they were quick to learn to ski.

Óðr's Journey and Freyja's Pursuit

Another of the gods mentioned in the ancient literature is Óðr, but once again we know very little about him. My question concerned Freyja's relationship with her wandering husband, Óðr . . .*

Freyja had two daughters, Hnoss and Gersemi.† Both were very beautiful. The name Hnoss means "jewel," and Gersemi means "treasure." Their father was Óðr, and he was a wanderer. He left Vanaheim after his daughters were born, and Freyja has cried tears of gold ever since he left, knowing that he was never going to return.

Grieving, she went to seek Óðr from her seiðhjallr, the high platform used by a seeress. There she lay fully outstretched in order to go on a spirit journey to find him.‡ He had been gone only two days, and she had no idea in what direction he had gone or where he was going. She could not find him in her trance journey this way, so she sat upright on her platform with her hands clasping her knees and relaxed into a trance in order to see into the future—maybe that way she could find where Óðr was going. But again she searched to no avail. So she went back to crying. Her daughters were very concerned. They also spent time on the seiðhjallr trying to find their father.

One day, Gersemi called her mother to the platform. She had seen her father. They both lay out with their hands touching, and in a trance they journeyed together so that Gersemi could take her mother to where he was. He was in Midgard, traveling on the road toward Jötunheimr, the land of the giants. Freyja was overjoyed and quickly harnessed her cats, jumped in her chariot, and flew to see him. However, by the time

---

*Óðr means "the frenzied one." We learn of him in the Gylfaginning of the *Prose Edda*.
†We learn of Freyja's daughters and the meaning of their names in the Gylfaginning of the *Prose Edda*.
‡Recall that from Felicitas Goodman's research on ecstatic postures we know that the posture of lying with outstretched arms is a spirit journeying posture and that of sitting and clasping one or both knees is a divination posture.

she got to the road to Jötunheimr—it took her less than a day to get there—he was no longer on the road. She couldn't imagine where he had gone. After several days of searching, she returned home in deeper grief.

Once Freyja saw Óðr from her high platform, this time traveling south toward the hot, fiery southern region of Muspell. Again she harnessed her cats and went after him, and again she could not find him. She spent some time wandering, and in her wandering through Midgard she met people. They all had stories to tell her, and she would listen to all of them. So many women were in pain because they could not find their lover or because they could not get pregnant. In these cases, Freyja had the power to grant them their wish. Sometimes their warrior husbands were away fighting. She would promise these wives that she would harness her battle boar* and go to the battlefield to protect their husbands. Thus, she became known as the warrior goddess. Some of their concerns were with problems and unfairness caused by a neighbor. These kinds of problems were not within her power to resolve, but still she showed compassion and was a sympathetic listener. She would tell them to carry their concerns to the god Forseti,† the god of justice and the son of Baldr and Nanna. Over time, from her seiðhjallr or while on her journeying in Midgard, Freyja saw more and more altars of stone built to honor her. Even though these journeys were undertaken out of her own personal grief, she was pleased to see how much human beings loved her.

On these journeys Freyja would often seek lodging in the homes of the humans of Midgard, and all were quick to open their doors to her. The families were also quick to give her a bed, usually with a young man in it if there was a young man in the family. If the family did not have a young man, they might borrow one from a neighbor. So on these journeys Freyja was never lonely. On one particular journey she met a young man, a warrior of the local king, and she fell in love with him. His name was Óttar. With him she did not feel the grief of loss of her husband.

---

*Freyja is famous for riding her battle boar, Hildisvíni, as told in the "Lay of Hyndla," found in the *Poetic Edda*.
†We learn of Forseti as the god of justice in the Gylfaginning of the *Prose Edda*.

Óttar was a great warrior, and Freyja learned that he was a descendant of Sigurd, the dragon slayer. She was especially concerned when he went to battle and was always there to protect him. On one occasion, another warrior, Angantyr, challenged Óttar to a duel over who had the best ancestry. Freyja went to the giantess-goddess and vǫlva Hyndla to learn of Óttar's ancestry to insure that he could win this challenge. His ancestry was impeccable, she learned. Yet men cannot live forever. When Óttar died, Freyja imbued her battle boar with his spirit so that she could live with him forever.*

Probably the most famous story of Freyja's hunt for Óðr was the time that Frigg, from her high platform, saw Óðr traveling south through Sweden. She promptly sent a messenger to Freyja with the news. Freyja at that moment was tending to the needs of Hildisvíni, her boar. When she heard the news, she immediately jumped on the boar's back and grabbed the reins. In just a few moments she was across Bifröst, the flaming rainbow bridge that reaches between Asgard and Midgard, cruising south through Sweden. She had a strong feeling that this would be her day, and at that moment she saw someone she was sure was Óðr. She yanked on the reins and Hildisvíni was quick to put his hindquarters down and his feet out to come to a sliding halt. In landing, he dug a long trench, pushing the earth ahead of him, thus digging what would become known as Vättern Lake. Yet Freyja's sorrow and tears of gold were to continue, because the person she saw was not Óðr, but in fact nothing more than a rock formation that can still be seen on the shore of the lake. Her tears formed the dark pools of black water, the skogstjärn, known as "the tears of Freyja," found so plentifully at the end of this lake. Many centuries later, people continue to search for this rock formation that Freyja thought looked like Óðr.

Some say that Gefjon,† when plowing the land that formed the

---

*The story of Freyja's love for Óttar and the challenge given him by Angantyr is in the "Lay of Hyndla" in the *Poetic Edda*.

†Gefjon, a seeress and goddess, is a member of both the Vanir and the Æsir. She was associated with the plow, virgins, and good luck. Her story is recorded in the Ynglinga saga of the *Heimskringla*.

island of Zealand, also plowed and pulled the land that is now Lake Vättern out to sea, to the east of Sweden, to form what will someday be known as the island of Öland, but now we know differently.

Óðr never did return, but Freyja's grief and compassion for people gave her a purpose as a goddess of the Vanir. Her daughters continued at her side, and when she became part of the Æsir they remained with the Vanir to carry on her work. Her wandering in search of Óðr brought her in closer contact with humans than the other gods and made her a much loved and worshipped goddess, prayed to by all people.

Calling on Moðir

Njord was recognized as the leader of the Vanir. What happened to the memory of his mother, the Great Mother, Moðir?

During the early times before the rise to power of the Æsir, Moðir was the most important goddess, the mother of all. With the rise of Odin and the death of Moðir, she was shamefully forgotten. While she lived, Odin knew that most of the goddesses and a few of the gods had turned to her with their concerns. He had seen the image of Moðir carved in stone by Ullr that Frigg had kept wrapped in a silken cloth in her chest, and he knew how she valued this object. He had heard his wife mumbling prayers to Moðir. He knew that Moðir's death had left a void in the lives of these goddesses and gods. To fill the void caused by Moðir's fall from power, Odin tried to put Freyja and Frigg in her place by showing them respect and occasionally calling on them for advice, but still he made them lesser gods than himself.

In earlier times, the people built altars to Moðir and placed gifts to her on these altars. The people loved her because of her great compassion. She was the Great Mother. Each family kept a carved stone image of her in their home like the one kept by Frigg, an image with a big belly and large breasts showing Moðir's love and essence in producing life. They would pray to her in times of trouble, and she would answer these prayers if she found them appropriate. Sometimes prayers were not appropriate when people would ask for things that were not best for themselves or their family. She was all-knowing, and she knew what was best.

Moðir did not have a battle boar or cats to take her to the world of humans. She did not need to make such journeys because she was able to watch over the people and hear their petitions from her position in the Sky World. From there she could watch the gods and goddesses, too. She could watch her nephews, Odin, Vili, and Vé. She saw how they took after her brother, Borr.* She appreciated what they did in creating much

---

*We know about Borr and his three sons, Odin, Vili, and Vé, from the Gylfaginning of the *Prose Edda*.

of the world, but she was greatly hurt by how they treated her own children, grandchildren, and great-grandchildren, for she loved them all and saw value in them all. She knew that in the end there would be a final battle, and that love and patience would win. She knew she would not be there for this final battle, but she believed that she would be remembered.

The war that occurred when the Æsir attacked the Vanir was a time of much calling on Moðir. Freyr's primary position among the Vanir was as a warrior to protect them. He sang and cast spells to arm the trees, calling "Praise be to Moðir," and "Thank you, Moðir." Moðir was the source of all their magic. All the gods and goddesses of Vanir called out, "Moðir, why are they attacking us?" Both Freyr and Freyja went out to face the enemy in their chariots pulled by golden boars.* As they patrolled the front lines, they called, "praise be to Moðir," and in calling her name they were insured of holding the line. On these patrols, Freyr would often direct his sword to attack the Æsir warriors that were gaining an advantage. Freyja, as a warrior among the Vanir on her mission to the front line, would call songs and spells to hold their line, sometimes moving stones into the reach of the trees. The spells and songs always included praise and thanks to Moðir.

When Freyja, Freyr, Njord, and the other gods of the Vanir went to live with the Æsir, they did not forget Moðir. They prayed to her with everything they did, knowing she would understand and hear them. They would call to her more quietly, but nevertheless they would call to her, in thanks and with requests in their struggle to bring the magical powers of love, compassion, and curiosity to the Æsir. When Freyja journeyed to Midgard or when she journeyed from her seiðhjallr she would ask, "What would Moðir want?" Moðir was not forgotten by the Vanir as she was by the Æsir and the people of Midgard. When the

---

*Freyr's golden boar Gullinbursti ("golden bristles") was made by the dwarfs Eitri and Brokk, the sons of Ivaldi, in their cave forge, as recorded in chapter 5 of the Skáldskaparmál of the *Prose Edda*. Freyja's war mount, Hildisvíni, "battle swine," fashioned by the dwarfs Dain and Nabbi, also had golden bristles such that it could lead her way even in the dark, as told in the *Poetic Edda*, in the poem "Hyndluljoð."

Vanir gods and goddesses journeyed through Midgard, they constantly reminded the people of her love and compassion, but slowly she was forgotten in Midgard, too, and in her place humans worshipped Odin, Thor, and Freyja.

Even at the time of Ragnarǫk, Móðir was not forgotten. Njord never forgot her as he stood back near the edge of the sea when the fires of the giant Surtr grew so hot, and he saw each of the gods of the Æsir dying. Then he called out, "Móðir, how could this be happening?" Even so, he knew that the new world after the death of the gods would be a world that his mother would appreciate.

In the final battle, Freyja retreated to the sea along with Frigg to watch. Sif was the last to retreat—only after the death of Thor did she follow the others. Frigg was proud of the Æsir god of vengeance, Víðarr, for his strength in tearing apart the wolf Fenrir, thus avenging the death of his father, Odin, but she believed that the rightful heir to Odin was her son, the gentle Baldr. They all remembered the compassion and love of Móðir. In the final battle, they heard the voice of Freyr calling out above all others, "Móðir, I'll do what I must," when he faced his death at the sword of Surtr. This was Freyr's first real battle in which he had to fight himself, and his last, and he brought praise from his grandmother. She was proud of him in doing his duty as a warrior, knowing that he could not win, but his loss was painful to her.

Freyr's Power of Illusion

In learning about how the Vanir fought against the Æsir, there was more to their magic than so far described, but this other element of magic missing from the record is more difficult to understand. I asked a question to learn about this other kind of magic and received an answer from Freyr: that it involves the power of illusion . . .

After Freyr learned from Bragi, god of poetry, the power of singing and spell-casting, and after Bragi and Idunn had left the Vanir, Freyr continued to refine these powers. From his power of observation he realized that if he squinted his eyes, what he saw became somewhat blurred and could appear different. He also realized that things looked similarly blurred when in a trance, and he knew he could put people into a trance with his singing or chanting. Adding the beat of a drum, like the way the heart beats, made his singing and chanting work even better. In this way, Freyr caused the warriors of Einherjar to see the armed trees as armed warriors. When he learned of the approaching army of the Æsir, he quickly went into action and armed the trees around Vanaheim. He harnessed Gullinbursti, his golden boar that had been made in the forge of the dwarves, to his chariot and flew out over the battle line in this attack. From his chariot he sang his chants while beating his war drum, the chants that put the Einherjar warriors in a trance and made them think that the trees were armed warriors. Freyja joined him in her warrior state in chanting to the Einherjar, first from behind their lines and then, switching places with her brother, from in front of their lines. With trees appearing as armed warriors on either side and the songs of Freyr and Freyja before and behind, the Einherjar in their confusion believed they were surrounded by a mighty army.

Patrolling the battle line from his chariot, Freyr could see places in the line where the Einherjar began to gain the advantage, and it was in those places that he directed his sword that would fight by itself. In this way his and his sister's power of illusion continued to confuse and demoralize the Einherjar.

Both Hnoss and Gersemi, the lovely daughters of Freyja, loved their uncle Freyr, but they also frequently wanted to scream at him because of the constant pranks he played on them. He was forever using his power of illusion to annoy them. He would stand behind them and call their names, and when they turned he would not be there, yet from the other side of them he would call again. These pranks gave Freyr much practice and helped him refine his power of illusion. The Vanir's ability to change shape was another example of the power of illusion. Freyr would borrow his sister's falcon skin, put it on, and convince his two nieces that a falcon could talk. One god among the Æsir, Loki, was quick to embrace this power when he learned it from Freyr, and he used it often.* Stories of Loki changing shape include his changing into a fly,† an old lady,‡ a salmon,§ and a seal.¶

Freyr became very good at making himself look like an old man. Generally, the god in his natural state appeared young, strong, and alert. But when he let his face totally relax and sag, when he let his eyelids droop and his shoulders and posture sag, he could quickly change his appearance to that of a dimwitted old man. One day, as he sat in this guise along the road just outside of Vanaheim, his nieces saw him. They did not recognize him and thought of him as some wandering old man, so effective was his illusion.

After the attack by the Æsir, Freyr decided he wanted a new golden harness for Gullinbursti to go with the boar's golden bristles. He went to the cave of the dark elves to ask Eitri and Brokk to make him such a

---

*In chapter 1 of the Skáldskaparmál of the *Prose Edda,* Loki borrows Frejya's falcon skin to travel to the hall of the giant Thjazi to retrieve Idunn.
†Loki became a fly to enter Sif's bedroom to cut off her hair, as told in chapter 5 of the Skáldskaparmál of the *Prose Edda.*
‡Loki turned himself into an old lady to deceive Frigg into telling him about the one substance that could harm Baldr, i.e., mistletoe, as recorded in the Gylfaginning of the *Prose Edda.*
§Loki shifted shapes to be a salmon in an attempt to avoid being captured by the Æsir, as told in the Gylfaginning of the *Prose Edda.*
¶Loki took the shape of a seal in his duel with Heimdallr over Freyja's necklace, Brísingamen, as told in the *Laxdæla Saga.*

harness. He told them about the power of illusion, and they were excited about adding it to their storehouse. First, he demonstrated this power when he arrived: When Eitri had his back turned for a moment, Freyr sang a spell that made the dwarf think Freyr was behind him to the right. When he turned to face Freyr and found that he was not there, he turned with a start to find Freyr on the other side. Brokk laughed hysterically at the joke. Eitri asked Freyr how he did that, and that was when Freyr told the dwarfs about the power of illusions. He also told them how the Æsir could not beat them in battle because of this same power possessed by the Vanir. The dwarfs were eager to gain this power and asked Freyr to say his spell again so that they could collect it in a jar.

This Freyr did, though he knew that this power was different from the other powers and could not be collected. Each and every illusion and spell had to be made especially for the situation and the person. A particular spell works only in a very specific situation. Singing a spell or creating an illusion for an angry person is quite easy because the anger distorts and blinds how a person sees. Creating an illusion for a frightened person is also very easy because in fear he is very susceptible to seeing monsters, raging fires, or other frightening things. The greedy person is susceptible to illusions of price, value and quality, as evident in the greed of the dwarfs. The person in love is susceptible to illusions of returned love or rejection and illusions about the cost of love, as Freyr so well knew from his foolish payment of his sword. To be skilled in casting spells and illusions takes an exceptional ability of observation and understanding of the person on whom the spell or illusion is cast.

When Freyr next had the opportunity to visit the cave of the dark elves, he heard much grumbling from the dwarfs known as the sons of Ivaldi. The power of illusion was among the many powers of the Vanir, but it was a power that could not be collected by the elves.

Freyr's Journeys to Midgard

The stories of Nordic kings mingling among their people while dressed in disguise are fascinating and often quite funny. Knowing that the Nordic gods and goddesses enjoyed doing the same thing, I asked about the adventures of Freyr on his trips to Midgard . . .

When Freyr found it necessary to go to Midgard he did not want humans to recognize him, so he went in disguise. He was quick to make himself look like an old man by letting his face, eyelids, shoulders, and posture sag. He would also dress as a farmer or merchant. He would not dress as warrior because that would give away his disguise, since an old man would not be dressed as a warrior.

As Freyr traveled through Midgard, he inspected the fields of farmers and noticed the weather. He would cause the rain to fall or the sun to shine as needed to help the farmers with their crops. He could perhaps have done these inspections more conveniently from a seiðhjallr, but women were better in the art of seiðr, and he was certainly not a woman. Anyway, he enjoyed traveling and did not like being stuck at home.

On one trip to Midgard, Freyr came as an old beggar man to a fortified settlement with a guard at the gate. His trick of making a person think he was standing in one place when he was actually in another could sometimes get him into trouble, and this was one of those times. He tricked the guard in this way, sneaking by him to get into the settlement. The guard was quick, though, and turned and grabbed Freyr. When grabbed, Freyr stood erect and appeared to be a virile, strong young man, thus intimidating the guard. He demanded that the guard usher him to the king.

Coming before the king, he revealed himself as the god Freyr. Traveling as an old beggar, the clothes he wore were not the most presentable, so the king at first did not believe him. He asked Freyr many questions, asking first about the way he traveled. Freyr always hid his golden boar and chariot in the deep woods, knowing that if some outlaw found the boar, the outlaw's life would be very short. This stranger in front of the king knew that the boar's name was Gullinbursti and was the creation of Eitri and Brokk, two dwarfs. The king of this fortress was nephew to King Alf the Old and knew that King Alf's grandson Óttar was the earthly lover of Freyr's sister, Freyja. Thus, the king's questions went to this relationship and the ancestry of Óttar.* Freyr knew that Óttar was a descendent of Sigurd, the slayer of the dragon Fafnir, and also a descendent of King Harald Wartooth. This convinced the king that the stranger must be who he said he was.

The king apologized profusely about the guard's behavior, explaining that because of what was going to be a poor harvest, the people of the settlement were worried about the coming winter and knew that there would not be enough for every beggar who came to the gate. The king had thus instructed the guard to stop strangers. Freyr had noticed the poor condition of the fields outside of the wall and had already called for the needed rain. That it was already raining outside helped support Freyr's claim. The king was happy to provide Freyr food and lodging for the night in his opulent hall but did not provide a woman for his bed, knowing of Freyr's faithfulness to Gerðr.

On another occasion, after Freyr left Gullinbursti in the deep woods and was walking toward another settlement, to his surprise outlaws stopped him along the road. What would outlaws want from an old man whose clothes were those of a beggar? The outlaws knew all the beggars in the area and saw that this man was a stranger, and being a stranger, must be traveling and thus not as poor as he appeared. Freyr was about to ask them what they thought they could get from an old beggar man when they grabbed him, ready to take anything they could find. Freyr commanded his concealed sword to fight them off. The sword made quick work of the situation in protecting the god, and Freyr continued on his journey.

Even though Freyr traveled in disguise, after revealing himself to

---

*The story of Óttar's ancestry is found in the Hyndluljoð of the *Poetic Edda*.

the king, who was nephew to King Alf the Old, word spread that Freyr traveled as an old beggar man and from then on beggars were generally treated with respect. The poor would congregate at the gates of the settlements where merchants and warriors would pass, and kings would order their servants to take the leftover food from the royal meals to the gates to feed those who sat there. Along the roads that beggars traveled were found many piles of stones erected as altars to the god Freyr by the beggars of Midgard, and on those altars were various gifts—sometimes the blood of a rabbit or some other animal that the beggars were lucky enough to catch, other times a few grains of barley that the beggars found in the fields. The farmers also erected fancier altars to the god on which to call for rain and sunshine for their crops. Freyr was one of the most respected and loved of the gods, third to only Odin and Thor.

Freyr's Journeys to Jötunheimr

Being enamored with these stories of the power of illusion, I asked for more and was given the time-tested story of Útgarða-Loki, the giant and ruler of the castle Útgarðr, in Jötunheimr, home of the giants . . .

Freyr often journeyed to the land of the giants. He had a good relationship with them because he showed them respect and was not their enemy, unlike Thor. Also, both he and his father had formed alliances with the giants by marrying giants: Freyr had married Gerðr, and Njord had married Skaði. Freyr thought the Æsir, and especially Thor, were very foolish in their antagonism toward the giants. Unlike the Æsir, Freyr was always welcome in the halls of the giants.

Yet Thor's grandmother and Odin's mother was a giantess, Bestla.* Loki's mother, Laufey, and father, Fárbauti,† were of the race of giants. Angrboða,‡ Loki's mistress, and Gríðr, the mistress of Odin, were also giantesses. The giantess Gríðr helped Thor against the giant Geirröd.§ Even with all these close interrelationships to the giants, the Æsir, especially Thor, were constantly fighting with them. Freyr often commented that Thor, the strongest among the gods, must doubt his own strength, being so threatened by the strength of giants. What other explanation could there be for why he would go out of his way to fight them?

On one trip to the land of the giants, Freyr met Útgarða-Loki, an intelligent giant who had a great interest in magic, especially the magic of the Vanir. Freyr enjoyed finding someone of like interest. He enjoyed sharing his skills in magic and was a born teacher, especially to those who

---

*As recorded in the Gylfaginning of the *Prose Edda,* the frost giantess Bestla was the mother of Odin, Vé, and Vili.

†As recorded in the Gylfaginning of the *Prose Edda,* the giants Laufey and Fárbauti were the parents of Loki.

‡As recorded in the Gylfaginning of the *Prose Edda,* Loki made frequent trips to Jötunheimr, where he sired three children with the giantess Angrboða.

§Thor relied on help from the giantess Gríðr in his journey to the court of the giant Geirröd, as described in the Skáldskaparmál of the *Prose Edda.* On this journey he traveled with Loki, but without his hammer, his belt of strength, or his iron gloves. Thus, he required assistance from Geirröd.

learned quickly. Útgarða-Loki was quick to learn how to make people think he was in one place when in fact he was in another. He was quick to learn to shape-shift and to learn how to make others think things were what they were not. He was sensitive to the feelings of others, to their anger, vanity, fear, greed, and love; he knew how these emotions blind a person and distorted the way one sees the world. On this visit from Freyr, the giant enjoyed hearing the stories of Freyr's use of the power of illusion, and he practiced to hone his own skills in using illusion.

When the day came that Útgarða-Loki was ready, it happened that Thor and Loki came for a visit.* Before they arrived, he saw them coming and changed his shape to appear much larger than he was. As a giant among giants, he gave himself the name Skrýmir. As the gods journeyed and night approached, they found a large but strange hall in which to bed down. The next morning, they saw a large giant asleep on the ground. When he awoke, he introduced himself as Skrýmir.† When the giant reached for his glove, they realized that the hall in which they had slept was the giant's glove. They then journeyed with the giant to the great hall of Útgarða-Loki. When night fell, they slept under the trees. During the night, Thor tried three times while Skrýmir slept to kill the giant with his hammer, Mjölnir, but Skrýmir used the illusion of not being where Thor thought he was and so escaped death. The next morning, Skrýmir gave Thor and Loki directions to Útgarða-Loki's hall and then went on his way in a different direction, but he got to the hall before them anyway.

When the gods arrived at Útgarða-Loki's stronghold, Skrýmir had changed his appearance back to Útgarða-Loki, and he challenged the strengths and skills of the gods by insulting them. Taking the bait, Loki challenged the giants to an eating contest to see who could eat the most or the fastest. The giant Logi accepted the challenge, and each contestant started at either end of a long bench filled with food. As they raced, they met in the middle. Loki had eaten the meat from the bones. Logi had

---

*The story of Loki and Odin's journey to the realm of the giants to visit the giant Útgarða-Loki, and their competitive games there, is recorded in the Gylfaginning of the Prose Edda.

†Skrýmir means "big-looking."

eaten everything—bones, table, and all. Later, they learned that Útgarða-Loki had used an illusion in creating Logi, who was actually a wildfire.

Thor challenged the giants to a drinking contest, stating that he could empty a drinking horn faster than anyone else, vowing to empty the horn in one try. The giants brought the horn to Thor and he drank. After three tries the contents of horn were only slightly lower. Again, Útgarða-Loki had tricked Thor with an illusion: the lip of the horn was actually the shoreline of the ocean. Now when the tide goes out, it is said that Thor is drinking from the sea.

With each contest, Thor's frustration and anger grew, making him blind to the task at hand. Útgarða-Loki, knowing that Thor was the strongest of the gods, challenged him to lift the giant's cat. Even giants in their childhood could lift a cat. When Thor took hold of the cat and began to lift, he struggled and struggled but could only lift one of the cat's legs off the floor, with the cat arching its back like a rainbow above Thor's head. This time Útgarða-Loki's illusion was that the cat was in reality Jörmungandr, the sea serpent, who encircles the great ocean that encircles Midgard and grew so large that he was able to surround the earth by grasping his own tail.

Next, the giant insulted Thor by suggesting that none of the giants in the hall would stoop so low as to wrestle with him except for one old female giant, Elli. As they wrestled, the more Thor threw his strength at her, the more steadfast Elli stood. The match ended when Thor fell to one knee. This time the illusion was that Elli, the old giantess, was in actuality old age, and no one can beat old age.

Only afterward, when Loki and Thor were leaving the hall of Útgarða-Loki, did the giant admit to the use of illusions and tell Thor how impressed the giants were with his strength and skill. When Thor heard this he raised his hammer to strike the giant, but in that moment Útgarða-Loki and his great hall disappeared.

Thor, in his blinding anger and frustration, was susceptible to such illusions, and it was from Freyr that Útgarða-Loki learned much of what he could do.

The Power of Shape-Shifting

In reading the many ancient Nordic stories, one magical power that was used by several of the gods and goddesses was shape-shifting. I asked how they acquired this power . . .

Freyja spent a lot of time sitting on her golden seiðhjallr. Because the seiðhjallr was a central fixture at Sessrúmnir, her golden hall of many rooms, she had the dwarfs make her a golden seiðhjallr, with golden steps to take her to the top of the platform. On this particular day she was sitting with her legs bent back under her, with the knuckles of her hands resting on the platform in front of her knees.* The time she spent on the platform was almost always in a state of relaxation and trance. Trance had become automatic with her. Today, she first noticed that her center of harmony began to vibrate and tremble. Then she found herself bounding across a field to pounce on a field mouse. She held the mouse under her paw until she caught it between her teeth to eat it. She realized in looking at the mouse that her paw was furry—that of a cat. Once the mouse was dispensed with, she sat back and started licking her fur, cleaning herself. *Wow,* she thought, *I've become a cat.* She was very familiar with cats since she used them to pull her chariot.

The next few times Freyja went to her seiðhjallr, she again sat with her legs under her and the knuckles of her hands resting on the platform in front of her, while thinking of being a cat. Sure enough, she would find herself somewhere doing what cats do, sometimes stalking, sometimes preening, and at other times just lying in the sun. The next time she tried this she thought of another animal she knew well, her battle boar, and the next thing she knew she was not a boar but a sow in the field, digging for roots with her snout. She did not like being a pig, getting her nose dirty digging in the dirt. Later she thought what she would most like to be was a bird that could fly and soar anywhere. Though she

---

*Felicitas Goodman has identified this posture from prehistoric and primitive art as a posture for shape-shifting.

meditated on being a bird, somehow it just didn't happen, and she was disappointed. She did not have the familiarity with birds that she did with cats and boars. But the next time she left her hall she found on the doorstep several falcon feathers, and these gave her an idea.

Freyja hurried back to her platform where she held the falcon feathers between her fingers as she rested her knuckles on the floor in front of her. This did the trick. She became a falcon and was able to soar like a falcon. She told this to Frigg because they thought a lot alike and shared their experiences. They both were excited about what they could do from their platforms. Frigg tried it and had the same experience. Both goddesses were inspired about what they could do while flying. Because they both were experiencing the life of a falcon, they searched for more falcon feathers and made for themselves a falcon-feathered cloak.

When Freyja now traveled to Midgard, she did not have to worry about hiding the cumbersome chariot or about what to do with her cats. Her falcon-feathered cloak was quite attractive and she could carry that with her. This made her journeys easy and aided her in her search for her wandering husband, Óðr. One time this search took her over Lejre, on the island of Zealand in Denmark, where she saw her friend Gefjon, the goddess of plowing.

When she went to live with the Æsir, Freyja took this knowledge with her, and sometimes she and Frigg would travel together as falcons. The Æsir gods showed little interest in most of her powers, but the power of shape-shifting was one that became important to Loki at least. He already knew a little about it from Frigg, but Frigg had tried to keep it a secret. In contrast, Freya's position among the Æsir was to teach them the magic she knew from being of the Vanir, and here Loki was a willing pupil. Loki often borrowed Freya's falcon-feathered cloak. He used it to travel among the giants to rescue Idunn when she was held captive by a giant,* and he used it to fly in search of Thor's hammer when a giant had stolen it.†

---

*The story of Idunn being held captive by a giant is told in chapter 1 of the Skáldskaparmál of the *Prose Edda*.

†The story of the time Thor lost his hammer, Mjölnir, is found in the poem "Drymskviða," in the *Poetic Edda*.

But Loki was an impatient sort. He did not want to take the time to fetch a feathered cloak or climb onto a high platform. After much practice at shape-shifting, he found that he did not need to use a platform and he did not need to use feathers, either. He could change shape anytime, anywhere, and shape-shifting was very useful in playing his tricks. He shifted his shape to become a fly to get into Sif's bedchamber to cut her hair. Then, when he went to the cave of the dark elves to have them make new golden hair for Sif as ordered by Thor, he distracted the dwarfs from their task by becoming a stinging fly and pestering them to distraction.* He changed into a flea to get Freyja to roll over in her sleep so he could steal her necklace.† He changed into a frisky mare in order to distract a stallion from the work it was doing in building a wall around Asgard.‡ This distraction saved Freyja from having to marry the wall-builder. To rescue Idunn, Loki was able to change her into a walnut so that he as a falcon could carry her back to Asgard.§ He shifted his shape into that of an old woman to gain the secret from Frigg that mistletoe was the one substance that did not give its assurance to not harm Baldr. And near the end of his life, Loki shifted shapes to become a salmon in an attempt to avoid being captured by the gods.

Thus the god who became most adept at shape-shifting was Loki, but his source of knowledge was Freyja and the Vanir, the gods and goddesses of magical powers.

---

*The story of Loki becoming a fly to pester the dwarfs to distraction is found also in chapter 5 of the Skáldskaparmál of the *Prose Edda.*

†Kevin Crossley-Holland, in his book *The Norse Myths,* pieces together the scant stories of Freyja's necklace, Brísingamen, and tells of how Loki became a flea in order to steal it from her.

‡The story of Loki becoming a mare in order to distract the horse of the giant master builder in his reconstruction of the wall of Asgard, and as a result giving birth to Sleipnir, Odin's eight-legged horse, is told in the Gylfaginning of the *Prose Edda.*

§The story of Idunn becoming a nut in order for Loki, as a falcon, to carry her away from her captivity is told in chapter 1 of the Skáldskaparmál in the *Prose Edda.*

The Lay of Gefjon and the Kings of Denmark

Two major tribes or dynasties of the ancient Nordic people were the Skjǫldungs and the Ynglings. The Ynglings were from what is now Sweden and their center was at Gamal Uppsala. The Skjǫldungs were from what is now Denmark and they were centered at Gammel Lejre. I have visited both archaeological sites. From the ancient poem *Beowulf*, the first king of the Skjǫldungs was Scyldr Scefing, who had been abandoned on the shores of Denmark. I have long wondered where he came from and how he happened to be abandoned. In trance, it was explained to me . . .

The Vanir goddess Gefjon is most famous for her four huge oxen sons conceived by a giant from Jötunheimr. When King Gylfi of Sweden offered her as much land as she could plow in one day and one night, she hitched these oxen to her plow and dragged a great piece of Sweden out into the sea. She dragged the land from what future generations would call Lake Mälar to form what is now the Danish island of Zealand. The truth of this claim can be observed by comparing the size and shape of Lake Mälar to that of Zealand. As the goddess of virgins, Gefjon welcomed all women who died as virgins to her realm and cared for them at the place called Gratabjǫð, "weeping fields."* Gefjon divided her time between caring for these virgins and caring for her sanctuary in the land of Denmark, the land she dragged from Sweden. It just so happens that Gefjon married a human, Scyldr, the king of Denmark. The ancient stories tell of how Scyldr had been abandoned on the shores of Denmark as an infant, and grew to become its first king.† It just so happened that

---

*Gefjon's role in caring for women who died as virgins is told in the Gylfaginning of the *Prose Edda,* but now we learn where they are cared for after death.

†Scyldr, the first king of Denmark and the beginning of the line of Danish kings, is named in the Old English story of *Beowulf.* But now we learn how Scyldr happened to be abandoned on the shores of Denmark. A deeper understanding of this Old English story is found in my first book, *Grendel and His Mother.*

when Gefjon dragged this land from Sweden, Scyldr was separated from his family, which was left behind in Sweden. When Gefjon found him as an infant she nurtured him so that he grew into healthy manhood, and he was blessed by the goddess to become king. A successful king requires the strength and power of a warrior, so Gefjon, wanting the best for the youth who was to become her husband, had him fostered as a child to Odin, whom she knew would train him well. Thus, Scyldr has also been called a son of Odin. When Scyldr returned home to become king, his strength was such that all the warriors of Denmark soon pledged their allegiance to him. With a good many retainers, he proceeded to either go to battle with neighboring kings to easily win their allegiance or to gain their pledge of allegiance without having to battle.

Scyldr valued Gefjon's magic and learned to use much of it himself. He could journey short distances using the practice of seiðr, and he could look into the future. He would retire to his private sleeping quarters, an alcove off his great hall, and there he would practice the powers of seiðr to learn what was going on in his own and neighboring kingdoms while his retainers slept in the great hall. It was just these powers that made him a great king, but his retainers and the kings who were subservient to him also expected him to be a great warrior. They all worshipped Thor, the warrior god, and did not understand the power of magic.

Through his powers gained from the practice of seiðr, and through the greatest powers of all—the power of observation, the sound a cat makes when it walks, and the power gained by centering himself in his hvilðgarðr, his center of harmony—he had great intuition in under-standing others. This intuition and his compassion for others gave him an exceptional advantage. He could see by using the practice of seiðr when other kings were raising forces to use against him, and he took advantage of this knowledge in going to battle. But he knew that gain-ing the kings' allegiance through friendship and mutual support was much more reliable than gaining their allegiance through armed com-bat. Even though his champions were ready for battle, he maintained their allegiance through his compassion for them and his generosity in bestowing gifts on them. He also allowed his warriors to hone their skills in battle with competitions between themselves and with the retainers of other kings.

One time, when the king and Gefjon were talking while in bed together, he asked her how he could reconcile the difference between these two approaches to life, the approach of gaining allegiance of others through battle and the approach of using magic. Gefjon explained to him that it was his humility in being a warrior and his understanding and valuing of magic that provided him with the power of magic. A warrior's pride, his vanity in his strength as a warrior, prevents him from understanding and using magic. It was Scyldr's humility as a warrior that made him the greatest king of Denmark.

Soon all kings of Zealand were pledged to Scyldr and supported him with their annual tribute, making him the foremost king of the island and respected by kings from across the water. He was greatly blessed by the goddess Gefjon and raised their son, Beowulf, to become an even more powerful king after him. Thus, the dynasty of the Danish Skjǫldungs began.

Scyldr's son Beowulf and his grandson Healfdene themselves grew to be great kings. They each understood this power of humility, and in turn they had the blessing of their mother and grandmother, Gefjon.

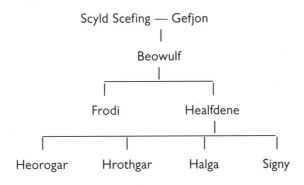

Lineage of the kings of Denmark

The Lay of King Healfdene

Not all who died went to Valhalla or Hel, places for the dead that have been extensively described. What was life after death like for those warriors who were taken by Freyja and for those women who died virgins and taken by Gefjon?

As the goddess of all women who died as virgins,* Gefjon takes these women to Gratabjǫð, the "weeping fields," in her realm. Gefjon's realm is adjacent to but separated from Freyja's realm by a deep gorge, Harmagil, the "gorge of sorrow." A person peering into this chasm and sniffing the air can see and smell the yellow clouds of sulfur rising from the realm of Hel. The virgins who die reside along Gefjon's side of the chasm.

Though the warriors who die a valiant death are accepted by Odin to live at Valhalla, where they play out their vanity every day by fighting, the warriors who die in their first battle are not poisoned by the experience of victory and so journey to Freyja's realm to reside on Gæfuleysabjarg, the "cliff of lucklessness," along her side of the gorge. These warriors, who had prayed to Thor and who wore an amulet of Mjölnir around their necks when going into battle, were awestruck by Freyja's beauty when she greeted them upon their deaths. Their innocence to what the Vanir would consider the false power of victory in battle allowed them to reside in the realm of Freyja. She visited them frequently to assure them that they were not lost to the excess of vanity. There, along Harmagil, the virgins and warriors faced one another and could see across the spans. During the day the virgins sat along their edge and sewed or wove, and the fallen warriors sat opposite, sharpening their swords and axes. At night the servants of the goddesses built fires along the gorge to warm their charges, but tears would put out these fires.

---

*We know from the Gylfaginning of the *Prose Edda* that Gefjon is the goddess of all women who die virgins, but now we learn what happens to them after death, and about Gratabjǫð.

These dead warriors' vanity, though less than that of the fallen warriors in Valhalla, was still such that it prevented most of them from appreciating the power of real magic. Still, during those long days and nights, an occasional warrior was able to set aside his grief and vanity, and with the right frame of mind, by practicing patience, curiosity, and gentleness, discover for himself the magic of seiðr. Sometimes this magic would come to him in a dream. If he was open enough to such magic, he could learn to journey to the other side of the chasm to meet the virgin for whom he longed. Attaining this magic required that a warrior let go of his vanity. Some of the warriors would strut back and forth waving their swords or axes as a warrior might in an attempt to woo a virgin. Some of the virgins would sit and brush their long golden hair or sit in seductive ways to show their love for a particular warrior who was out of reach, only adding to their frustration and grief. Only the ones who discovered the magic of seiðr could transcend their life of grief in death and travel to Griðbustaðr, the "dwelling place of peace," but this magic required going against all that was learned in being trained as a warrior. These warriors of Gæfuleysabjarg had plenty of time—indeed all they had was time—to learn to quiet their minds, but grief and pride were their greatest hinderances. Still, these warriors were at least given this chance, while the warriors who won in battle only thought about future wins. Their pride, vanity, and arrogance prevented them from ever reaching Griðbustaðr. Many of the virgins were sufficiently adept in seiðr to attain Griðbustaðr, but their unfulfilled lives as virgins caused them to maintain their vigil along Harmagil. On the occasion that a warrior succeeded in crossing Harmagil, Gefjon provided a place for the warrior to stay for the night with his chosen virgin, after which they would ascend together to Griðbustaðr.

King Healfdene had a brother, Frodi, who had his own kingdom to rule.* King Healfdene was a very powerful and good-natured king, as was his father, King Beowulf, and his grandfather, King Scyldr Scefing, the hus-

---

*We know two different stories of King Healfdene, one from the old English story of *Beowulf* and the other from the story of "King Hrolf and His Champions," in *Eirik the Red and Other Icelandic Sagas*. Here we learn more about the nature of Healfdene and his journey to Griðbustaðr because he knew the practice of seiðr.

band of the goddess Gefjon. Gefjon, being Healfdene's grandmother, stood by him in his kingly activities. He had four children, his sons Heorogar, Hrothgar, and Halga, and a daughter, Signy, who was married to a certain Jarl Sævil. Having grown up in the great hall of his father, Healfdene knew the power of going to his center of harmony to practice seiðr.

Frodi, Healfdene's brother, was as greedy and harsh as Healfdene was kind and good-natured. He greatly envied his brother and plotted to kill him. Frodi arrived in the darkest of night, burned and destroyed all of his brother's property, and killed Healfdene. Healfdene's three sons had been given to Regin, a lifelong friend of Healfdene, for fostering, and Regin deeply loved the boys.

Upon his death, Healfdene journeyed to Gæfuleysabjarg to reside in the realm of Freyja. Because of his gentle nature and because he was the grandson of Gefjon, it was not long before he journeyed to Griðbustaðr, the "dwelling place of peace" for those who understood the magic of the Vanir.

After the death of Healfdene, Frodi forced all of the inhabitants of Healfdene's realm to swear allegiance to him.* He would have killed Healfdene's three sons, but they were living on a secluded island with their foster father. Frodi became obsessed with trying to find these three boys and sent out search parties throughout the realm to find them, but these searches were fruitless. He called on the sorcerers of the kingdoms for their aid in finding them, but, again, all attempts failed, as they were being protected by Gefjon's watchful eye. When those who searched came to the secluded island, as they did on more than one occasion, the boys were forewarned and hid well.

With Gefjon's aid, Healfdene's sons outlived Frodi, and Hrothgar became the greatest and most famous king of Denmark, continuing the Skjoldung dynasty of Danish kings due to his ability as a warrior and, more importantly, his gentle and compassionate nature.† The Skjoldung continued to worship Gefjon at her sanctuary on Zealand.

---

*We know the story of Frodi from the story of "King Hrolf and His Champions," in *Eirik the Red and Other Icelandic Sagas.*
†The story of famous King Hrothgar is found in *Beowulf.*

Why Baldr Didn't Go to Griðbustaðr

The question that I now needed to ask was, "With Baldr's peace-loving nature and knowledge of magic, why did he not go to Griðbustaðr?" Vanadisdottir explained . . .

In the beginning, when people died, they journeyed to Griðbustaðr, the "dwelling place of peace." They had worked hard in life, supported one another, loved Moðir, and lived in peace, thus they deserved a place of peace after death.

Moðir watched her nephew Odin grow. She watched him create a new world, a beautiful world of mountains, valleys, animals, and vegetation, but also a world of warriors, of people seeking strength and power, a world of valor, a world no longer of peace. In this new world, the lack of valor was despised, while the strong and brave warrior was greatly respected. The warrior was to be respected even after death, and thus Odin created Valhalla, a place where these warriors could continue to fight and demonstrate their strength. Moðir was disappointed in her nephew's love for the valor that is gained through physical strength and violence. He was still her nephew, and she loved him, though he could not see or appreciate the valor found in acts of compassion.

Loki, one of the gods of the Æsir, was not disappointed, but he recognized a problem. He saw the inconsistency in the Æsir loving the gentleness of Baldr, Odin's one son with Frigg, and at the same time loving strength, power, and valor. It was Loki's way to play tricks on the gods to confront them on their inconsistencies. He thus went off, and with the evil giantess Angrboða, "distress-bringer," sired three children. The third child, a daughter, was Hel. Half of her body was beautiful but the other half was rotten with decay, just as half of Odin's world was beautiful and half rotten with violence. When Odin saw this monster from his high seat in Asgard, he had her brought to him and he threw her into Niflheim, the underworld. There she was to rule the dwelling place of those who died of illness and old age. Thus under Odin, the decent people who worked hard and lived in peace throughout their lives fell into great disrespect. It was this splitting apart of the people that eventually led to the death of Odin and the others who respected valor but showed little or no respect for the magic found in the beauty of the world.

Moðir's disappointment grew. Her nephew's disrespect caused her such great pain that she gave up the will to live. Yet her son, Njord, his children, and the others of the Vanir carried on her legacy in understanding magic using love and compassion. There was still some hope. Freyja and Gefjon combined their powers of naming, and together they named Gratabjöð the "weeping fields," Gæfuleysabjarg, the "cliff of lucklessness," and the deep gorge Harmagil the "gorge of sorrow." These names were a message to all the people: that striving for valor through violence brings sorrow, to both virgins and warriors, sorrow that caused Moðir, the Great Mother, intense grief. Yet Gæfuleysabjarg provided an avenue for these warriors who died in their first battle to attain Griðbustaðr, "the dwelling place of peace," if they could quiet their minds and give up their pride. The compassion of these two goddesses gave hope to the people.

Baldr had a series of dreams that the Æsir interpreted to be a prediction of his death. Frigg, fearing the death of her son, went on a journey to gain the assurance from all substances that none would harm Baldr. These substances included fire, water, all metals, stones, trees, diseases, animals, birds, and snakes. Frigg returned to Asgard with this assurance but was confronted by her stepson Víðarr, asking why she couldn't do the same thing for him.* He pleaded that his life was in greater danger than Baldr's, since he was a valiant warrior. Frigg knew well that Baldr was different, that everyone loved his gentle and compassionate ways. She knew that Víðarr valued his strength and ability to fight. So that he would not feel bad about her favoritism, she told him that it was because he could take care of himself in battle that he did not need such an assurance.

---

*We know of Frigg's journey and the assurance she received from all substances except mistletoe from the Gylfaginning of the *Prose Edda,* but now we learn here of Vidar's jealousy and why Baldr went to Niflheim.

After Frigg returned with her reported success, the others of Asgard began testing Baldr's invulnerability by throwing everything imaginable at him. Freyja, watching this, wondered what Baldr must be thinking. Perhaps he was thinking, *For once I'm stronger than all others. They must be envious of me.* This would have been a new feeling for Baldr, not his usual feeling of humility, but the feeling of a warrior who had won his first battle, a feeling of pride.

When Baldr fell to Loki and Hǫðr's dart of mistletoe and all were grieving his death, Freyja thought that he deserved to go to Gæfuleysabjarg, the "cliff of lucklessness," considering that this testing could be considered his first battle, even though she felt that he actually deserved to go directly to Griðbustaðr, the "dwelling place of peace," considering his gentle and compassionate ways. Thus, Freyja approached Odin with this request.

As much as Odin loved his son, however, to him it would be an insult to go to Gæfuleysabjarg, a place for losers, so Baldr started his journey to the realm of Hel. As far as Odin was concerned, Griðbustaðr did not even exist. Thus Baldr resided in Niflheim, the realm of Hel, until Ragnarǫk.

The Lay of Freyja and Her Daughters

With their magical powers, why were the Vanir unable to change the attitudes of the Æsir? Though I did not find the answer to that question, I had a humorous vision of what might have happened. Maybe the Vanir, in valuing each person, believed in self-determination and that such change should not be coerced but needs to come from within. Freyja and her daughters Hnoss and Gersemi humiliated the warriors of the two kings—something not very Vanir-like. When Freyja showed up as a falcon, I thought at first it was going to be Loki. What Freyja and her daughters did was much more Loki-like, and so it was a surprise to me that the falcon was their mother, Freyja . . .

Hnoss and Gersemi were taking a walk through the fields of Midgard when they came to a field where the champions of two kings were fighting one another. The two virgin goddesses sat down on a hillside near the battle to watch. Noticing their beauty, the warriors began to fight harder to win their attention. The goddesses sat with their heads together, giggling about the warriors' antics and silliness. Hnoss, with a smile on her face meant for her sister, said, "Watch this," as she cast a spell causing the sword of one of the retainers of one king to turn into a piece of rope. This gave the advantage to his opponent, who thrust his sword at the warrior holding the piece of rope. At that moment the rope took to the air and flew into a knotted noose around the opponent's neck, lifting him off the ground. As he dangled in the air, the two girls began to laugh harder.

Not to let her sister outdo her, Gersemi said, "Watch this," as she flung a mud puddle just behind another champion who was about to step backward. As he stepped backward and sank into the puddle of mud, his opponent jabbed his sword in the air, striking at nothing and falling forward into the same puddle. Again the two girls howled in laughter.

The two girls then looked at each other and smiled, each knowing what the other was thinking. They began to sing a soft song as the men continued to fight. As the song drifted down over the warriors, the warriors' swords and axes began to move more slowly. The men looked even more silly as they fought in slow motion. The two girls were enjoying their afternoon but soon tired of watching the fight go on in slow motion and so switched their song. As two of the fighters' swords clashed, the swords stuck together. The men tugged and tugged to pull them apart, to no avail. They quickly gave up, dropped their swords, and began to wrestle. Once their hands touched, however, they stuck together, and as they twisted and turned, their bodies stuck to wherever they touched. Soon the men were lying on the ground so stuck together that they could not move. Another warrior fell over them and got stuck too. The harder he tried to pull away, the more stuck he became. Soon there was a large number of warriors stuck in this pile, all unable to fight. The girls roared hysterically.

In all the commotion, only the two sisters noticed a falcon fly up and land between them. When the falcon looked up into their faces they immediately knew it was their mother, Freyja. They could see her smiling and laughing in a falconish way. Then she whispered to her two daughters, "I'll show you how to do it." As each warrior fought his opponent, he began to slice away a part of his opponent's body—an arm or a leg—or gashed him in the side. At first each of the champions rejoiced in their apparent victory and in their ability to hack down the enemy. But their opponent kept on fighting as pieces of his body flew. Nothing could stop the enemy. Then their helmets flew off, and the champions of both kings could see that they were fighting someone with empty eyes, someone dead. They could see that they were fighting themselves, themselves in death. How could the dead be fighting? No one is able to kill the already dead. Some of the retainers of both kings turned and ran screaming upon seeing themselves in death. Others threw themselves to the ground, their eyes staring in terror. Freyja's spell brought the battle to a quick end.

When the warriors began to gather in their own camp some distance from their opponent's camp, Freyja changed herself back into her goddess form, wearing her necklace, Brísingamen. In this form, each of the warriors recognized her and knew that what they had experienced with such terror was her magic. The two kings came to her in homage, with their warriors standing back in awe. All knew what Freyja stood for, and some of the warriors took off their Mjölnir amulets and threw them to her. She waved them off with a shake of her head and a look of compassion, telling them, "Carry Thor's hammer as a reminder that with each swing of your sword or ax, you are cutting off a part of yourself. Let it be a reminder to see yourself in what you thought was your enemy."

With that, Freyja, Hnoss, and Gersemi turned into falcons and flew off.

That evening, the two kings and their men shared the camp and ate together. Together they built an altar to Freyja and made sacrifices to her. Peace came to the two kingdoms.

Idunn's Travels to Midgard

The goddesses of the Vanir realized that more and more humans were becoming enamored with the Æsir, and the men were beginning to value too highly their swords and axes. The question I asked was, "What did the Vanir do about this?"

To pass time, most of the gods and goddesses traveled around Midgard. They often went in disguise so that the humans would not recognize them, and in this way they learned how the humans felt about them. The goddesses of the Vanir were talking one day, comparing their observations, and realized that the humans were turning more and more to the Æsir in facing their daily needs. With this new awareness the goddesses felt that it was important to travel among the humans to remind them of the powers of their magic. With this goal, Idunn journeyed to Midgard, something that she did often and always enjoyed. She was always looking for more new uses of plants and would collect them and carry them in her medicine basket.

On this particular trip she came to a farm and was watching a young boy romp in the fields. He was a handsome and energetic boy. Idunn saw a patch of *nælde,* stinging nettles, in the field, and he was running right toward it. She knew what was coming, and sure enough a moment later the boy was crying. From her experience Idunn had found that *burre,* burdock, generally grows close to nœlde, and sure enough she noticed this big-leafed plant growing nearby. She called the boy over and showed him the plant, then took a leaf and rubbed it on his leg until his leg was green from its juice. She also had him look closely at the stinging plant so that he would recognize it again, pointing out to him the square stem with little hairs all over it. The boy thought what she did was magic.

As Idunn sat with him, she asked him his name. It was Thjálfi,*

---

*As Thjálfi and his sister grew older they would become servants to Thor, as told in the story of Útgarða-Loki found in the Gylfaginning of the *Prose Edda.*

and he was the farmer's son. He told her that everyone thought he was a very fast runner and he ran off to demonstrate it to her. When he came back he told Idunn that his mother was going to have another baby, and he would have a brother or a sister. At that point, Thjálfi's mother came out and welcomed the stranger to their humble farm and home. As they walked to the house, Thjálfi's mother tried to quiet him because she wanted to hear the news from the stranger, but he had to tell her about how the stranger made the stinging on his leg go away.

Since it was evening, Thjálfi's mother invited Idunn to spend the night, and after a simple meal all went to bed. Before sunrise Idunn heard Thjálfi's mother call out in pain from the first contractions of childbirth. The family was pleased that Idunn was there to help. Even though the farmer had helped with Thjálfi's birth, he still feared that he might not know what to do. But as with Thjálfi, this birth was quite easy, especially with Idunn's help. Afterward the goddess gave the farmer's wife tea of *røllike,* yarrow, and *hyrdetaske,* shepherd's purse, to help stop the bleeding. The family was happy in welcoming a daughter, Röskva, into the family, and Thjálfi was so excited about his sister that he ran off, running a great distance to tell the neighboring farmers, mostly his aunts, uncles, and cousins, about his sister and about the visitor who had magically stopped the stinging on his leg.

A couple of days later, Idunn continued her travels and soon came to a large hall, the hall of a king. Outside of the hall the king's retainers were fighting. A group of a dozen large, hairy, almost-naked men were wrestling and making loud growling noises. Idunn knew that these men, acting like bears, were berserkers. Some were competing with one another in lifting a large boulder. While waiting to lift the boulder, one of the men was rubbing his arm. Idunn could see it was swollen. Not far away were some servants tending a large kettle of boiling water. Idunn obtained from them a cup of boiling water to make a tea from *kamille,* chamomile, *guldpil,* willow, and *hyrdetaske* to reduce the swelling and decrease muscle spasms. As she approached the berserkers, they all stopped in wonder to watch the beautiful woman, but when she offered the tea to the man who was rubbing his arm, he proudly brushed her away, telling her that he didn't need it.

As she turned to leave, the queen of the household came out to greet her. The queen recognized Idunn by the basket of herbs she carried—as always with several golden apples in it—and was quick to embrace her. The queen was waited on by a priestess of Idunn who was learning much about her plants. The queen quickly sent one of the servants to fetch the priestess, and the three sat on a couple of benches in the priestess's garden. Idunn was pleased to discover that she was not forgotten among the people, and she enjoyed teaching the queen and priestess about some plants and herbs they did not know. Both were concerned, though, about a wounded warrior who lay in the great hall with a high fever. When they told Idunn about him she went to see him with her basket of herbs. She selected a couple of fresh large leaves of *kulsukker*, comfrey, soaked them in warm water, and wrapped in them the leaves of *vejbred*, plantain, *guldpil*, and *røllike*. She tied this poultice to the champion's wound and gave him a drink of *hvidtjørn* to help him sleep.

Idunn spent that night and the next several days with the queen and priestess. They went on long walks together to find new herbs. She showed them how to hold and dream the plants to know what they could do with them. In the meantime, the king's champion awakened, his fever broken, and he was alert and healing. The priestess and queen were concerned about how the power of Idunn's magic was being lost, and the queen agreed to let the priestess travel with Idunn for a few days to meet with the women in nearby kingdoms. The kings and their retainers were very skeptical, priding themselves on their strength, toughness, and ability to deal with pain. They often pushed away the idea of using such herbs, but in serious situations they let their women treat their wounds. They saw that the wounds healed, but they did not want to admit that such magic helped. Holding these beliefs, the king's champion also had faith only in himself and believed that he could deal with any sort of pain. Idunn knew intuitively that the man was embarrassed about needing her help. She said to him, "You are strong, but you will eventually lose the battle with the strongest warrior of all, whose name is death. Your greatest power over death is magic, and with the wound you received, the magic you need is found in the life of these plants. These plants died to give you a longer life. They should be valued and appreciated. You eat to be strong. You can use some of the same plants you eat to stay healthy and to beat death as long as you can." In saying this, Idunn revealed to him the power of her intuition.

Thus Idunn continued on her journey, sharing her wisdom and magic. She won adherents to her beliefs and knew that her knowledge would not be forgotten.

The Goddesses' Power of Intuition

How did Baldr happen to become so sensitive to others, and why do others not see the power of this trait? Maybe if we knew the answer to these questions there would be more people with Baldr's qualities . . .

In treating the ills and wounds of gods, goddesses, and humans, Idunn had learned of their fears, pain, embarrassment, and anxieties. She was able to look at them and use all her senses to see, hear, taste, smell, and feel as they do. She was able to see changes in their color and the way their chests rose and fell with their breathing, hear their voices, smell their sweat and their breath, feel their tension, and even taste the air around them. With practice, this kind of sensing became automatic, so that she knew exactly how people felt. Her powers of perception gave her great intuition—another magical power.

Each of the goddesses, in their stalking for understanding had developed this power of intuition. Those goddesses who had children learned this power of intuition in raising and protecting their children. Skaði learned it from Freyja and Freyr, her stepchildren. Freyja learned it from Hnoss and Gersemi. Frigg learned it from Baldr.

By watching her children and by caring for them, a mother can tell how her child feels. It is this understanding of feelings that gives one the power of intuition. A child loved by a parent also begins to learn this magical intuition. Baldr was special because his father, being the highest of the gods, had little time for him, so he was raised mainly through motherly love. Other male children were usually sent out to be fostered by men, who taught them to fight, to be strong, and to hide their feelings.

When Baldr was young, there was a time when he asked his mother why he did not fight like other boys. She explained to him that he was learning a different kind of power, the power of magic, a magic much greater than fighting and being strong. Frigg took him out to watch the other boys fighting and wrestling. She pointed out to him one boy who was thrown hard to the ground. She asked Baldr how that young boy felt. He told his mother that the boy could not catch his breath because he had the wind knocked out of him, that he was embarrassed for letting the other boy gain that advantage, and that he was scared that the other boy would jump on him when he was down and could not breathe. The boy who was down quickly rolled over and tried to crawl away, but his opponent grabbed him by the feet and pulled him back.

She then asked Baldr how the boy who threw the one that was down felt. He replied that the boy was smiling and that he felt proud of himself. She then asked Baldr what he wanted to do, and he said that he would like to pick up the boy who was thrown to the ground and give him some time to get his wind back. Baldr was already gaining the power of intuition, a power that fueled his compassion for others, a power that caused others to love him. With these thoughts he knew he had a greater power than that of fighting and being physically strong. The boys who were fighting did not understand the power of intuition and compassion.

Skaði knew that Freyr had had the same kind of thoughts as Baldr as he was growing up. He could see other boys fighting and knew he did not want to fight, so he spent his time learning the magical powers of the Vanir. His father, Njord, was busy being the leader of their gods and goddesses and so did not have the time to train Freyr to be a fighter and to hide his feelings. Freyr, too, learned the power of intuition at a young age.

Odin had many powers, one being the power to see long distances from his high seat, Hliðskjálf, which was also his seiðr platform. From it he could see to all corners of the world, but he developed only this one practice of seiðr, to see into all realms. He did not learn to journey long distances or see into the future using it. He relied on the three most important norns,*

---

*Norns are female beings who rule the destiny of gods and men, somewhat like the fates in Greek mythology. According to Snorri Sturluson's interpretation of the "Völuspá," the first poem of the *Poetic Edda,* the three most important norns, Urðr, Verðandi, and Skuld, come out from a hall standing at the Well of Urðr ("well of fate") and draw water from the well and take sand that lies around it, which they pour over Yggdrasil so that its branches will not rot. These norns are described as three powerful maiden giantesses whose arrival from Jötunheimr ended the golden age of the gods. Besides these three norns, there are many other norns, both benevolent and malevolent, who arrive when a person is born in order to determine his or her future.

Urðr, Verðandi, and Skuld, to see into the future and to learn from the past. He lacked the power of intuition in most areas except in fighting. When fighting, Odin's intuition told him of his weaknesses and strengths and how his opponent was about to move. This intuition was automatic and did not require thought. Otherwise, he lacked intuition in most all other areas—in not understanding women, and especially in not understanding the Vanir.

Odin's lack of intuition was obvious when he courted Billingr's daughter.* When she made of fool of him by rejecting him, he called out, "Men cannot trust a woman's word. Men should never rely on a woman's promise. Women have hearts full of caprice and fickle minds." Odin was no match for Billingr's daughter in the use of intuition. He did not understand that her intuition and her deception were her way of surviving. Knowing intuitively that Odin would not take "no" for an answer, she told him to come to her bed at night. When he arrived, he found all of Billingr's warriors waiting for him. He had been deceived. So Odin came back at dawn when the warriors were asleep, but then found only a bitch leashed to the maiden's bed. With intuition he would have known that this young woman wanted nothing to do with him, and he would not have made such a fool of himself.

---

*The story of Billingr's daughter and how she made a fool of Odin is found in the *Poetic Edda,* in the poem "Hávamál."

Ullr's Travels

The visits of the gods and goddesses to Midgard have always provided fascinating stories. I asked how the ski god Ullr related to the humans of Midgard, and was given the following story . . .

Ullr preferred winters to summers because he could travel faster over the snow using his skis. Like the other gods, he enjoyed visiting the humans who inhabited Midgard. The people especially enjoyed Ullr's visits because he was likely the only god they would see during the wintertime, and he would bring them news of the world.

On one of Ullr's journeys he visited a farmer and his wife who were settled in for the long winter on their farm. Ullr was invited to spend the night, and after dinner the family sat and talked. Ullr heard about how the family's winter supplies were holding up, and that they believed they had enough to get through the winter. He told them about their neighbors and about the terrible flooding far to the south because of a warm spell that had melted much of the snow. As the conversation went on, the farmer ventured to tell Ullr about a major concern of his: His father lived in a small cabin beyond the woods to the north. He lived alone and was getting old. His family was worried about whether he could survive the winter. He did not have a lot, but he never wanted to burden his son and never complained about how little he had. The son knew that his father was not afraid of dying, but if he died he would be sorely missed by his three young grandchildren. Ullr agreed that when he left he would go north to visit the farmer's father.

The next day, Ullr left the farmer and his family early, traveling north on his skis. After he crossed the fields he came to a forest. While skiing through the woods he saw a wolf, and with his bow he shot the wolf, thinking that the old man would appreciate some meat during the winter. Ullr had become a skilled woodworker and carried some basic tools of woodworking with him. He saw a *hvidtjørn,* a hawthorn tree, nearby and knew it was the best wood for skis because it was so hard.

He cut off a good branch and split it to make a wide single ski in order to have a way to drag the dead wolf along with him. While working on the ski he heard the yip of a wolf pup. He went to investigate and found a small cave where the wolf had lived and discovered she had two young pups. He felt very bad about killing their mother, so he took the pups, bundled them up in a fur, and put them on the ski, too.

He then continued his journey to the old man's cabin. When he got there he called out but no one came to the door. He knocked but no one answered, so he went in. There in the darkness of the cabin he found the old man in bed, covered in blankets. The cabin was cold and the fire had gone out. The old man, however, was still alive. Ullr put his head near the old man's and could hear him breathe. The man opened his eyes and whispered that he had fallen ill a few days earlier and could not go out to get wood for the fire. He thought it was about his time anyway, so he went to bed to die.

Ullr started a fire, got some water boiling, and cut off a few pieces of meat from the dead wolf to boil into a broth. He then fed the broth to the old man, who quickly began to regain his color. He also fed some of the stew to the two wolf pups, who ate the meat greedily. Because of this behavior of the pups he named them Geri and Freki, both meaning "greedy" or "ravenous."*

The old man and Ullr talked. Ullr told him that his son and grand-children were concerned about him and that he should let Ullr take him back to his son's house. Ullr wouldn't take "no" for an answer and went out and found another hvidtjørn tree; he cut another decent-size branch, and from this he made a pair of skis. The old man watched and knew that he did not have the strength to ski to his son's home. But Ullr had noticed a large box that the old man used to hold firewood. He took the box and lashed it to the skis, and thus Ullr invented the first sled. He bundled the old man in the box, along with the two pups,

---

*As you may recall, Geri and Freki were Odin's two wolves, described in the poem "Grimnismal," in chapter 11 of the *Poetic Edda*. From this story you now learn how these wolves were named and became Odin's.

Geri and Freki. Then he tied to the back of the box the ski with the rest of the meat lashed to it, and he retraced his tracks back to the farmer's house, dragging the old man and the wolf meat.

When they arrived back at the farmer's house it was quite dark, but a fire was glowing inside. The travelers were warmly welcomed, and the old man's son was relieved with this reunion, and that his father was still alive and safe. His wife was happy with the wolf meat and took care to freeze it.

The next day, Ullr started his return journey to Asgard with Geri and Freki. When he arrived he was welcomed back among the Æsir and greeted by his mother, Sif, and stepfather, Thor. The next thing he did was to ask for an audience with Odin, and he offered him a gift of the two wolf pups. Sif was pleased that Ullr paid homage to Odin in this way since Ullr's primary allegiance had always been to his grandfather Slœgr, believing that this grandfather gave him his creativity. She knew that Odin, being more interested in gold and swords, had no interest in the beauty of Ullr's woodwork. Odin did take an interest in the wolves, however, and soon was the only god who could feed them. You already know that as these two pups grew they did not leave Odin's side.

In Memory of Moðir

The following hypnotic trance experience did not come as a result of any particular question; only with my curiosity did I decide to visit Moðir's great hall, Moðirasalr, to see what it was like . . .

The great hall in Vanaheim, was the central meeting place of the Vanir. At one end of this hall was a large comfortable chair with many animal skins to make it soft and warm for Moðir when she was alive. There she would sit and watch her children, grandchildren, and great-grandchildren come and go. They would all come to her with their cares and concerns. She always had wise answers to their concerns. They would bring her meals, making sure she was comfortable and that she had everything she needed. Sometimes they found her asleep in the chair and would not want to wake her, but then her eyes would open a crack and they would know that she was ready to hear their problems. When she died she was greatly missed and her children, grandchildren, and great-grandchildren would still go to her chair, which remained exactly as it was, with warm animal skins; there they would still ask questions and express their concerns, and her answers would still come to them.

After Moðir died, after her children, grandchildren, and great-grandchildren lit the funeral pyre, and after her remains rose up in smoke, they named the great hall Moðirasalr. The hall was large, with three large firepits down the center to keep it warm. Around the edge were long benches for everyone to sit on. The firepits were also used for cooking, so the great hall always smelled good. The roof of Moðirasalr was held up by large pillars made of the trunks of trees. It was Ullr, her grandson, who spent many hours in the great hall doing what he loved the most, which was woodworking. He spent hours carving beautiful designs on the pillars that held up the roof, designs of animals and gods. Many of the carvings were stories of Moðir. Everyone who came into the great hall of Moðir admired these carvings. He used many kinds of wood, but he knew that the wood of the *eg,* or oak, was the hardest and would last the longest. The Vanir used some gold ornamentation to add the final touch in making the great hall beautiful, but they valued the natural beauty of wood, especially Ullr's carvings.

Ullr's aunts and uncles, his cousins, and the rest of this large family would come to him to carve special memorials for them, such as carvings to remember a wedding or the birth of a child. His carvings became special to everyone. The most popular was his carving in memory of Moðir, depicting the goddess with a large belly that had given birth to them all and large breasts to nurture them all. This carving was in everyone's home, in a place of honor. When anyone wanted to talk with Moðir, if they were not in her great hall they would go to the special places that held these carvings and talk to her there. Her answers would still come to them. Ullr would often go to her for inspirations for what to carve. They led a good life, and Moðir was always a peaceful inspiration to them. Even in death she continued to nurture them and make their lives beautiful. The Vanir gods and goddesses of Asgard—Njord, Freyr, Freyja, Frigg, Ullr, and Kvasir—made regular return journeys to Moðirasalr to pay their respects to Moðir. Only Sif stayed at home, but even she had hidden among her belongings a carving of Moðir. Yet Odin and Thor held no memory of Moðir.

After the war with the Æsir, as a condition of the truce, the Æsir gods Hœnir and Mímir came to live with the Vanir. Neither god at first understood who Moðir was or why she was so important. They thus showed her no respect. The Vanir tried to explain to them who she was, but they paid no mind. To them she was only an old woman with no strength or power. They just didn't understand. Without Njord, who now lived among the Æsir, the Vanir had no leadership. The Æsir sent the Vanir the indecisive god Hœnir in the mistaken belief that he would make a good leader, but he was insensitive to what was important to the Vanir and lacked the intuitive knowledge that the disrespect he paid to Moðir would turn all against him. Instead, Hœnir decided to prove his leadership by sitting in the Great Goddess's high seat at the end of the hall, the seat that had remained empty in honor of Moðir. The gods, furious that he would dare desecrate her chair, grabbed Hœnir and threw him out. He did not have the strength or confidence of a leader, and with this humiliation he left.

Mímir remained in the hall. In his great wisdom he could see that the carving of Moðir was very important to all the the Vanir. He realized that it carried a special power for them. He had seen them go to her chair or to her statue and talk to her with great reverence. Watching this, he began to believe that if her image was destroyed, her power over the Vanir would be destroyed. After Hœnir left the hall humiliated, Mímir took a wooden carving of Moðir and threw it into the fire. When Ullr saw such disrespect, he swung his ax at Mímir in rage, severing his head from his body.*

The Vanir had never experienced such disrespect, or such rage. Ullr was just as shocked by his own behavior as he was of Mímir's, but he loved Moðir so much that he tried to explain that it was the only thing he could have done. He called a meeting of the Vanir to decide what they should now do. They believed that with the exchange of the gods between the Æsir and the Vanir, they had gotten the worse deal, and they decided that they needed to send the head of Mímir back to the Æsir, and so they did. Odin preserved Mímir's head in a well near the root of Yggdrasil and would go to it with his concerns and questions. Because of Mímir's wisdom, Odin became dependent on this severed head for secret knowledge and counsel. To Odin, Mímir's head became what Moðir's carving had been to the Vanir, except Mímir did not have the intuition and compassion of Moðir.

---

*The story of Odin receiving Mímir's severed head is told in chapter 4 of the Ynglinga saga of the *Heimskringla*. We now learn who severed his head and why.

Baldr Visits Moðir

Did Baldr ever meet his great-aunt Moðir, I asked . . . ?

As Baldr grew as a god, he appreciated more and more the power of magic, of intuition, of moving into his center of harmony, and of stalking like a cat in watching the world. He learned how to journey and see into the future with the practice of seiðr. He was content with this magic and had no interest in fighting like his father, though he still showed Odin respect.

In hearing the stories of the Vanir, Baldr began to feel an urgent need to meet his great-aunt Moðir. Frigg was planning a journey to visit Moðir, and so Baldr asked if he could accompany her. Frigg was pleased that he felt this need. When they arrived and entered Moðirasalr, Baldr was impressed with the beautiful simplicity of the hall, which was not gaudy like the halls of the Æsir. Moðir was sitting on her chair lined with furs. She smiled widely when she saw Frigg approaching and reached out her hand to her. Frigg kissed her hand as Moðir asked who the young gentleman with her was. Frigg explained, "It is your great-nephew, Baldr." Moðir had heard of Baldr and held out her hand to him in pleasure. Baldr was awed by Moðir's presence and the brightness of her countenance. She beckoned for her two visitors to sit, and she wanted to know all of what Baldr had been learning. He was eager to share with her what he had learned about the powers of magic. She listened intently and then told him that she thought he was ready to learn more.

Baldr told Moðir that he had journeyed to see her before using the practice of seiðr, and that he could see into the future. Moðir suggested that he might be just the person to journey to Gæfuleysabjarg, the "cliff of lucklessness," along the abyss Harmagil, the "gorge of sorrow," to present himself to the warriors who fell in their first battle. She received his promise that he would not tell them the secret of how to journey using the practice of seiðr, because that is something they could and needed to discover for themselves. However, he could, just by his presence and his ability to listen to them, show them the power of compassion and intuition that would help them if they desired to acquire this ability. In his presence they might just slip into the center of harmony, and from there it would be a much shorter step to seiðr travel. Moðir truly wanted to save the warriors from their life of torment on Gæfuleysabjarg and wanted them to find peace. To her, their need for power was a destructive and insidious trap of unhappiness.

Baldr's instruction then began. Moðir had him climb onto her seiðhjallr, her high platform, and there he stood straight with his arms across his chest as if hugging himself, his left arm above his right arm.* Moðir drummed rhythmically while Baldr went into his center of harmony. Soon he was traveling, lights flashing by him, until he alighted on the edge of a cliff. He was somewhat surprised to discover the warriors there could see him and talk with him. Before when he had traveled by seiðr he could not be seen or heard. He assumed that the difference was that these warriors were dead. Several of the warriors gathered around him in their torment. They wondered why he was there, as he was neither dressed like nor appeared to be a warrior. He was too pale and smooth, too soft, not rugged-looking. One warrior recognized him as Baldr, but that made it even more perplexing as to why he was there. They knew that gentle Baldr is nothing like his warrior father. They asked him what brought him to Gæfuleysabjarg.

"Moðir, the great, compassionate Mother, asked that I visit you, to let you know that she cares." The warriors did not recognize the name Moðir. Baldr explained: "She is Odin's aunt and she cares about you just as Freyja, her granddaughter, cares about you. That is why Freyja brought you to her domain after your death in your first battle." They had no idea that Freyja's father, Njord, was a cousin of Odin. But with that explanation and introduction, Baldr asked to hear their stories.

The warriors began to talk, more about the maidens they could

---

*This posture, according to the research of Felicitas Goodman, is used to journey to the realm of the spirits of the dead.

see across the gorge and their love for them than about their first and last battle. Talking about that battle was an embarrassment to them. Baldr listened with empathy. As their stories unfolded, some did tell about their battles, and Baldr was able to understand their embarrassment, though he showed no judgment of them. They were surprised that Odin's son was not disappointed by their failures in battle. When evening came and the fires were lit, they continued to talk as they sat around the fire. There was a sense of peace, a sense of harmony. The warriors had dropped their feelings of competition. Later they slept peacefully. In the morning, Baldr continued to listen to the stories of more and more of the warriors, and the feeling of peace and harmony came over more and more of them. Baldr had done what was needed. He did not expect to see any of them leave on their journey to Griðbustaðr, the "dwelling place of peace," not yet, but they were closer to being able to do so. He told them that he would come back frequently to visit. Then he felt a tug on his shoulder and his eyes opened to see his mother, Frigg, standing next to him.

As they climbed off the platform, Moðir had a big smile for him. She already knew what had happened, but Baldr, with a sense of peace and harmony within, told her of the experience and that he had promised the warriors that he would visit regularly. Moðir explained that where he went was in Freyja's realm and that he should tell Freyja when he was going to visit, for she, too, would be pleased.

Baldr Meets Nanna

When and how did Baldr happen to meet the Vanir goddess Nanna, who became his wife . . . ?

Upon Baldr's return from meeting the warriors in Gæfuleysabjarg, as his mother, Frigg, talked with Moðir and visited with other friends, Baldr withdrew in thought, reliving his recent experience at the cliff of lucklessness, Gæfuleysabjarg. He sat on a bench not far from Ullr, watching him while he carved on one of the support pillars of the great hall. He was thinking of the fallen warriors, of how his father would be proud of him were he a warrior, and of how his father did not understand the power of magic and compassion.

Baldr strongly felt the love, compassion, and creativity that filled Moðirasalr as he sat in the Great Mother's hall. Baldr knew that Odin saw him as special and loved him too. He respected his father and appreciated his judgment as a leader. He looked up to his father as the others of Asgard looked up to him, but as his understanding of magic had grown, he felt a little sad or sorry for his father. The energy in Moðirasalr was calming, peaceful, and loving. In Odin's hall, Valaskjálf, the "shelf of the slain," the energy was loud, aggressive, and boisterous. Even in speaking the names of the two halls he thought that Moðirasalr sounded softer and more pleasing. As he sat there struggling with his thoughts, someone came and sat down beside him. He could feel concern and curiosity coming from her. He looked up to see a beautiful young goddess next to him. A smile came to his face as he shook his head free of these thoughts.

The goddess reached out and put her hand on Baldr's knee while looking into his face. She didn't need to say anything—he knew what she was thinking and felt a need to explain himself. He told her about his thoughts about his father, and she quietly said, "I know," and added, "Odin's aunt feels the same way. What you did on your journey to Gæfuleysabjarg is the most you can do to help your father. He most certainly is not going to change. He is always going to be a warrior, but he might occasionally be able to experience feelings of peace and harmony if you can listen to him with the empathy you felt for the warriors of Gæfuleysabjarg."

Baldr understood what she was saying and understood her ability to read his mind as he read her mind. That is the power of empathy, but it still surprised him that he had found someone who could do it as naturally as he could. He had not been to Vanaheim in person before. When he had visited through the practice of seiðr, others could not see him to empathize with his thoughts and feelings. He remembered that he had not asked this beautiful young goddess's name, but he did not need to; he somehow knew it was Nanna. With that thought, they both laughed. He knew little else about her.

Nanna stood up and took Baldr's hand, pulling him to his feet, and together they walked. She wanted to show him around Vanaheim. She took him to one of her favorite places, Idunn's herb garden. The flowers, butterflies, and other insects flying around the flowers were beautiful. Again Baldr felt the same peace he had felt in Moðir's hall as he learned of Nanna's love for Idunn and her garden. At the edge of the garden were Idunn's apple trees. Nanna picked an apple and gave Baldr a bite of it, saying to him, "May we both stay young and in love." And that they were. As they sat there on a bench in the garden, they could see the Vanir coming and going from the great hall. One of the goddesses approached them and put her hands on their shoulders with a smile. It was Freyja. They sat there until sunset, when Nanna beckoned Baldr to her bed.

The next morning, Frigg awakened them and told Baldr it was time to go. Both Nanna and Baldr knew by now that he could go but they would not be apart. They knew they could be together anytime by meditating in unison from their seiðr platforms. Journeying together in this way, they could see, touch, and smell each other. They could hear each other, too, but that was not necessary. In their love, they each knew what the other was thinking without speech. But, before Baldr left, Frigg called on the goddess of marriage oaths, Vár, and before her Nanna and Baldr swore their eternal love for each other. They touched, smiled, and Baldr left with his mother.

Upon returning to Asgard, Baldr made it a point to listen empathetically to his father whenever he had a chance, which was not often. But he knew what would happen: Odin sought him out more and more frequently. When he had something that worried him or a decision to make, he often came to his son Baldr. Somehow, telling his son about his concerns always made him feel better and more at peace with his decisions. This is what created the special bond between Baldr and his father.

Baldr listened this way to everyone who came to him, and as a result he was loved by everyone. He often journeyed to Gæfuleysabjarg to listen to the fallen warriors, but most of all, many times throughout each day, he was with Nanna. From that first night together she was with child, and their son, Forseti, was soon born.

The Lay of Borr and Moðir's Dream

We know very little about many of the gods, goddesses, and giants of ancient Norse mythology, and so many of my questions have been directed toward learning more about these beings. One god, Borr, the brother of Moðir and the father of Odin, is one of those gods about whom I requested more information . . .

Moðr, the Great Mother of the Vanir, discovered and taught much of the magic used by the Vanir. This magic was based on three fundamental principles: coming into one's center of harmony; stalking with the sound a cat makes when it walks; and the intuition gained in listening, observing, and stalking. Other magic, such as the practice of seiðr and shape-shifting, came from these fundamentals. Moðir also had the power of dreaming, and many of the gods and goddesses came to her with their dreams. She also learned many things from her brother, Borr. She and her descendants learned from Borr how to fill their basic needs by hunting, cooking, and building shelters. She appreciated her brother for teaching her these skills to survive, yet it was her power of magic and the use of the three fundamental principles that were her real strength.

On the other hand, Borr, the son of Búri and the father of Odin, did not follow these principles. He was strong—as strong as many of the giants. Through his travels he discovered other things. Borr had no sheltered place in which to live. Ymir, Búri's father, a frost giant, just wandered the earth to eat and would lie down to sleep wherever he might be. His son, Búri, lived the same way. It was Borr who found other ways to live. He first found a cave and discovered fire as a source of warmth and for cooking. He learned how to hunt with a spear and how to herd animals into a trap to slay them. He found a straight tree branch and sharpened it to use as a spear. Later he found flint, which he could shape into a sharp point and tie to the end of his spear so that it could penetrate the skin of an animal. When he killed an animal, he used the animal skins for warmth and the meat for food. In his wanderings and hunting he met Bestla, the daughter of a giant, with whom he had his three sons, including Odin. He found ways to provide shelter and food for his family. As the family outgrew the cave, he built a shelter of wood and thatch. He was a good provider for his family.

At first, Borr lived near his sister, Moðir. One night, Moðir was asleep in her bed when she awoke feeling something or someone stepping on her belly. Jumping up and screaming, she saw a dark elf bending down, looking into her face. Moðir was beautiful, and she heard the words coming from the dwarf Afskræmi's hideous face, "I love you." Her scream was heard by her brother, who came running. When he got to her room, Borr saw Afskræmi tugging at his sister's nightclothing.

Borr grabbed Afskræmi and tied him to a tree outside of the hall. The boundf dwarf was soon terrified to see the sun rising, knowing that he was about to turn into stone. This stone remains today as a reminder of Borr's care for his sister. Moðir was confused. She thought she should thank Borr for protecting her, but she also knew that the other dwarfs would hold Borr as the cause of their grief and anger. Borr was powerful and had no problem restraining a dwarf, but Moðir valued the friendship of the dark elves and understood their anger at Borr. She did not know why Borr just did not let Afskræmi go after telling him that what he did was wrong. She tried to talk to Borr, but he just did not understand. It was then that he left to go off on his own. He was hurt by not being totally appreciated by his sister. Moðir struggled. She had compassion for her brother, too.

Soon after Borr left, Moðir had a dream. Wolves were very common around Moðirasalr. She dreamt that a cat was stalking and had crept into the mouth of a wolf and down into its belly. There it lived for many eons. The wolf's belly was warm and provided sufficient food for the cat, though it was dark. Then came a time when the wolf was torn apart and the cat again lived in the sunlight, or *dagan*.*

---

*In the final battle, Ragnarǫk, Odin is swallowed by Fenrir the wolf, but to avenge his father's death, Odin's son Víðarr puts one foot on the wolf's lower jaw, and with his hands against the roof of its mouth, tears the wolf apart. This story is told in the Gylfaginning of the *Prose Edda*.

Moðir sat in her chair in her hall and called her family around her to interpret the dream for them. "There will be a time when those of us who believe in magic will not be appreciated or understood. The power of our magic and compassion will be lost in the darkness. But have no fear. We will survive and there will be a time when we will again return, the time of Nydagan, the New Dawn, and the sunrise will be appreciated."

Borr built a hall. He expanded the hall many times for all his family, and all felt secure. He was proud of his sons, especially Odin. He watched with pride Odin's incredible strength and the even greater strength of his grandson Thor. After Odin left the great hall, Borr enjoyed visiting his son and watching the warriors in Valhalla practicing and fighting, demonstrating their strength and skill. He appreciated their adeptness in hunting. He knew that when his time passed and Odin would take his place as a leader, he would be a great one. He had faith in Odin. He had neither faith in nor understood the power of the magic of his sister Moðir. Yet he led a simple life and did not have enemies. He did not feel a need to fight others or to fight the giants. He was married to a giant and he considered giants his friends. Like his sister, as he grew old he sat in his hall and was a source of inspiration to his descendants.

The Lay of Borr's Son Odin

In learning more about Borr, my next question, put to Vanadisdottir was to learn more about Borr and his relationship with his children, particularly Odin, as nothing has been written about how Odin related to his father . . .

When Borr left the hall of his father and left his sister, he wandered the world. One day he saw ahead of him a beautiful giantess. She saw him coming and felt vulnerable, fearing him as he approached, but she knew she could not get away and did not want to appear foolish by running. As he approached she felt quite anxious, but when Borr came to her he treated her with respect. As they talked he told her that he was Borr, the son of Búri and the brother of Moðir. He told her he was wandering because he had left their home when Moðir did not appreciate him for killing a dark elf who was sexually harassing her. Moðir felt the dwarf should have been given his freedom after receiving a lecture about his behavior. Instead Borr held him until he was turned to stone by the sun.

Bestla felt safe with Borr. She explained that she was wandering because that is what giants do. She suggested they wander together, and she appreciated his strength and success in hunting and in protecting her. Borr found a cave in which they stayed during inclement weather, and Bestla appreciated the fires he built to warm the cave. Then he did something she did not understand at first. He started collecting wood and thatch. He built her a home, a place for them to live. She had never had a home, but soon after the home was finished she gave birth to their first child, Odin. Borr took it upon himself to hunt, to keep their hall in good repair, and to keep the fires burning. They had a good life.

Odin was the first of Borr and Bestla's three sons. He was very large, three times larger than other boys his age, and very strong. He enjoyed fighting with his spear, Gungnir, and practiced with his two brothers, Vili and Vé.

The story about Gungnir, Odin's spear, you have likely heard involves how Loki persuaded the sons of the dwarf Ivaldi to make the spear for Odin in their forge in the cave of the dark elves. Loki has been given credit for having this spear made for Odin,* but that is not the true story. The spear is much older than Loki, having been made when Odin was young. The real story is that Odin and his brothers happened on the cave of the dark elves in their wanderings. Upon entering the cave they found the blacksmith sons of Ivaldi in despair. Their forge was fueled by red molten rock flowing from the center of the earth, but a boulder had fallen from the ceiling of the cave into the mouth of the fissure from which the molten rock flowed, thus blocking the source of heat to the forge. Odin and his brothers saw this problem and were able to lift the boulder to open the fissure. In payment for his help, the dwarfs made Odin his famous spear.

The three brothers, Odin, Vili, and Vé, would often go out hunting together and they were often successful in the hunt. Bestla appreciated the meat the three youths brought home, for they ate a lot and she was never sure whether she cooked enough. One time when the three brothers were out hunting they came across a frost giant, their great-grandfather Ymir, and Odin, with his spear, killed the giant. The brothers had found him sleeping on a hillside, and they had little respect for a giant who did not know how to get in out of the cold. They came home to Borr laughing, thinking that it had been fun to kill the giant.

Though Borr was proud of his sons in most all of their activities, he did not understand why they had to kill Ymir. He had no quarrel with the giant. When Ymir fell at the hands of his great-grandsons, the whole world began to change, with new rivers, new mountains and valleys, new trees and vegetation. The world changed, probably for the better. Yet Borr did not understand Odin's competitive need to test his strength and to test the strength of others. In his view, the strength to throw a spear to kill a deer or some other animal was sufficient. Soon

---

*The story of Loki persuading the dwarfs to make the spear Gungnir is told in chapter 5 of the Skáldskaparmál of the *Prose Edda*.

after the death of Ymir, Borr had a dream about his son. Odin was standing on the rim of an abyss named Ginfreka, "the wolf's mouth," looking down, unable to see the bottom. From this chasm he smelled sulfur and saw its yellow fumes rising. The earth shook, and a great chunk of the rim broke and gave way into the chasm, with Odin falling into the great jaws of the wolf. From this dream Borr knew that Odin would die in the throat of a wolf. He believed that Odin's death would be related in some way to the death of Ymir, and he told Odin that he should not have killed the giant. He did not understand the evil committed by Odin in killing Ymir, other than knowing it would turn all the giants against him.

In hearing this from his father, Odin felt humiliated and decided it was time to leave home. At first he wandered for a few years, until he met Frigg. He decided to settle down with her and build a hall for them to live in. In his wanderings he had fathered other children: Thor with Fjorgyn; Vali with Rindr; and Víðarr with the giantess Gríðr, a giantess who befriended Thor. He also fathered Bragi, the god of poetry; Hermóðr; the blind god Hǫðr; and the great sacrificing warrior Týr. He brought these sons to his hall, and there they were raised along with Baldr, Odin's son with Frigg, and their fame grew.

Forseti's Blessing and Loki's Silence

With my continued curiosity about the many deities about which very little is known, I asked to learn more about Forseti, the god of justice . . .

Forseti, with Nanna as his mother and Baldr as his father, matured into the same, if not greater, beauty as his parents. He spent much time in the hall of Moðir and learned at a very young age the spirit travel at which both of his parents were so adept. In this way he spent a lot of time with his father and with both parents when they were together, though Nanna and Baldr often wanted to be alone when they were together. From the time he spent at Asgard, Forseti quickly learned that the Æsir were much different from the Vanir and that the best way to deal with these differences was just to listen and show compassion. Forseti grew in great wisdom and discernment. He easily learned all the magical powers of the Vanir and found peace and harmony in them.

One day he was called before his beloved Moðir in her very old age. She reached out to take his hand in hers, and he kissed her proffered hand. It was at this time that she gave him his commission: "You have grown to be wise and you make good judgments. You listen well to people and show them exceptional empathy. You are much needed among the gods and people to show that same judgment when they cannot agree. It will be your commission to offer such judgments when others call on you. Go and be a wise judge."*

With Moðir's blessing, Forseti knew his place was not among the Vanir, for they lived in peace and without conflict. Instead, his place was with the Æsir, where conflict abounded. Thus, he moved to live with his father. There it did not take long for the gods and goddesses to start coming to him as they did to Baldr. Empathetic listening is magical in its ability to attract others. When someone came to him

---

*From the Gylfaginning of the *Prose Edda* we know that Forseti's role as a god was to offer judgment in conflict, but now we know how he received his commission.

complaining of a conflict with someone else, he would ask the two parties to come to him together. He had the intuition to ask the right questions that led them to the right answer. His intuition also told him when someone was being dishonest, and he had the ability to lead them to tell the truth. Word spread of Forseti's skill in resolving conflict, and even Odin would go to him for advice.

One time when Forseti was in Valaskjálf, Odin's hall, Odin beckoned Forseti to approach his high seat. Odin had a concern. He was feeling guilty about the piece of whetstone imbedded in his son's head. If you recall, after Odin won the horse race against the giant Hrungnir, he invited the Hrungnir into the hall, where they sat and drank together. When Thor entered the hall and saw the giant, he was enraged that Hrungnir was granted this hospitality and challenged the giant to the duel in which Thor was injured.

Forseti listened with care to his story. Odin was wondering about his wisdom in being so welcoming to the giant. Forseti understood Odin's concern and assured the high god that reaching out with friendship and good hospitality could never be wrong. He could not tell Odin, though, that it was all Thor's fault—that Thor's blind temper and hatred for the giants was the cause of his injury. Odin might have difficulty hearing such criticism of his son. Forseti did tell Odin that Thor seemed to lose no strength because of the injury, though he may have an occasional headache, and added that it might be helpful to remind Thor that he is related to the giants and would benefit by becoming their friend. Yet as much as he might wish it, Forseti saw no possibility of Thor giving up his war on the giants.

What brought Forseti the most respect was the way in which he dealt with the guile of Loki. When the sea giant Ægir brewed ale in his new ale vat and invited all of the Æsir, apparently neither Baldr nor Forseti were there, or at least Loki had no insults for them if they had been there. Were they above such insults?

On another occasion, however, Loki did have an opportunity to insult Baldr and Forseti. He found the father and son sitting in Idunn's garden, talking. To Baldr he said, "Baldr, you, so gentle and compassionate, are a hypocrite in showing compassion to your father and brothers. They are strong and warriors. You are not like them. How sweet it is of you to sit in a garden while the others are sweating, swinging their swords. Behind your back they deride you for not being strong and brave. Yet you listen patiently and lovingly to them."

To Forseti Loki then said, "You, too, are so compassionate. You listen to others' woes, and they respect your judgment, but not your strength. You are a weakling, and all of Æsir laughs at you. They belittle you and take advantage of you. Where is your judgment in defending yourself?"

Listening to Loki, Forseti felt compassion for him. He knew Loki looked at the world much as he did, with the intuition to see inconsistencies and the nature of conflicts, the weaknesses and deceptiveness of others; but unlike Loki, Forseti realized that alienating others with insults was not the way to resolve conflict. Showing compassion for such weakness and inconsistency gives the other the strength to find a more effective path to accomplish what he or she may want. He said to Loki, "You see the world much as I do. You see the weaknesses and deceptiveness in others; you recognize how these issues cause them to suffer, and you try to rescue them with your honesty, but they couldn't care less."

Loki was silent, maybe for the first time. Forseti again appreciated the power found in showing compassion. Idunn was in the garden at the time and overheard Forseti and Loki talking. She told Bragi, the god of poetry, about the discussion. Bragi then created a ballad to tell the story of Loki's rare silence.

The twisted mustached god　　　*Comes face-to-face with Baldr's son*
You are weak, you don't fight　　*Others deride you behind your back*
Forseti beckons him to sit　　　*Sit down here with your concerns*
Loki dances before Forseti　　　*Fleet of foot and ready to run*
His nervous feet know not what　*No, not now, I'd rather stand to do*
You, Loki, and I think alike　　 *You see deceit, you see lies*

What they do makes no sense   *The bear-skins fight with mindless strength*
You tell them of their craziness   *His feet slow down, he bends to sit*

Next to Forseti Loki sits   *From then on nothing's spoke*
What you tell makes them mad   *Beneath a viper you are tied*
To listen may seem weak   *Compassion may make me the fool*
From your dart my father dies   *But in the end love will rule*

Forseti's Justice

Wanting to learn still more about Foreseti, I asked about what he had learned while journeying among the humans in Midgard . . .

Forseti journeyed to the island of Zealand. There he wandered, visiting with kings, jarls (earls), warriors, and farmers. He spent some time with King Healfdene, who was the chief king of the island. There he saw that Healfdene was a wise and just ruler. He had strong and fearless warriors, but he also had love and compassion for his people. The king himself went to the sanctuary of Gefjon, the goddess of plowing, as did his father and his father's father before him. He knew that he was of the lineage of Gefjon and believed that he was her grandson. He knew her stories of how she raised his grandfather and was the mother to his son, Healfdene's father. Thus, Healfdene remained faithful to the family lineage. Forseti was pleased that Gefjon was remembered.

The warriors and berserkers of Healfdene were fearless, and it was Thor who gave them their fearlessness. Thor had little compassion. Compassion, he thought, would diminish his fearlessness. When fighting, warriors could not think about what was just and unjust. Those thoughts would interfere with their resolve to win in battle. It was the king's job to decide what was just and unjust, and they knew their king, Healfdene, was a just and good king. They honored him.

The farmers worked hard supporting their families and did not resent giving their share of what they produced to the king, for he was a good king who protected them well. For an abundant crop, the farmers worshipped Freyr, while the farmers' wives looked to Freyja and Gefjon to protect their family and the land. Thus, all of Healfdene's subjects led lives of contentment.

During his travels Forseti came to a jarl of the land. This jarl collected tribute from his farmers and paid tribute to King Healfdene. He was a just jarl, and his retainers, surfs, and farmers respected him. The jarl and his family were productive, and they were proud of their young son. He was of an age when he could be fostered to some family who would raise him as their son. In fostering a son to a family, a bond between these families was formed, for mutual support and to ensure peace. The jarl and his wife held a concern that they took to Forseti. The father wanted his son to be fostered by a family that worshipped Thor, because he worshipped Thor, as did his father, who was a warrior. The mother, who worshipped Freyja and Gefjon, wanted her son to be fostered by a family that worshipped Freyr, Freyja, and Gefjon. The mother and father could not agree, though they did agree that both families under consideration were good families and an alliance with either family would be valuable.

Forseti asked the father how he happened to be a jarl when his father was a warrior. Forseti learned that the jarl's father had died in his first battle and he was left fatherless. His mother was of a good family whose father was a jarl, so it came about that he was raised to become a jarl, and when his grandfather died he was the only male heir, so he became jarl. Yet he often thought of how his father dreamt of being a great warrior, and he wanted to give his son that chance. His widowed mother worshipped and sacrificed to Freyja, knowing that her husband was a charge of Freyja, having died in his first battle.

Forseti asked the father about the qualities of Thor that he valued and wished for his son. The jarl acknowledged that Thor was strong and fearless, the qualities hoped for by a warrior. He asked about the qualities of Freyja and Gefjon. The mother and father reported that these goddesses were loving and compassionate. They understood the needs of people and fulfilled these needs when asked.

Forseti asked who King Healfdene worshipped. They answered, "Gefjon." He asked what qualities the king learned from Gefjon. They said fairness and justice. Forseti then asked what qualities they most wanted their son to have. The father put fairness and justice before being strong and fearless. He then knew that the family that worshipped Freyja and Gefjon was the right family for the son. He knew that warriors could not afford to think of fairness and justice in battle. They were happy that

Forseti was able to listen to them and lead them to the best answer.

After spending the night with this family, Forseti traveled on to meet other people and other families. He helped many find the correct answers to their concerns and conflicts. Sometimes the conflict was about boundaries between farm fields. In each case, Forseti listened and asked the right questions. Questions about who owned the land before and where the line went, or what the field was going to be used for, or what the terrain naturally dictated, were all questions that would lead to the best answer. Sometimes a family's concern was about who a son or daughter was going to marry. Questions about the characteristics of the families and the daughter or son in question, and sometimes about what each person wanted for the future, were asked. Often the questions were about the petitioner's knowledge about the gods and goddesses. All were questions that would lead to finding the right answer.

Thus, as Forseti journeyed throughout the realms, his fame in being a wise and just arbiter grew. His influence was such that many of the leaders of the people sought to emulate him and pay homage to him as they did to his father.

The Lay of Slœgr

The answer that came from my next question was that creativity and beauty comes out of compassion and love, not aggression and physical strength. What I requested, though, was to learn more about Slœgr, Moðir's husband and Njord's father . . .

Njord's father was Slœgr. His name means "crafty." He was sometimes called Skapari, "creator." Slœgr was the father of the Vanir. This giant was very creative and became a skilled ironsmith. He built a hall from the trees and grasses of the area for his wife and child, with a large firepit in the center to keep them warm. He learned how to work with iron and made the first ax so that he could cut wood to burn in the firepit. Moðir was a good cook, but it was her husband, Slœgr, who made her the spit that she turned over the fire to cook the meat. He made her kettles that hung over the fire, in which she cooked soups and stews. He made her knives to cut with, forks to stab with, and spoons to scoop with when she was cooking. He made himself a spear for hunting. He stayed busy making things and became especially skilled in making things with iron.

Slœgr watched his son grow and made Njord toys. He made him a small hammer like the big one he used on his anvil. Slœgr was a giant of a man, with giant lungs, and he could blow hard. He had to blow hard to make his fire glow hot enough to soften the iron to hammer it. But in his creativity he figured out a way of blowing on the fire so that he would not get dizzy: he made the first bellows, and Njord enjoyed helping him by pumping the bellows. When his father made Njord his own bellows, Njord found many other things to do with them. He would go out and use them to blow leaves from under trees, or go to the water's edge and blow up waves. As the world developed and men learned to make ships and became sailors, he would blow the wind to fill the sails to make the ships move. Njord's son, Freyr, had a magical ship, Skíðblaðnir, made by Ivaldi, one of the dark elves, which whenever the sail was raised a wind would be there to fill it. It was Njord with his bellows who was always there for his son when he would put his ship in the water.

As the Vanir grew in number, Slœgr's skill became more and more in demand. He taught others the skill of blacksmithing, but he was still the best smith and was always involved in special projects, making special things for special people. Ullr looked up to Slœgr as his mentor in creativity. The tools that Ullr so much prized in doing his carving—his iron chisels, his knife, his ax, and other wood splitters—were all made for Ullr by Slœgr and came from his forge. Slœgr was a powerful man with a powerful arm for swinging his hammer in forming these tools on his anvil. But though he was strong, he was very gentle. He was confident in his strength and did not need to prove it. As he watched Ullr grow in his own creativity, Slœgr was proud of having made him his tools. Ullr would come to him at times with a special need, and together they would create the tool.

Slœgr's tools were very practical; whatever Ullr made was very beautiful. Ullr's creations that at first were practical, such as his bow and arrow and his skis, later were made with great beauty. He so much enjoyed the texture and grain in the wood that he used the texture and grain to enhance the beauty of whatever he made. Slœgr appreciated this beauty and thus began making things of great beauty himself. As Ullr made the pillars in the great hall beautiful, Slœgr made iron plates to hold together the rafters to the pillars, and these plates were objects of beauty. He made the hinges that allowed the doors to the hall to swing smoothly, and he decorated these hinges. As he grew old and as he trained others to make the tools that were needed, Slœgr had more time to make things of great beauty.

The women of the Vanir liked to wear brooches and jewelry that were usually made by the dwarfs of the cave of the dark elves, because the dwarfs had gold and precious stones to work with. But Slœgr sometimes would make them brooches of iron. It was one such brooch that Moðir wore to hold her cloak because it was simple and she appreciated simplicity, but she loved it especially because it was made with love by the god she loved. Moðirasalr was alive with creativity. Out of the love, compassion, and sensitivity of those who dwelled there came the creative urge to express their love in beauty, whether in the song and poetry of Bragi or in the iron and wood of Slœgr and Ullr. Others, too, joined in with leather and needlework. The women of the great hall were always spinning wool, weaving fabrics, and making beautiful clothing and tapestries. This creativity was the outgrowth of their compassion and magic; it was a gentle and quiet creativity. It was the way the Vanir saw the world—with sensitivity, intuition, and the power of stalking like a cat.* The goddesses of the Æsir were creative and loved beauty, like the goddesses of the Vanir, but it was the gods of the Vanir who were most different from the gods of the Æsir. The gods of the Vanir were sensitive, gentle, creative, and compassionate. They were not warlike, aggressive, and powerful, like the gods of the Æsir.

---

*Riane Eisler in her book *The Chalice and The Blade,* describes the goddess society as found in the Mediterranean area as being exceptionally creative; here we find this same creativity in the North.

The Lay of Heimdallr

We know about Heimdallr's acute hearing and that he was the guardian of the gods and of Bifröst, the shimmering rainbow bridge between Midgard and the upper world. We also know that Heimdallr and Loki killed each other at the final battle, Ragnarǫk. As the guardian of the gods, Heimdallr sees Loki as the enemy. But we know nothing about how Heimdallr became the guardian of the gods, thus I asked for information . . .

Nine maiden sisters gave birth to Heimdallr. Though they loved him dearly as a son, being good mothers they realized that he needed the influence of a man, so they arranged with Njord to be his foster father. Therefore, during his younger years he was raised among the Vanir.

Living with the Vanir, Heimdallr had the opportunity to develop certain powers of magic. Of the sixteen powers, the ones he developed best were that of going into his center of harmony and the power of stalking, or observation. He learned to listen so well that he could hear the grass growing on the earth and the wool growing on sheep. His vision became such that he could see a distance of a hundred leagues, day or night. In going into his center of harmony, he could find such quietness within himself that he needed very little sleep—less sleep than a bird.*

As Heimdallr grew, he watched Freyja and her brother Freyr grow. Freyja and Freyr were very close, and Heimdallr felt left out. Freyja was beautiful and was the center of attention among all the young gods of the Vanir. Heimdallr, being only a foster child, stood to one side and watched. He knew these young men were all competing for Freyja's attention, and he was concerned for her safety. Freyr was one of these

---

*The description of Heimdallr, his vision and sense of hearing and his lack of a need for sleep, is given in the Gylfaginning of the *Prose Edda*.

young men, and though he, too, was concerned for Freyja, he didn't think this attention and competition was a problem and just laughed at Heimdallr's concern. One day one of these young men cornered Freyja in Idunn's garden while another youth stood watch to see if anyone was coming. Heimdallr, with his power of vision and hearing, knew what was happening. He quickly called to Freyr as he ran to the garden to rescue Freyja. He came to the watchman, who blocked his way. Heimdallr, being very large for his age, pushed him away and entered the garden. By then Freyr had caught up with him and stopped him. Heimdallr told Freyr that his sister was in danger and beckoned to him to follow. Freyr grabbed him by the arm and told him he was being ridiculous.

Nevertheless, by the time they got to Freyja the other youth had her on the ground and was straddling her. She seemed to be enjoying the attention she was getting, and Freyr couldn't control his laughter. Heimdallr stood in shock. By then all were laughing at Heimdallr, who turned in embarrassment and left the garden. He knew what was going on was wrong, but everyone was laughing at him. He had taken it on himself to become the protector of his foster sister, Freyja, and did not understand why she, too, thought what was happening was funny.

So, as Heimdallr grew, he did not feel part of the Vanir. Like so many boys, he began to want what he could not get, and so he became obsessed with the power of the gods of the Æsir. The Vanir did not value the power of the sinew of the bear. As a man, Heimdallr felt he should be the protector of others and stand up against what he thought was wrong. The Vanir believed that this power worked against all the other powers that they so much valued, so they did not encourage their youth to develop it. When Heimdallr was told that developing this power was not recommended, he lost interest in all the other magical powers and became obsessed with the power of the sinew of the bear. When he reached the age of choice, he decided to go live with the Æsir in order to become adept in fighting and developing the power of the sinew of a bear. He wanted to be strong to protect others.

When Heimdallr came to Asgard, Odin called him to audience.

He told Odin what he had learned from the Vanir—that he could hear the grass grow, he could see a distance of a hundred leagues day or night, and needed less sleep than a bird—but he also told Odin that he wanted to learn the strength of the Æsir: he wanted to learn how to fight. Odin agreed that he could become part of the Æsir but commissioned him to become their watchman because of his keen eyesight and hearing and his need for little sleep. Odin recognized that these qualities would make Heimdallr the perfect watchman, and he gave him a horn to blow that everyone could hear if he should see danger lurking. No one could disagree with Odin when he commissioned them to do something. Though Heimdallr was disappointed that he was not going to be trained as a fighter, he was happy to play an important part in protecting the Æsir. His job of watching for danger seemed to be a mindless job, but he remained faithful to the Æsir and performed his role as watchman resolutely.

The Lay of Ullr's Drawings

After my trip to Tanum, Sweden, where I had the opportunity to examine the many petroglyphs there, I posed the question, "Why did the ancient people of Sweden draw such pictures?"

Odin, the high one, hung on a tree for nine long days and nights to learn the runes and the power of the runic alphabet.* Ullr and the Vanir learned to draw not runes, but pictures, and discovered power in these pictures—the power of telling and remembering stories in pictures.

Many of the stories of the Vanir were recorded in the pictures that Ullr carved into the pillars of Moðirasalr. He depicted the skillful Slœgr making kettles and tools in his forge. He showed Idunn picking apples from her tree and herbs from her garden. He showed Freyja listening to fallen warriors and Gefjon listening to young virgins. He showed Njord blowing into the sails of ships at sea and Freyr in his travels through Midgard. Ullr showed the trees defending Vanaheim, and Bragi, skaldic god of poetry, singing to the warriors from high above. His favorite theme, though, and he carved it often, was of Moðir listening with compassion to everyone who came to her. These stories remembered in pictures inspired everyone.

Ullr also carved and drew stories as he wandered. In his wanderings he carried with him his bow and arrows. One time when he traveled across Midgard, hunting as he went, he saw a large buck. He placed an arrow on the bow string, pulled it back, and let it go. The arrow flew true into the side of the deer, striking its heart. The deer fell. Ullr gutted it and dragged it a short distance to a cave that he had seen earlier.

Arriving at the cave, he found a group of hunters camping for the night. They had a large fire blazing and accepted Ullr into their camp when he offered to share the deer with them. They hung it over the

---

*The story of how Odin learned the power of the runes while hanging on a tree is told in the "Havarmal" in the *Poetic Edda*.

fire to cook as they sat and shared hunting stories. Using his tools, Ullr started drawing pictures in the soft walls of the cave, showing a hunter pulling back the string of a bow, arrows flying, and one arrow hitting a deer in its side. He showed the falling deer and showed the hunter gutting it. The hunters watched him drawing these pictures in amazement. The hunting party was using spears, and none of them had learned how to use a bow and arrow. One hunter tried drawing a picture of building a fence of brush and branches and showed the hunters herding a deer into this trap so they could spear it to show how they did it. Ullr praised the hunter for drawing and all of them for their ability to hunt with spears, but he told them that some of them might want to learn how to use a bow and arrow.

He then took them outside the cave and showed them how to use the bow and arrow. It was not dark during this summertime of long evenings, and he let them each try his bow to shoot an arrow. They all could see that it would take practice to hit a deer with an arrow, but they were excited about learning. The next morning, Ullr drew more pictures suggesting that they build their fence and use the spears that they were used to, and he would use his bow and arrow. He would help them make bows and arrows in the evening after the hunt, but that would take some time. The hunt was successful exactly as it was shown in the pictures. With Ullr's help, the pictures were magical.

That evening and for the next several evenings after that, Ullr helped the hunters make bows and arrows. He showed them the kinds of wood he liked to use, especially yew, and how to split the wood. He set up a target and helped them practice, telling them that their spears were important, too. Each morning more pictures were drawn. One showed a canyon with rock cliffs on either side with a brush fence built across it. Some of the hunters stood behind the fence with their spears. Others were shown up on the canyon walls with their bows and arrows, and still others were shown behind the herd of deer, herding the deer into the canyon. That day they killed six deer, the ones they had herded into the canyon.

The next day, Ullr wished them well as they left for home carrying a good supply of meat for the winter. At home they told their families about the hunt, about Ullr, and about the drawings he made using their own drawings. They used a nearby cave wall as an altar to Ullr, making offerings to the god of their drawings and asking him for continued success.

After they left and Ullr continued on his journey, the hunters began their hunt each morning with drawing pictures. The caves became temples to the god Ullr, and the pictures were their offering to the god. In this way they ensured the success of the hunt.

As Ullr moved on, teaching the ways of hunting and the way of using a bow and arrow, more and more cave walls and rocks on the hillsides became altars for making offerings to Ullr. The magical pictures brought the hunters success in their hunt. Pictures became a powerful way of teaching.

Pictures began to be used for other things, too. It did not take long for travelers to learn to tell one another how to get from one place to another by drawing pictures—pictures of mountains, streams, rocks, and trees, pictures that showed the way to go. Idunn drew pictures to show others what herbs to pick. Children drew pictures to learn how to do the things they needed to learn to become adults. Seamen drew pictures of the sea serpent Jörmungandr to let others know of the dangers of the sea. Pictures had become a powerful way to remember history and to teach others for the future. That is why where pictures are found, Ullr is being worshipped.*

---

*Many such pictures drawn on rocks can be seen on the west coast of Sweden, near Tanum. One of my favorite rock carvings is of Thor being pulled in his chariot by his goats, drawn with elegant simplicity.

Idunn, Freyr, and the Giants

The giants were a great ally to the Vanir, but what happened to this relationship after the demise of Vanaheim? I wanted to explore this question and did so in a series of trance experiences . . .

One day, the giant Thiazi, the father of Skaði, approached Vanaheim asking for Idunn. He came in the form of an eagle because that was the fastest way for him to travel. He knew Idunn was a healer and needed her skill. His wife, Kona, was sick. She was very hot and had pain in her stomach. He was worried. Idunn packed up her basket. She tied a rope around the eagle's neck and got on its back, holding onto the rope. It took very little time for them to get to Thiazi's hall, Thrymheim, high in the mountains.

Idunn found Kona in bed. She was hot and complained of pain in her stomach. For these symptoms Idunn brewed up some tea made from isop, kamille, and røllike to help Kona's stomach and alleviate her fever. She fed this tea to Kona, who drank it willingly. Idunn stayed for a few days until she knew that Kona was getting better before Thiazi took her back to Vanaheim. Because of Idunn's love and compassion, she became a good friend to Thiazi and Kona.

Some time later, after Idunn moved to live with Bragi among the Æsir, Kona became ill again during her pregnancy. Again Thiazi wanted Idunn, but he knew that he could not go to Asgard because he feared Thor; whereas the Æsir saw Thiazi's actions as evil, the Vanir saw them as compassionate.* Thiazi thus devised a way to get Idunn outside the wall. He saw that Odin, Loki, and Hœnir were camping for the evening and were roasting an ox. Watching them while in the form of an eagle from his perch in a tree not far away, Thiazi used magic to

---

*This story is very similar to the story of the theft of Idunn's apples as told in the Gylfaginning of the *Prose Edda,* but in this case seen very differently, through the eyes of the Vanir.

keep the fire from touching the ox, thus preventing it from cooking. The gods became more and more frustrated while the eagle laughed to himself as he perched in the tree. After some time, the eagle spoke up and told the gods that if they would share the ox with him he would let the fire do its job. On this they agreed. But Thiazi was famished and ate and ate. Soon Loki became angry with him and struck him with a stick. Again Thiazi used his magic to make the staff stick both to him and to Loki's hands, so Loki could not get free. He then flew, dragging Loki, who was screaming for him to stop, along the ground. Eventually he promised Loki that if he could bring Idunn outside the walls of Asgard, he would let Loki go. Loki promised.

Upon returning to Asgard, Loki told Idunn the story that he had found an apple tree outside the walls and wanted her to see it. She eagerly followed him outside the wall, only to be greeted by her friend the eagle, who picked her up and took her back to his hall, Thrymheim, in the mountains. She was gone for some time to treat Kona for her ailment, while back at Asgard the gods began to grow old rapidly because they did not have Idunn's apples to keep them young. They were worried and wanted to find Idunn, not knowing where she was. Loki agreed to go find her if Freyja would loan him her falcon skin so he could fly. When he arrived at Thrymheim, the giant was not there. He was out collecting herbs for Idunn. Loki quickly turned Idunn into a nut, took her in his talons, and started to carry her back to Asgard.

Thiazi saw them leave and took flight as an eagle in pursuit, but they had a good head start. Thiazi got closer and closer in the race back to Asgard. The gods saw them coming and built a fire inside the wall. Loki beat Thiazi inside the protective wall, with Thiazi right on his tail, but Thiazi could not stop in time and flew into the fire to meet his death.

The gods dragged his body outside the wall rather than let it rot and contaminate their holy ground. Idunn, now turned back into herself, saw what had happened and felt deep grief for Kona. She went to her garden and wept and wept. The giant's family and friends came to provide a decent funeral for Thiazi. They built a large fire some distance from the divine walls and carried the corpse to the fire, all wailing and mourning his death. The noise of their wailing got the attention of the gods, and one god in particular understood the grief of Thiazi's family and friends. Freyr went to Idunn's garden to get Idunn, and together they left the walls to grieve with the giants. Freyr and Idunn listened to the stories they told of Thiazi's goodness. He was a good husband and a good father. God and goddess told some of their own stories of how Thiazi was a good friend to the Vanir and how he had helped protect the Vanir when they were attacked by the army of the Æsir. The giants held nothing against Freyr and knew that Idunn was a good friend to Thiazi and Kona. They appreciated Idunn and Freyr joining them in their grief over the death of a good giant.

As the giants' three days of mourning went on, the giants became hungry. Freyr left and returned later with three oxen for them to roast. The giants were grateful. When the giants were ready to leave and return to Jötunheimr, Freyr went with them to help carry the giant's ashes to the top of the mountain surrounding their land. It was on this mountain that the ashes of the giants were thrown—a mountain made of the ashes of the giants when they died. Freyr respected the giants and they appreciated his respect. Thus, Freyr and the giants formed a bond of friendship.

Upon hearing of her husband's death, Kona had traveled with the other giants, even though she was still weak. She still needed Idunn's help. Idunn returned with Kona, to Thrymheim, to nurse her back to health.

Upon leaving Asgard, Idunn told the gods that they need not worry. No harm would come to them by growing a little older while she was gone over the next few days, and that hopefully with age comes wisdom, something that might benefit them. She then left with Freyr on the back of his golden boar in the direction of Thrymheim.

Baldr Grieves Hrungnir's Death

I continued to explore the relationship between the Vanir and the giants after the fall of Vanaheim . . .

When Freyr and Idunn returned with red eyes from grieving the death of Thiazi, the others of the Æsir shook their heads in wonder, not understanding these Vanir in their midst. Not long after Thiazi's death, Thor faced the strongest of all the giants, Hrungnir, and killed him, even though Thor, too, was injured in the battle, having been trapped under Hrungnir's leg. Although to the Æsir Freyr's grief over Thiazi's death may have been acceptable because Thiazi was the goddess Skaði's father,* when Freyr explained to Odin that he intended to go to Jötunheimr to grieve the death of Hrungnir, heads really did shake. Only Baldr understood why Freyr needed to go, and he asked to go along with him.

When Odin heard this he was concerned and called the two gods to audience. With the explanation that the Vanir and the giants were longtime allies and that Freyr wanted to continue this relationship, which would also be to the advantage of the Æsir, Odin answered, "Do what you must."

With Odin thus weakly giving his permission, Baldr and Freyr left to journey to Jötunheimr. When they arrived, Freyr was welcomed, but strange looks were cast in the direction of Baldr, whom they knew was Thor's brother and Odin's son. Baldr, though, was quick to express empathy by saying, "You don't understand why I am here when my

---

*One person, in reading the manuscript of this book, questioned, "How could Skaði, being Thiazi's daughter, be used as an excuse?" I countered, "It excused Freyr's role in mourning Thiazi's death because Skaði was married to Njord." But the argument continued: "Skaði was allowed to marry Njord in compensation for Thiazi's death, so it had to be sometime after Thiazi's death." This once again proves that the logic of myth and the logic of the unconscious mind are both time-free and as such go beyond the rational way of thinking; *B* comes after *A* in rational logic, but in the symmetrical logic of the unconscious mind and mythology, *B* may come after *A,* before *A,* or at the same time as *A.*

brother killed Hrungnir." He could see that they were now listening with open ears. "I feel it was wrong for Thor to kill Hrungnir and want you to know that not all the Æsir think of the giants as their enemy." With that comment, the giants withheld their opinions about whether or not Baldr should be among the mourners, and he joined them in their wailing and grief. He could understand their feelings of insecurity, since the strongest of them had been killed, leaving the rest not knowing what lay in store for them.

When the funeral pyre was lit and Hrungnir was returned to ashes, Baldr, too, helped carry the ashes to the top of the mountains surrounding Jötunheimr. While spreading the ashes he offered a eulogy:

Hrungnir	*A towering ash*
Holds the whetstone	*His shade protects*
The tree has fallen	*His shade is lost*
His stone shattered	*Hones fearsome swords*
The High One's son	*Shows respect*
Carries these ashes	*To honor Hrungnir*
The High One's son	*Stands on ashes*
Plants new trees	*For protective shade*

He stayed to talk with the giants, assuring them that Njord, Freyr, and all of the goddesses except for Sif, Thor's wife, agreed with him that they should be friends and not act as if the giants were a threat, as Thor did. He pointed out to them that Odin had invited Hrungnir into his great hall for a drink of mead and that even he hoped there could be peace. In this way Baldr became a friend to the giants. This bond later made it possible for Frigg to receive assurance from all of the giants that they would weep for Baldr after his death. There was one exception, since the giantess Thokk would not weep, but all believe that Thokk was Loki in disguise and intent on inflicting more pain on the Æsir.

When Baldr returned to Asgard and told Odin about his friendship with the giants, Odin understood the advantage of being friends, but he knew that he could not change the beliefs and attitudes of Thor.

After that, Baldr journeyed frequently to Jötunheimr and sometimes took Forseti with him to show the giants friendship. The giants learned to ask Forseti for advice in settling their disputes and appreciated his skill in resolving conflicts.

The Lay of the Giants

As we continue to better understand the relationship between the Vanir and the giants, we learn that the *jötunns,* or giants, speak a different language, so I asked how Baldr learned this language . . .

Baldr returned from Jötunheimr, the giants' land, with a lot to report. The experience for him had been profound. He had occasionally seen a jötunn creeping around in the moors and fens in the borderlands between Vanaheim and Asgard, but he had never been close to one as had Thor and many of the other gods and goddesses. Thor, being the son of Jorð, a giantess, knew the language of the giants. Some of the other Æsir who had parents who were jötunns knew their language too. Most of the gods and goddesses of the Vanir, with their powers of stalking, observation, and intuition, had easily learned their language as well. The giants' language was very different in that they spoke using their hands, arms, and facial expressions. The vocal sounds they used in speaking were very guttural and limited. Since Baldr did not understand their language, Freyr acted as the interpreter when he spoke to them, explaining why he was at Hrungnir's funeral and gave his eulogy. He was very glad that he had gone to the funeral. He had learned a lot about the giants and knew that he, too, could learn their language, and he knew that doing so would help in showing them respect.

Baldr was telling all of this to Nanna and to Forseti, who, like him, had not had much contact with jötunns. He was impressed with the giants' size and strength but surprised that they lived mainly in caves. He had heard stories that they were wanderers and would sleep whenever they got tired or when nighttime came, lying down wherever they might be. Though he had heard stories about the halls of the giants, he had learned that these halls were not like the halls of the gods or humans, but rather more cavelike. Giants still wandered, but with the coming of the gods and humans their lives had changed, and now they congregated in the place called Jötunheimr, to live apart from the gods and humans. In Jötunheimr they found many large caves where they could live. Baldr, Nanna, and Forseti knew their ancestors were giants, since Odin's grandfather and Moðir's father had been the giant Búri. Even without understanding their language, Baldr saw that the jötunns had the same feelings as the gods and humans. They could feel grief, they could become angry, and they could laugh and make jokes. They also remembered their ancestors. He had learned from Nanna that the jötunns had fought in the war between the Vanir and the Æsir on the side of the Vanir because of the mutual respect between the Vanir and the giants. In Baldr's compassion for everybody and everything, he could feel close to them in their grief. He knew he had to include them among his friends. Nanna and Forseti supported this decision.

Baldr made frequent spirit journeys to Jötunheimr to watch the giants to learn their language, and it did not take him long. While watching them, he at first wished there was a way that they could better protect themselves, especially from Thor, since they lived so out in the open. It was true that they would often lie down wherever they were to sleep, and their caves were too open. Where they lived was forested, but the giants were not very protective of the trees. Wherever they walked they would pull up trees to clear the way. One day he was talking with Bragi about how to protect the giants and suggested that Bragi could teach them to sing to the trees. Maybe if they learned that the trees could protect them they would become more gentle with them. Bragi had already learned, though, that the jötunns were tone deaf and could not sing.

One time when Baldr was spirit journeying, he watched Thor fly over the mountain surrounding Jötunheimr and saw that the giants saw or knew he was coming and quickly disappeared into the depths of their caves, hiding the cave entrances with large boulders. There appeared to be no giants at all in the land. It shocked Baldr how fast the word spread and how they all vanished so quickly. The way Baldr traveled, none of the giants could see him, nor did they know he was in the area, so they stayed out in the open where he could see them. This he mentioned to Bragi, who explained to Baldr that the giants had a way of communicating that no one could see or hear. Somehow they had a way of reading one another's minds without a word being said, especially at a time of an emergency; and anyway, Thor was so noisy in the way he got around, with his cart bouncing and banging around making thunder, that who could not know he was coming? They both laughed at his image of Thor. With this understanding, Baldr worried less about his friends, the giants.

Once Baldr felt comfortable with using their way of talking he went to visit the giants and was welcomed in one of their caves. He found their families lived quite comfortably around a central fire, just as Baldr lived, and he enjoyed a meal with them. They explained to him that they did not have a great worry about Thor because they could get away from him, and only when a giant got stuck outside his cave was he in danger, and that did not happen very often. Their ability to hide the entrances to their caves was part of their ability to use illusion and shape-shifting. Actually, they somewhat enjoyed the game of hiding from Thor and watching him stomp around in frustration at finding no jötunns to fight. They laughed in telling how one giant got left outside the cave when Thor came and kept him busy by throwing boulders to make him think that the giant was in one place when he would be in another, until he found a place to hide.

Baldr gained a lot of confidence in the giants' abilities to protect themselves and from that time on he did not worry.

The Survival of the Vanir

Now that we come to the final battle, my last question (for the time being) was who survived, how did they survive, and then what . . . ?

It was Moðir's prediction. She saw Odin, her nephew, leading the Æsir in the foolish direction of seeking power through physical strength, the power of the sinew of a bear. She knew this direction would lead to failure. She grieved the pain that this direction would cause, but she knew it would not be the end.

She was friends with the giants but grew too old to venture out to visit them, so they came to visit her. Two of the giants were Fárbauti and Laufey. They would talk about their son Loki. He was a god unto himself. Moðir couldn't help but laugh in hearing stories of his pranks and mischief. She was afraid for Loki, believing that he would go too far, yet his pranks were to make fun of the gods, especially Thor. He was a god after Moðir's heart in that he could see the foolishness in the gods' actions and had the audacity to make them face this foolishness. Yet the gods did not learn. Loki's confrontations brought the Æsir gods the conflict and tension that gave them emotional energy, that gave them life. When he finally went too far, when he caused the death of the most beloved god, Baldr, they imprisoned Loki, tying him to three boulders using the entrails of his son that had turned to iron.* There, the venom of a viper dripped on him, causing him to writhe and quake the earth. Yet his wife, Sigyn, tried to protect him by catching the poison in a bowl. With Loki thus restrained, life as the gods knew it came to an end, replaced by six years of torment and endless cold. The gods had no clue as to the cause of the endless winters.

It was Njord who best understood the cause. "Loki brought life to the people of Midgard, to the gods and goddesses of the Æsir. Loki was a mirror in which we saw our lives, in which we could see who we are,

---

*The story of the binding of Loki is found in the Gylfaginning of the *Prose Edda*.

both our integrity and our lack of integrity. Loki showed us the tension between the strength found in compassion and the strength found in insensitivity, between magic and the sinew of the bear, between peace and war, between creativity and death. Once this tension was restrained by the entrails of its son, all that was seen in the mirror was the endless winter of insensitivity, brute strength, war, and death. Loki's restraint ended the warmth of life."

To the gods of the Æsir, Njord's words sounded undecipherable, like a riddle, but there were still those who knew and had faith in compassion, magic, peace, and creativity.

It was time for the final reckoning. Moðir could see the end from her seat in Griðbustaðr, the dwelling place of peace. She could no longer watch this suffering of endless cold. She called on Surtr from the fires of the south, Jörmungandr the serpent from the sea, and Fenrir the wolf from his island. She called on and opened the gates of Hel. She called on Loki. All broke free and came. For the suffering to end, it was the only way left.

We all know what happened: In facing one another on Vígríðr, the battlefield, Surtr killed Freyr, who was without his sword. Garmr, the guardian dog of the gates of Hel, and Týr faced and killed each other. Thor killed Jörmungandr, but as the serpent died, his poison killed Thor. Odin was swallowed whole by Fenrir the wolf, but then the wolf was torn apart by Odin's son, Víðarr. And in the end, Loki and Heimdallr faced each other and both died. Moðir heard wailing coming from her friends in Jötunheimr, from Fárbauti and Laufey, the parents of Loki. They could see the final battle, too.

In the end, with the war that the Æsir call Ragnarǫk, the world burned with the fire of Surtr, and Njord retreated to the sea. He knew that the new world after the death of the Æsir would be a world that his mother could love. She held hope for and had predicted this new world, Nydagan, the New Dawn. Freyja retreated to the sea along with Frigg to watch. Idunn, Bragi, and Ullr all followed. Sif followed the others only after the death of Thor. Forseti saw his father coming and only a few steps behind him was Nanna. He waited, holding back to greet Baldr. Frigg was proud of Víðarr's stength in tearing apart Fenrir, thus avenging the death of his father, but she believed that the rightful heir to Odin was the gentle Baldr. They all waited by the sea. The gods and goddesses all remembered and called on the compassionate Moðir. Among them only Freyr had fought in the battle. Moðir was proud of him in doing his duty as a warrior while knowing that he could not win. Still, it hurt to lose her grandson.

Valhalla was no more. Freyr, Týr, Thor, Odin, Loki, and Heimdallr had no place to go. Showing compassion, Freyja led them to her realm and Gæfuleysabjarg, the cliff of lucklessness. It didn't take long for Freyr to find the key to Griðbustaðr, the dwelling place of peace, since he knew well the power of practice of seiðr and how to find his way there, to reunite with his grandmother. Eventually, Loki and Heimdallr also made the journey. Yet Odin and his two faithful sons may still be on the cliff overlooking the abyss of Harmagil. Baldr holds the hope that his father and two brothers, Thor and Týr, will someday find their way.

Soon, out of the flames and scorched earth, came Forseti with a smile on his face, followed by Nanna and Baldr. They were all together again with a hope for building a new world. They all turned to Baldr to find direction as Baldr reached for Nanna and pulled her to his side, for they would lead together.

11

THE TEACHINGS OF THE VANIR

Though the end of the Ice Age and the beginning of the era of agriculture and animal husbandry was more recent for the people of the North, 10,000 years ago has been considered the time of this transition. The time before this transition was thought to be much closer to paradise than any time since. In the North, that time was characterized by veneration of the Great Mother, Moðir. When people began to control the earth through the practice of agriculture and the domestication of animals, the respect for and veneration of Moðir began to diminish. The larger animals, especially horses and cows, but also sheep and goats, began to represent a person's wealth. To increase wealth and thus power, the size of a person's herd and the land needed to support the herd had to increase accordingly. The raiding of herds and the taking land that belonged to others became a way of life, the way to gain wealth, prestige, and power. The patriarchal world as we know it emerged with the rise of a few to the status chieftain and later king, itself a prelude to the eventual rise of nations warring against nations to amass wealth, land, slaves, and power. To justify this way of life, the religion that proclaimed that man shall have dominion over the earth grew, and the world became a world where heroes were defined by their physical prowess. Heroes of ancient times went to Valhalla after death to be with Odin; heroes now wear the ribbons of military valor or the ring of a Super Bowl victory. As those destroyers of the earth once lived in great halls and castles, they now live in mansions built by corporate wealth.

Many today realize that this so-called progress, with its destruction of the earth, is no longer viable, and that a new world is being born. The Vanir who venerated Moðir are the ones who can show us the way to this New Dawn.

The gods and goddesses of the Vanir loved and cherished Moðir because of her trusting, nurturing and empathic nature, of her valuing and seeing the good in everybody and everything. This loving energy was infectuous—everyone experienced it and related to one another in this same loving manner and found personal value and strength in their own self-confidence because of it. When Freyja was brought before Odin, she felt this strength in her center of harmony. She was not intimidated by his booming voice of authority and was able to express herself effectively. Moðir's loving energy brought harmony to her people and to their relationship with the earth, with all its flora and fauna. This life was closer to paradise than at any other time in history.

This love, compassion and empathy opened each person to listen and observe in all relationships, and to learn from all situations in life. To truly listen and observe, trust in the nurturance of Mother Earth is needed. When we try to control others and the earth we begin to experience the fear of the lack of control, and with this fear we begin to hear and see only that which we expect in our distrust of others, thus making honest listening and observing truly impossible. The love of Moðir taught Freyja to trust, thus opening her to watch her cats and learn the power of the sound a cat when it walks. When reminded by her father, Njord, to watch the world under the sea, she learned of the power of the breath of a fish. When her brother, Freyr, watched Odin's warriors fight, he learned of the adhesive power of the spittle of a bird, and likewise Njord observed the planted strength of the roots of a mountain as he watched these warriors in battle. When Skaði, Njord's wife, responded to Loki's harangues at Ægir's feast, she demonstrated the power of the beard of a woman with a joke that brought about laughter from all. From the power of observing and listening without fear, the skills of the harmonious way to live are learned. But during the era of the Æsir, the control of life and the earth through strength as is seen in the sinew of a bear was the one strength valued above all others by Odin and Thor, and this strength has been valued by the heroes of all succeeding generations, to the detriment of the earth for the last 4,000 years.

We need to listen to and observe not only other humans, but all of nature as well. Much is to be learned from everything in our environment. When we realize this, we are no longer separated from it, we no longer put ourselves above it, and we are again part of nature and a part of our Great Mother, Mother Earth.

Over the last 10,000 years we have lost this love and compassion, and we have lost the magic given us by Moðir. We have forgotten her magic, but this magic is again becoming available to us, especially through the power of trance, whether hypnotic or ecstatic posture work. Hypnotic trance induced by the yes-set was simply the way of life during the era of Moðir, with her affirming mindset toward everything that we experience in life. Ecstatic trance induced by rhythmic stimulation of our nervous system, by the chants of Bragi—stimulation that quiets competing and interfering thoughts—along with the postures, taught by Freyja, allows us to listen and observe the spirits of Mother Earth, to again ensoul our world, to open us to a deeper level of experiencing our world, past, present, and future, near and at a distance.

Freyja finds this power of magic, of seiðr, while sitting on her high platform. Through her power of listening and observing she learns that particular body postures allow her to look into the future, while other postures allow her to journey to distant places or to shape-shift to experience the world as a falcon or other fauna. The songs and rhythmic chants of Bragi help induce ecstatic trance, which can be used to influence one's mood and facilitate healing. This power of song and chant is also learned by Freyr and Baldr. Baldr, in his relationship with Nanna, learns that through these powers of trance he and Nanna can communicate and be together even when physically apart from each other. These powers of trance are available to us today when we open our mind to them and practice them. Then, from the power taught us by Idunn, of listening to the flora around her, we learn of the power of healing found in plants. As we wander the forests and fields of the world we find these plants that can heal us and provide us with the sustenance we need to live. Again, experiencing these plants while in trance shows us what they have to offer us.

The new world can also provide us with a new sense of creativity—the creativity of Slœgr, Moðir's husband, and of Ullr, the son of Sif. Ullr shows us that the spring in a branch of yew makes it the perfect material for a bow for hunting, and that the rib bones of a large animal can be used to ski when strapped to one's feet. The creativity in art of both Slœgr and Ullr is seen in the carvings and furnishings in the great hall of Moðir, the creative beauty that exists in the world of paradise.

The loving creativity of this world of Moðir can also show us new ways to get along with others. This creativity shows Freyr and Baldr the strength in befriending and allying with the giants, and the senselessness of relating to them as enemies as Thor does and as do the many people today who show hatred toward the people and beliefs of other cultures. Even though the giants live a very different life, much can be learned from them, too. Similarly, Forseti finds his ability to make wise judgments when listening to the problems of others through his power of listening and observing at the deeper level of feelings and emotions.

If we open ourselves with a sense of quiet harmony we can see and hear from beyond ourselves, to see, hear, and benefit from the earth's spirits. If we embrace them, if we patiently open ourselves in trust to truly listen to and observe them, if we let go of our need to control and our need for power, we can experience the true magic of living in paradise.

As I write these last words, the days grow longer. The snow has melted and I have seen the first Skovjordbær or wild strawberry. I look forward to Nydagan, the new dawn. I look forward to again wandering the fields collecting the plants to heal and planting the plants for the Great Mother to sustain us.

VANADISDOTTIR, PRIESTESS OF FREYJA

EPILOGUE

Now is the time for the rebirth of innocence, for the rebirth of compassion, creativity, and magic, for bringing alive the enchanted earth, for the return of the Great Mother, for the rebirth of Baldr. The compassionate gods and goddesses have survived. All of this is within you and me. The timeless Great Mother is alive within us. The timeless Baldr is alive within us. The Great Mother is not out there somewhere in impersonal space. She is personal and real, residing within each of us, if only we would let die the Odin and Thor within us, the gods of violence, revenge, war, and fear. The death of *Homo aggressus,* of those who do not respect life, will allow the new strain of humanity, *Homo pacem,* to come forth, the humanity that embraces the Great Mother and reclaims at a deeper level our origin in magic, compassion, creativity, and innocence.

Ragnarǫk, the timeless final battle, happened centuries ago, years ago, last week, and yesterday. It is happening today and will happen tomorrow and next week. This battle is within you and me. Now is the time to let those gods and monsters of retribution die in order to embrace the Great Mother, the gods and goddesses of the Vanir within us. The rebirth of Baldr comes with each sunrise, with each spring, and with the rebirth of compassion and cooperation.

We awaken each day to the morning headlines to news of murder and suicide, of war, terrorism, and heroes who become heroes by fighting and brute force. This has been our cultural mythology, a mythology that has said we must stand up with strength to face and kill our enemy or those who threaten us to survive and maintain our self-esteem. But this is false strength, false self-esteem. For those of us of Nordic ancestry, this cultural mythology has been handed down through the generations from the ancient stories of the Nordic gods Odin and Thor. These cultural myths have been sustained by the heroes of our many wars and sporting competitions, from literature, movies, and now video games.

Now is the time to rewrite our negative personal myths, to replace them with the positive myths of compassion and love that bring us greater personal health and creativity. Such writers as Stanley Krippner,[1] Stephen Larsen,[2] and Lewis Mehl-Madrona[3] each have written books on rewriting our personal myths. Rewriting our negative personal myths is also central in the current popularity of cognitive therapy.[4] Our cultural myths can also change and are changing to support a culture of greater compassion and creativity. Such writers as Marion Zimmer-Bradley,[5] with her rewriting of the King Arthur stories, and Jean Auel,[6] with her stories of an earlier time of the goddess, do just that.

The stories of living with compassion and creativity, of valuing life and love, are available to us. Central to the beliefs of Christianity is the belief of love, of forgiving your enemy, of "turning the other cheek," of "forgive them for they know not what they do"—beliefs that are in fact realistic, effective, and possible, yet few Christians embrace these teachings. We see this "magic" of compassion and love in the news stories of persons who show forgiveness, compassion, and acts of kindness. This compassion was shown the American people after 9/11, but the United States squandered its international support for these inspired acts of compassion with its subsequent acts of aggression. We now learn that the threads of these beliefs in magic, compassion, and love are also found in the ancient myths of the Germanic and Nordic peoples. *Baldr's Magic* traces the thread of this magic and compassion through our Nordic cultural fabric by bringing back to life the goddesses and gods of the Vanir.

There are those who write of the goddess culture that came before the more recent culture of worshipping omnipotent masculine gods. The archaeologist Marija Gimbutas leads the way for us to find these myths of compassion, peace, and creativity that have their roots in the ancient goddess culture. Gimbutas' understanding of the archaeological finds of 6500 to 3500 BCE in Southwest Asia and the Mediterranean are recorded in her book *The Goddess and the Gods of Old Europe: Myths and Cult Images.* Her research describes a culture that appreciated the Great Mother. The writing of Riane Eisler, in her book *The Chalice and the Blade,* brings to us a greater understanding of the beauty and compassion of the ancient Mother Goddess. Jean Auel, in her historical fiction series about the earth's children, beginning with *The Clan of the Cave Bear,* has popularized the belief in the Great Mother. Now *Baldr's Magic* brings us to a new depth of understanding of the Mother Goddess, this time from the myths of the ancient Nordic people.

*Before there were the gods there was the Great Mother
   Goddess.
Before there was Odin and his son Thor there was Moðir.
Before the aggressive nature of the Æsir there was the
   compassion and magic of the Vanir.
Before the sinew of the bear there was the sound a cat
   makes when it walks.*

In a more concrete sense, this rebirth of Baldr is happening in my world, in Penns Valley, in central Pennsylvania. This New Age is here, blooming in many ways. In the late 1960s and early '70s there were three communes, people who came together to creatively build a new life and work in love and cooperation. I was part of one of those communes. We grew much of our own food and celebrated life together. Though the communes no longer exist, most all of us still live in the valley and our numbers have grown to several hundred. From us has sprouted the Penns Valley Conservation Association, which works to protect our watershed, our Great Mother. From us has grown the Pennsylvania

Association for Sustainable Agriculture, a statewide network of small farmers and farmers markets. Though we are not the hunter and gatherers of the magical era, we are seeking ways to sustain ourselves without assaulting the earth. From us has grown Pennsylvania Certificated Organic, the organization that certifies as organic the farms and their products throughout our state and beyond. PCO has become a model for other organic certifiers. All three groups were born in and thrive in Penns Valley.

Many of us teach alternative ways of living that show our love for the Great Mother Earth and seek to sustain her. I teach the way of ecstatic trance using the Cuyamungue Method to revive the ancient powers that are a real way of healing and connecting with one another, even at a distance of miles or years. Others in the valley teach many other alternative ways of healing and experiencing the spiritual life. We come together in such places as the Green Drake Art Gallery and Art Center, the St. Luke's Cultural Center, the Elk Creek Café and Aleworks, and the IngleBean Coffee House, places in the town of Millheim that our network of friends has created, places where we meet and create together. I am one of several local growers of hops for the aleworks. We gather in the Brownlee barn, around campfires and in our homes, groups of people who feel love for one another and who are having a major influence on others in our valley who may not think like us. We are not an organization; we are people of the valley, each with something different to contribute and with different resources to offer, and we recognize and value what the others contribute. We celebrate this life through music, art, work, and actions tht show our love for the Great Mother, Mother Earth, at such events as our annual Labor Day Crickfest and our weekly Wednesday evening peace vigil. Our numbers are reaching a critical mass, and they cannot be turned back. We do not have all the answers for what this new world will be like, but we know that we are at its beginning. There are many communities like ours all across the country and in other countries around the world, doing similar, creative things. We have much to learn, and we know we are not alone as we reach out to one another. We are experiencing this New Dawn, Nydagan, now.

> *We are moving from a world of greed to a world that sustains the Great Mother Earth.*

> *We are moving from the loneliness of a world that attempts to settle conflict through violence to a world of cooperation and nurturance, a world that values diversity.*

> *We are moving from a world that is cold and empty in its overly rational approach to life, to a world filled with the energy and spirits of the past, present, and future, to teach us and provide us with the creativity to lead us effectively into this New Dawn, Nydagan.*

The time is right for us to understand in a much deeper sense the magic of the Vanir. We are moving into a new era of civilization, an era of time-free transparency, an era of *Homo pacem,* an era of appreciating the enchanted earth, an era of appreciating the Great Mother— the time of the return of Baldr.

NOTES

PROLOGUE: OUR RELATIONSHIP TO THE GREAT MOTHER

1. Goodman, *Ecstasy, Ritual, and Alternate Reality*, 17–18.
2. Mason, *An Unatural Order*, 28–30.
3. Gebser, *The Ever-Present Origin*.
4. Cunliffe, *Europe between the Oceans*, 76–78.
5. Ibid., 126.
6. Ibid., 126.
7. Ibid., 213.

CHAPTER 1. THE LOST POWERS OF THE NORDIC PEOPLE

1. Hasenfratz, *Barbarian Rites*, 62.
2. Ibid., 64–65.
3. Gebser, *The Ever-Present Origin*, 297.
4. Price, "Viking-Age Sorcery," 5–6.
5. Hasenfratz, *Barbarian Rites*, 76–89.
6. Ibid., 90–123.
7. Eisler, *The Chalice and the Blade*, 71.
8. Ibid., 69.
9. Gebser, *The Ever-Present Origin*, 60.
10. Ibid., 99.
11. Ibid., 87.
12. Ibid., 99.
13. Clow, *The Mayan Code*, 115.

14. Calleman, *The Mayan Calendar,* 220.

15. Snorri Sturluson, *The Prose Edda;* and Hollander, *The Poetic Edda.*

16. Simek, *Dictionary of Northern Mythology,* 351.

17. Anna Malmborg, "Norse Religion—A Complicated One," 14.

18. Simek, *Dictionary of Northern Mythology,* 172.

19. Gebser, *The Ever-Present Origin,* 297.

20. Calleman, *The Mayan Calendar,* 196.

CHAPTER 2. THE POWERS OF ECSTATIC AND HYPNOTIC TRANCE

1. Hasenfratz, *Barbarian Rites,* 64–65.

2. Clow, *The Mayan Code,* 90.

3. Gore, *Ecstatic Body Postures,* 6–8.

4. Ibid., 32–35.

5. Sheldrake, *The Presence of the Past,* 112.

6. Laszlo, *Science and the Akashic Field,* 72–77.

7. Deloria, *The World We Used to Live In,* 68–69.

8. Waggoner, *Lucid Dreaming,* 78–79.

9. Erickson, E. Rossi, and S. Rossi, *Hypnotic Realities,* 58.

CHAPTER 3. NORDIC POSTURES

1. Anderson et al., *Att Föra Gudarnas Talan,* 25–50.

2. Goodman and Nauwald, *Ecstatic Trance,* 147.

3. Anderson, et al., *Att Föra Gudarnas Talan,* 78 (top right).

4. Ibid., 83.

5. Ibid., 85–87.

6. Sturluson, *Prose Edda,* 35.

7. Coles, *Shadows of A Northern Past,* 49, 195.

8. Ibid., 136.

9. Anderson, et al., *Att Föra Gudarnas Talan,* 78 (bottom, second from right).

10. Ibid., 75, 81, 89.

11. Anderson, et al., 81.

12. Ibid., 89.

13. Näsström, "Freyja—A Goddess of Love and War," 7.

CHAPTER 4. COMMUNING WITH ANCESTORS: AN OVERVIEW

1. Fry and Soderberg, "Lethal Aggression in Mobile Forager Bands," 270–73.
2. Sahlins, *Stone Age Economics,* 33.

CHAPTER 7. THE WARRIOR AND HIS FAMILY

1. Braden, *The Divine Matrix,* 54–55.
2. Goodman, *Where the Spirits Ride the Wind,* 20–22, 59.
3. Hilgard, *Divided Consciousness,* 209.

EPILOGUE

1. Krippner and Feinstein, *The Mythic Path.*
2. Larsen, *The Mythic Imagination.*
3. Mehl-Madrona, *Narrative Medicine.*
4. Beck, *Cognitive Therapy and the Emotional Disorders.*
5. Bradley, *The Mists of Avalon.*
6. Auel, *The Clan of the Cave Bear.*

GLOSSARY OF
NORDIC TERMS

Æsir: The race of warrior gods led by Odin that resides in Asgard.

Alf: King Alf the Old was the grandfather to Ottar, Freyja's human lover.

Alfheim: The underworld domain of Asgard inhabited by the light elves.

Alvis: The dwarf with whom Thor debates until daylight and thus is turned to stone.

Angrboða: "Anguish-boding." A giantess, the mistress of Loki, and the mother of Fenrir the wolf, Jörmungandr the sea serpent, and Hel, the being who presides over the place of the same name.

Asgard: The domain of the Æsir in the Sky World.

ask: The name given the ash tree by Idunn; also the world tree.

Auðumla: The cow that licks away the salty ice that gives birth to the god Búri.

Baldr: The most beautiful and gentle son of Odin and Frigg, who dreams of his own death, a death caused by the trickery of Loki. He returns after Ragnarǫk to become the god of gods.

baldrian: The name given to the valerian plant by Idunn.

berserkers: Warriors who work themselves up into a frenzy before battle and are thought to be invulnerable.

Bestla: The giantess wife of Borr and mother of Odin.

Beowulf: The son of Scyld Scefing, who became the second great king of Denmark.

Billing's daughter: The maiden who makes a fool of Odin by rejecting him in his attempts to court her.

Bolthorn: The giant father of Bestla.

287

Borr: The father of Odin, Vili, and Vé, the son of Búri, and the husband of Bestla.

Bifröst: The flaming, trembling rainbow bridge guarded by Heimdallr that connects the Upper and Middle worlds.

Bragi: A son of Odin and the god of poetry, the husband of Idunn.

Brísingamen: The most beautiful necklace, made by the dwarfs for Freyja in payment for her sexual favors.

Brokk: One of the two elves who makes the golden harness for Freyr's boar.

Búri: Odin's grandfather who is freed from the salty ice when licked by the cow Auðumla. He is the father of Borr and Moðir.

burre: The name given to the plant burdock by Idunn.

cikorie: The name given to the plant chicory by Idunn, sometimes a substitute for coffee.

Dottir: The daughter of Moðir, sister to Njord, and the mother of Freyja and Freyr.

Draupnir: Odin's golden arm ring that produces eight rings of gold every nine days.

Dvalinn: The dwarf who is turned to stone by the sun.

eg: The name given to the oak tree by Idunn..

Einherjar: Those Midgard warriors who die as heroes in battle and are taken to reside in Valhalla by the Valkyries, where they fight daily.

Eitri: One of the elves who makes the golden harness for Freyr's boar.

Elli: The giantess who in actuality is old age, as reported in the story of Útgarða-Loki.

Fárbauti: The giantess mother of Loki.

Fenrir: The wolf son of Loki who continues to grow to become a threat to the gods until it is restrained by a magical binding. This restraining of Fenrir costs the god Týr his hand.

Fjorgyn: The mother of Thor.

Fólkvangr: ("field of the host" or "people-field" or "army-field") a meadow or field ruled over by the goddess Freyja, where half of those that die in combat go upon death, while the other half go to the god Odin in Valhalla.

Forseti: The wise son of Baldr and Nanna and the Vanir god of justice.

Freki: One of Odin's two wolves that sit at his feet.

Freyja: The sister of Freyr and daughter of Njord. She is one of the fertility goddesses of the Vanir who goes with her father to live among the Æsir.

Freyr: The brother of Freyja and the son of Njord. He is one of the fertility gods of the Vanir who goes with his father to live among the Æsir.

Frigg: Odin's wife and mother of Baldr. She is originally of the Vanir.

Frodi: The greedy brother of King Healfdene who kills Healfdene and seeks to kill Healfdene's three sons in order to become king.

Gæfuleysabjarg: Literally, "cliff of lucklessness," the place of residence in Freyja's domain of those warriors who die in their first battle. This cliff overlooks Harmagil, the "gorge of sorrow," across which the warriors can see those women who died virgins.

Garmr: The monstrous dog chained to the gate of Niflheim. He breaks loose at Ragnarǫk to battle the god Týr.

Gefjon: The fertility goddess who plows the land from Sweden to form the Danish island of Zealand. She is the husband of Scyld Scefing, the first king of Denmark, and the caretaker of those women who die as virgins.

Geirröd: The giant who tries to kill Thor.

Gerðr: The beautiful giantess, daughter of Gymir, with whom Freyr falls in love but is unable to express his feelings except through his messenger, Skírnir.

Geri: One of Odin's two wolves that sit at his feet.

Gersemi: One of Freyja's two beautiful daughters.

Ginnungagap: The land between the North and the South that is mild and green, with soft air that thaws the ice of the North.

Gleipnir: The magical binding made by the dwarfs to restrain Fenrir the wolf.

Gratabjǫð: Literally, "weeping fields." The fields of the goddess Gefjon along Harmagil, "the gorge of sorrow," where those women who died as virgins can see across the gorge the warriors who died in their first battle.

Griðbustaðr: Literally, "the dwelling place of peace," the place where those who understand and practice the compassionate magic of the Vanir reside after death.

guldpil: The name given to the willow tree by Idunn.

Gullinbursti: Freyr's golden boar that pulls his chariot in battle.

Gullveig: The Vanir goddess who becomes addicted to mead, and when given the assignment to deliver mead to the Æsir, drinks most of it before she arrives. Because of this offense, the Æsir throw her into the fire, only to find that she does not burn, so they called her a *heiðr*, a witch.

Gungnir: Odin's spear.

Gylfaginning: The first part of the *Prose Edda*.

Gylfi: The king of Sweden who makes a deal with Gefjon that gives her the land that she plows out to sea that becomes part of Denmark.

Gymir: The father of the beautiful Gerðr. Freyr falls in love with Gerðr but is unable to tell her of his love, so he sends words of love through his messenger, Skírnir.

Halga: The son of King Healfdene, the third king of Denmark.

Harmagil: Literally, "the gorge of sorrow." From this gorge rises the smell of sulfur from Niflheim. It separates Gratabjǫð, "weeping fields," from Gæfuleysabjarg, "the cliff of lucklessness."

Healfdene: The grandson of the first king of Denmark, Scyld Scefing, who became its third great king. He was the brother of King Frodi and had three sons, Heorogar, Hrothgar, and Halga, and a daughter, Signy. Hrothgar became the fourth and most powerful king of Denmark.

Heimdallr: The Vanrir god who chooses to live among the Æsir, and who is given the position of guarding Bifröst, the rainbow bridge, because of his acute hearing. He could hear the grass growing.

heiðr: A witch. Gullveig is called this name when she does not burn when thrown into the fire.

Hel: The daughter of Loki and Angrboða whom Odin throws into the underworld to care for those who die not honorably in battle, but of illness and old age; also the place name of the underworld. Hel (sometimes called Helheim) is also the name of the underworld location ruled by Hel, the being.

Heorogar: A son of the third king of Denmark, Healfdene.

Hliðskjálf: The high throne of Odin from which he can see all that is happening in the nine worlds.

Hnoss: One of Freyja's two beautiful daughters.

Hǫðr: The blind son of Odin and brother of Baldr. He throws the mistletoe dart that kills Baldr.

Hœnir: A god of the Æsir who was thought to have leadership abilities so is offered to the Vanir in exchange for Njord and Freyr to insure the peace between the two races of gods.

Hrothgar: The fourth and most powerful king of Denmark and son of Healfdene.

Hrungnir: The giant who injures Thor in battle.

Hugin: One of the ravens that sits on Odin's shoulder, whispering in the ear of the god, bringing him the news of the nine worlds.

Hvergelmir: The wellspring in Neflheim that is the terminus of the underworld root of Yggdrasil, the world tree.

hvidtjørn: The name given the hawthorn by Idunn.

hvidløg: The name given to the plant garlic by Idunn.

hvilðgarðr: Literally, "the dwelling place of rest," the center of harmony within a person's body, just below the navel.

hyrdetaske: The name given to the plant shepherd's purse by Idunn.

Hyndla: The wise giantess from whom Freyja seeks to learn of the ancestry of Óttar, her human lover.

Idunn: The Vanir goddess who keeps the gods young by giving them the golden apples from a tree in her garden and who teaches all of the healing powers of plants and trees. Her husband is Bragi, god of poetry.

isop: The name given to the plant hyssop by Idunn.

Ivaldi: One of the dark elves who helps make the treasures of the gods.

Jarl Sævil: The husband of Signy, who is the daughter of the Danish king Healfdene.

Jörmungandr: The serpent son of Loki and Angrboða, who Odin throws into the ocean, where it grows to surround Midgard by holding its own tail in its mouth.

Jötunheimr: The domain in Midgard that is the realm of the giants.

jötunn: The Old Norse word for giant.

kamille: The name given chamomile by Idunn.

Kona: The giant Thiazi's wife, who gets sick and is made well by Idunn.

kulsukker: The name given the plant comfrey by Idunn.

Kvasir: The wisest of the gods who first brews mead from the spittle of the gods, making mead the drink of the gods. Also the god of the Vanir who is offered in exchange for Mímir, a god of the Æsir, to ensure peace between the Vanir and the Æsir.

Laufey: The father of Loki.

Loki: The trickster god skilled in shape-shifting and the father of Jörmungandr, Fenrir, and Hel. His confrontations with the gods because of their hypocrisy leads to his restraint until Ragnarǫk, the final battle that brings an end to the world. He is the cause of earthquakes.

Magni: A son of Thor and brother of Moði.

Midgard: The Middle World; our world as we know it.

Mímir: The Æsir offer the god Mímir to the Vanir in exchange for Kavasir to ensure peace between the Æsir and the Vanir. He is the wisest of the giants who is killed, after which Odin preserves his head in the Well of Mímir, consulting it as an oracle.

Mjölnir: The hammer of Thor that causes lightening when thrown by Thor and then returns to his hand.

mjoðr: The name given to the alcoholic honey-infused drink mead.

Moði: The son of Thor and brother of Magni who watches Freyja's cats silently land on the earth.

Moðir: The mother of the Vanir. She is the sister of Borr, who is the father of Odin, thus she is Odin's aunt. She is the daughter of Búri, the mother of Njord, and the grandmother of Freyja and Freyr. Her husband is Slœgr, the creative one.

Moðirasalr: The hall of Moðir in the realm of the Vanir.

Munin: One of Odin's ravens that sits on his shoulder, bringing him the news of the nine worlds.

Muspell: The realm of fire in the South, guarded by the giant Surtr.

mynte: The name given to the plant mint, used for tea.

Nanna: Baldr's wife and one of the Vanir.

Niðhogg: The dragon of Lower World that gnaws on the roots of Yggdrasil.

Niflheim: The realm of those who die of illness and old age and is ruled by Hel.

Njord: The god of the Vanir and father of Freyr and Freyja. The god of the wind and sea who marries the giantess Skaði.

nœlde: The name given the plant nettles by Idunn.

norns: Analogous to the Greek fates. The three most important norns, Urðr, Verðandi, and Skuld, who can see into the past to learn for the future, are advisors to Odin.

Nydagan: The New Dawn, the birth of the new age that is beginning now in the twenty-first century.

Óðr: Freyja's wandering husband.

Odin: The god of gods, the Allfather, and the father of Thor.

Óttar: Freyja's human lover whom she disguises as a boar.

perikon: The name given to the plant St. John's wort by Idunn.

purpur-solhat: The name given the plant echinacea by Idunn.

Ragnarǫk: The final battle between the gods and their adversaries that brings an end to the world and the rebirth of Baldr.

Ratatosk: The squirrel that runs up and down Yggdrasil, the world tree, carrying insults between Niðhogg, the dragon that gnaws at the tree's roots, and the eagle that lives at the top.

Regin: The foster father and protector of King Healfdene's three sons.

rejnfang: The name given to the plant tansy by Idunn.

Rindr: The mother of Odin's son Vali.

Skáldskaparmál: Meaning "language of poetry," the second part of the *Prose Edda*.

Scyld Scefing: The first king of Denmark and husband of the goddess Gefjon.

seiðr: The magic of the Vanir.

seiðhjallr: The platform on which vǫlvas sit that allows them to see or journey into the future.

Sessrúmnir: Freyja's hall in Asgard.

Sif: Thor's wife whose famous hair is cut off by Loki because of her vanity. Sif is originally of the Vanir.

Signy: The daughter of the Danish king Healfdene who marries Jarl Sævil.

Sigyn: Loki's wife who remains faithful to him until the end. When Loki is restrained with a poisonous snake hanging over his head, Sigyn protects him by catching the dripping poison in a bowl.

skogstjärn: Forest pond or forest tarn.

Skaði: The daughter of the giant Thiazi and the wife of Njord.

Skíðblaðnir: The ship of Freyr that always has wind for it sails but can be folded small enough to be carried in his pocket.

Skírnir: The messenger who carries Freyr's messages of love to the giant Gerðr, for which Freyr gives him his magical sword.

Skjǫldungs: One of the major ancient tribes of Nordic people of Denmark and Southern Sweden that was centered in what is now Gammel Lejre, Denmark.

Skuld: One of the three norns, or fates, and a goddess of destiny.

Sleipnir: Odin's eight-legged horse.

Slœgr: A giant whose name means "the creative one," who is the husband of Moðir and the father of Njord. He is a skilled ironsmith.

Surtr: The giant who guards Muspell.

Suttung: The giant whose father is killed by the dwarfs in their attempt to protect their mead. He seeks revenge for his father's death by trying to kill the dwarfs.

Svartafheim: The domain in the Middle World that belongs to the dark elves.

Thjalfi: The swift-running farmer's son who becomes Thor's servant.

Thiazi: The giant who kidnaps Idunn and who afterward is returned to the gods by the shape-shifting powers of Loki. Thiazi is killed in a fire in Asgard.

Thokk: A giantess thought to be Loki in disguise and who prevents Baldr's return from Hel.

Thor: The son of Odin whose mother is Fjorgyn. He is the husband of Sif. This warrior god brings lightning and thunder with the throw of his hammer.

Thrymheim: Skaði's mountain home where Njord lives half the time because she refuses to live by the sea. Also the hall of the giant Thiazi.

Thurd: A daughter of Thor and Sif.

Týr: The son of Odin and the god of war who sacrifices his hand in order to restrain Fenrir the wolf.

Ullr: The Vanir god of archery and skiing, the creative and inventive son of Njord and Sif, and the grandson of Moðir.

Urðr: One of the three important norns and a goddess of destiny.

Útgarðr: The domain of Útgarða-Loki, the giant skilled in deception who repeatedly tricks Thor.

Valaskjálf : Odin's great hall in Asgard.

Vali: A son of Odin whose mother is Rindr.

Valhalla: The realm in the Sky World that is the home to those who die valiantly in battle and is presided over by Odin.

Valkyries: The beautiful women who escort those who die valiantly in battle to Valhalla.

Vanaheim: The Upper-World realm of the Vanir.

Vanir: The race of fertility gods and goddesses that predates the Æsir. Because their powers are magical, their battles with the physically powerful Æsir are stalemates.

Vanadisdottir: Meaning "the daughter of the Freyja," a priestess of Freyja from whom in trance I received the ancient stories that comprise "The Lost Edda of the Vanir."

Vár: The goddess of oaths and marriage.

Vé: A son of Borr and brother of Odin and Vili.

vejbred: The name given to the plant plantain by Idunn.

Verðandi: One of three important norns and a goddess of destiny.

Víðarr: An Æsir god of vengeance. A son of Odin whose mother is the giantess Gríðr. He kills Fenrir the wolf to avenge Odin's death in the final battle.

Vili: A son of Borr and brother of Odin and Vé.

Vígríðr: The battle plain on which the final battle, Ragnarǫk is fought.

vǫlva: A seeress.

Well of Urðr: "Well of fate," the well in the Sky World guarded by the three norns that is the terminus of a root of Yggdrasil.

Yggdrasil: The world tree with roots in the Upper, Middle, and Lower worlds.

Ymir: The first giant killed by Odin and his brothers from whose body Odin creates the world.

Ynglings: One of the major ancient tribes of the Nordic people of Sweden, which was centered in what is now Gammel Uppsala, Sweden.

BIBLIOGRAPHY

Anderson, Gunnar, Lena Beronius Jörpeland, Jan Dunėr, Sara Fritsch, and Eva Skyllberg. *Att Föra Gudarnas Talan: figurinerna från Lunda.* Stockholm, Sweden: Riksantikvarieämbetes Förlag, 2004.

Auel, Jean M. *The Clan of the Cave Bear.* New York: Bantam Books, 1980.

Beck, Aaron. *Cognitive Therapy and the Emotional Disorders.* New York: International Universities Press, 1976.

Braden, Gregg. *The Divine Matrix: Bridging Time, Space, Miracles, and Belief.* Carlsbad, Calif.: Hay House, 2007.

Bradley, Marion Zimmer. *The Mists of Avalon.* New York: Ballantine Books, 1982.

Brink, Nicholas E. *Grendel and His Mother: Healing the Traumas of Childhood through Dreams, Imagery and Hypnosis.* Amityville, N.Y.: Baywood, 2002.

———. "Loki's Children: A Mythical Understanding of Hypnosis in the Process of Change." *Hypnos: Swedish Journal of Hypnosis in Psychotherapy and Psychosomatic Medicine* 22, no. 2 (1995): 154–58.

———. *The Power of Ecstatic Trance: Practices for Healing, Spiritual Growth and Accessing the Universal Mind.* Rochester, Vt.: Bear & Co., 2013.

Calleman, Carl Johan. *The Mayan Calendar and the Transformation of Consciousness.* Rochester, Vt.: Bear & Co., 2004.

Capra, Fritjof. *Tao of Physics: An Exploration of the Parallels between Modern Physics and Eastern Mysticism.* Boston: Shambahala, 2000.

Chambers, Raymond Wilson. *Beowulf: An Introduction to the Study of the Poem.* Cambridge, UK: Cambridge University Press, 1959.

Clow, Barbara Hand. *The Mayan Code: Time Acceleration and Awakening the World Mind.* Rochester, Vt.: Bear & Co., 2007.

Coles, John. *Shadows of a Northern Past: Rock Carvings of Bohuslän and Østfold.* Oxford, UK: Oxbow Books, 2005.

Crossley-Holland, Kevin. *The Norse Myths.* New York: Pantheon Books, 1980.

Cunliffe, Barry. *Europe between the Oceans: 9000 BC–AD 1000.* New Haven, Conn.: Yale University Press, 2008.

Deloria Jr., Vine. *The World We Used to Live In: Remembering the Powers of the Medicine Men.* Golden, Colo.: Fulcrum, 2006.

Eisler, Riane. *The Chalice and The Blade: Our History, Our Future.* San Francisco, Calif.: Harper-Collins, 1987.

Erickson, Milton H., Ernest L. Rossi, and Sheila Rossi. *Hypnotic Realities: The Induction of Clinical Hypnosis and Forms of Indirect Suggestions.* New York: Irvington Publishers, 1976.

Fry, Douglas P. and Partik Soderberg. "Lethal Aggression in Mobile Forager Bands and Implications for the Origins of War." *Science* 341, no. 6143: 270–73.

Gebser, Jean. *The Ever-Present Origin,* Noel Barstad, trans. Athens, Ohio: Ohio University Press, 1953.

Gimbutas, Marija. *The Goddesses and Gods of Old Europe: Myths and Cult Images.* Berkeley, Calif.: University of California Press, 1982.

Goodman, Felicitas. *Where the Spirits Ride the Wind: Trance Journeys and Other Ecstatic Experiences.* Bloomington, Ind.: Indiana University Press, 1990.

———. *Ecstasy, Ritual, and Alternate Reality: Religion in a Pluralistic World.* Bloomington, Ind.: Indiana University Press, 1990.

Goodman, Felicitas and Nana Nauwald. *Ecstatic Trance: New Ritual Body Postures: A Workbook.* Havelte, Holland: Binkey Kok Publishers, 2003.

Gore, Belinda. *Ecstatic Body Postures: An Alternate Reality Workbook.* Rochester, Vt.: Bear & Co., 1995.

———. *The Ecstatic Experience: Healing Postures for Spirit Journeys.* Rochester, Vt.: Bear & Co., 2009.

Hasenfratz, Hans-Peter. *Barbarian Rites: The Spiritual World of the Vikings and the Germanic Tribes.* Rochester, Vt.: Inner Traditions, 2011.

Hilgard, Ernest R. *Divided Consciousness: Multiple Controls in Human Thought and Action.* New York: John Wiley and Sons, 1986.

Hollander, Lee M., trans. *The Poetic Edda*. Austin, Tex: University of Texas Press, 1962.

Jones, Gwyn, trans. *Eirik the Red and Other Icelandic Sagas*. New York: Oxford University Press, 1991.

Krippner, Stanley, Michael Bova, and Leslie Gray, eds. *Healing Stories: The Use of Narrative in Counseling and Psychotherapy*. Charlottesville, Va.: Puente, Publications, 2007.

Krippner, Stanley and David Feinstein. *The Mythic Path: Discovering the Guiding Stories of Your Past, Creating a Vision for Your Future*. Santa Rosa, Calif.: Author's Publishing Cooperative, 2006.

Larrington, Carolyne, trans. *The Poetic Edda*. Oxford, UK: Oxford University Press, 1966.

Larsen, Stephen. *The Mythic Imagination: The Quest for Meaning Through Personal Mythology*. Rochester, Vt.: Inner Traditions International, 1996.

Laszlo, Ervin. *The Akashic Experience: Science and the Cosmic Memory Field*. Rochester, Vt.: Inner Traditions, 2009.

———. *Science and the Akashic Field: An Integral Theory of Everything*. Rochester, Vt.: Inner Traditions, 2007.

Magnusson, Magnus and Hermann Palsson, trans. *Laxdæla Saga*. New York: Penguin Books, 1969.

Malmborg, Anna. "Norse Religion—A Complicated One." *Viking Heritage Magazine* 2 (2000): 14–15.

Mason, Jim. *An Unnatural Order: The Roots of Our Destruction of Nature*. New York: Lantern Books, 2005.

Mehl-Madrona, Lewis. *Narrative Medicine: The Use of History and Story in the Healing Process*. Rochester, Vt.: Bear & Co., 2007.

Näsström, Britt-Mari. "Freyja—A Goddess of Love and War." *Viking Heritage Magazine* 1 (2002): 7.

Price, Neil. "Viking-Age Sorcery." *Viking Heritage Magazine* 3 (2004): 3–6.

Radin, Dean. *Entangled Minds: Extrasensory Experiences in a Quantum Reality*. New York: Paraview Pocket Books, 2006.

Sahlins, Marshall. *Stone Age Economics*. New York: Aldine Publishing Company, 1972.

Sheldrake, Rupert. *The Presence of the Past: Morphic Resonance and the Memory of Nature*. Rochester, Vt.: Park Street Press, 1995.

Simek, Rudolf. *Dictionary of Northern Mythology*. Cambridge, Mass.: D. S. Brewer, 1993.

Sturluson, Snorri. *The Prose Edda: Tales from Norse Mythology,* Jean I. Young, trans. Berkeley, Calif.: University of California Press, 1954.

———. *Heimskringla or The Lives of the Norse Kings,* Erling Monsen, ed. New York: Dover Publications, 1990.

Tarnas, Richard. *Cosmos and Psyche: Intimations of a New World View.* New York: Penguin Books, 2006.

Taylor, Paul B. and W. H. Auden, eds. *The Elder Edda: A Selection.* New York: Random House, 1969.

Terry, Patricia, trans. *Poems of the Elder Edda.* Philadelphia, Pa.: University of Pennsylvania Press, 1990.

Waggoner, Robert. *Lucid Dreaming: Gateway to the Inner Self.* Needham, Mass.: Moment Point Press, 2009.

Wright, David, trans. *Beowulf.* New York: Penguin, 1957.

INDEX

Page numbers in *italics* refer to illustrations.